New

BREAKTHROUGH

GERMAN

THIRD EDITION

Ruth Rach

Producer at the BBC World Service

Ruth has taught German at Sussex and Bath
Universities and has been involved in adult education
both as a teacher and researcher. She has written
several language books.

Brian Hill

General Editor
Professor of Modern Languages
Language Centre, University of Brighton

MACMILLAN

First edition published 1982 by Pan Books Ltd
First Macmillan edition published 1988
Reprinted three times
Second edition published 1992
Reprinted five times
Third edition 1996

Published by
MACMILLAN PRESS LTD
Houndmills, Basingstoke, Hampshire RG21 2XS
and London
Companies and representatives throughout the world

ISBN 0–333–63713–5 book
ISBN 0–333–63714–3 book and cassette pack
ISBN 0–333–63715–1 cassettes

A catalogue record for this book is available from the British Library.

10	9	8	7	6	5	4	3	2	1
05	04	03	02	01	00	99	98	97	96

Audio producer: Gerald Ramshaw, Max II
Actors: Tom Wesel, Dorit Berry, Erich Redman

Design: D&J Hunter
Printed in Hong Kong

Acknowledgements
The author would like to thank Agnes Scheuermann, Karin Bagan and of course little Jessica for their help with the recordings. Special thanks are due to my editor Helen Bugler whose dedication, thoroughness and enthusiasm were much appreciated.

The publishers wish to thank the following photograph sources: Helen Bugler pp. 13, 16, 63, 78, 95, 101, 113, 114, 115, 162, 168, 171, 182; Brighteye Productions p. 20; J. Allan Cash Ltd pp. 1, 46, 133, 165, 170, 174, 210; Wolf and Steffi Gröner pp. 27, 58, 74, 107, 182, 232; Rolf Kröger p. 19; Joachim Messerschmidt p. 172; Ruth Rach pp. 8, 9, 24, 49 foot, 62, 75, 80, 123, 141, 206, 208, 209, 224, 228; Zefa pictures pp. 7, 43, 164, 186.

The author and publishers wish to thank the following for permission to use copyright material: Deutsche Bahn AG for material from timetables, tickets and information leaflets; A&C Druck und Verlag GmbH for the extract from *Telemonat* on p. 223; Englisch-Intensiv for the advertisement on p. 29; *Frankfurter Allgemeine Zeitung* for the use of their masthead on p. 26; *Frankfurter Rundschau* for their masthead on p. 26; Fremdenverkehrsverband Bodensee Oberschwaben for the beer mat on p. 147, the beer logos on p. 150 and the photograph on p. 176; the German Wine Information Service, London, acting on behalf of the German Wine Institute, Mainz, for the illustrations and wine labels on pp. 148, 151, 157, 159, 167; Hotel Lipprandt for the photograph on p. 44; *Kieler Nachrichten* for the weather map on p. 184 and their masthead on p. 189; Leipziger Verkehrsvertriebe (LVB) GmbH for the tickets on pp. 70 and 72; Die Neue Sammlung, Staatl. Museum für angewandte Kunst, Munich for the brochure on p. 85; *Neue Zürcher Zeitung* for their masthead on p. 26; the Österreichische Post for stamps on pp. 96 and 97; Schwennau Stube for the advertisement on p. 55; SSF-Reisen GmbH for their advertisement on p. 29; das Städtische Verkehrsamt Ravensburg for the photograph on p. 93; Stadtwerke Weiden i.d. Opf. for the advertisement on p. 200; *taz, die tageszeitung* for their magazine cover 'Hin & Weg' on p. 226; Tiger Palast for the advertisement on p. 91; Tourismus Südlicher Schwarzwald for the pictures on pp. 82 and 90; the Tourismus-Zentrale Hamburg GmbH for the brochure illustration on p. 196; Ulm/Neu Ulm Touristik GmbH for the photographs on pp. 166, 167 and 195; the Wasserburg (Bodensee) Fremdenverkehrsamt for the pictures on pp. 38, 155, 163.

Every effort has been made to trace all copyright holders, but if any have been overlooked the publishers will be pleased to make the necessary arrangements at the first opportunity.

Contents

HOW TO USE THIS COURSE

Since the *Breakthrough* series was introduced in 1982, several million people world-wide have used the courses to learn a variety of languages. This is a completely revised edition: there are new recordings, new activities and new ways of presenting the material. We have talked to hundreds of learners about their 'Breakthrough' experiences and we have acted on what we were told to ensure the new course is even more enjoyable and useful.

Following this course will help you understand, speak and read most of the German you are likely to need on holiday or on business trips. The course is based on recordings made in Germany of ordinary German people in everyday situations. Step by step you will learn first to understand what they are saying and then to speak in similar situations yourself.

General hints to help you use the course

- Have confidence in us! Real language is complex and you will find certain things in every unit which are not explained in detail. Don't worry about this. We will build up your knowledge slowly, selecting only what is most important at each stage.

- Try to study regularly, but in short periods. 20–30 minutes each day is usually better than $3\frac{1}{2}$ hours once a week.

- To help you learn to speak, say the words and phrases out loud whenever possible.

- If you don't understand something, leave it for a while. Learning a language is a bit like doing a jigsaw or a crossword: there are many ways to tackle it and it all falls into place eventually.

- Don't be afraid to write in the book and add your own notes.

- Do review your work frequently. It helps to get somebody to test you – and they don't need to know German.

- If you can possibly learn with somebody else you will be able to help each other and practise the language together.

- Learning German may take more time than you thought. Just be patient and above all don't get angry with yourself.

Suggested study pattern

Each unit of the course consists of approximately sixteen pages in the book and fifteen minutes of recording. The first page of each unit will tell you what you are going to learn and will give some hints on language learning. You should follow the material at first in the order in which it is presented. As you progress with the course you may find that you evolve a method of study which suits you better – that's fine, but we suggest you keep to our pattern at least for the first two or three units or you may find you are not taking full advantage of all the possibilities offered by the material.

The book contains step-by-step instructions for working through the course: when to use the book on its own, when to use the recording on its own, when to use them both together and how to use them. On the recording our presenter will guide you through the various sections. Here is an outline of the pattern proposed:

Pronunciation notes

At the start of each unit there are some tips on pronunciation. One or two points are explained in the book, which are then picked up and practised on the recording. Remember that while good pronunciation of a foreign language is desirable, you will usually still be understood even if your accent is not quite accurate.

Conversations

Listen to each conversation, first without stopping the recording, and get a feel for the task ahead. Then go over it bit by bit in conjunction with the vocabulary and the notes. You should get into the habit of using the pause/stop and rewind buttons on your machine to give yourself time to think and to go over the conversation a number of times. Don't leave a conversation until you are confident that you have at least understood it. There are usually two or three conversations in each section, and three sets of conversations in a unit.

The conversations have all been recorded on location with native German speakers. They speak with the regionalisms, hesitations and corrections typical of spoken German. Don't be put off by this – we have made every effort to keep things clear and straightforward, and it is important to get used to German as it is spoken right from the start.

We have occasionally used the convention lit. = literally in the explanatory notes. This gives you a closer word-for-word translation alongside the 'correct' one to help your understanding.

Practice

This section contains a selection of listening, reading and speaking activities which focus your attention on the most important language in the unit. To do them you will need to work closely with the book and often use your machine – sometimes you are asked to write the answers to an exercise and then check them on the recording, at others to listen first and then fill in answers in the book. Again, use your pause/stop and rewind buttons to give yourself time to think and to answer questions.

You will also find practice exercises for speaking the main words and phrases which you have already heard and had explained. The book gives only an outline of the exercises, so you are just listening to the recordings and responding. Usually you will be asked to take part in a conversation where you hear a question or statement in German, followed by a suggestion in English as to what to say. You then give your reply in German and listen to see if you were right. You will probably have to go over these spoken exercises a few times before you get them absolutely correct.

Grammar

At this stage in a unit things should begin to fall into place and you are ready for the grammar section. If you really don't like grammar, you will still learn a lot without studying this part, but most people quite enjoy finding out how the language they are using actually works and how it is put together. In each unit we have selected just one or two important things. At the end of the book is a straightforward summary of the main grammar points.

Key words

This is a list of the most important words and phrases used in the unit. Pause at this section to see how much you can remember. Look first at the German and find the English equivalent. Then try it the other way round, from English into German. If you find there are some groups of words you have forgotten (don't worry – it happens to everybody!), turn back and have another look at the conversations and notes. These key words and phrases are likely to crop up later in the course so it's worth getting to grips with them before you leave a unit.

Did you know?

In this section you will be given some practical background information on customs, culture and life in German-speaking countries.

Answers

The answers to all the exercises can be found on the last page of each unit, if they have not already been given on the recording.

If you haven't learned languages using a recording before, just spend five minutes on Unit 1 getting used to the mechanics: try pausing the recording and see how long the rewind button needs to be pressed to recap on different length phrases and sections. Don't be shy – take every opportunity you can to speak German to German people and to listen to real German. Try watching German satellite television. It's even a good idea to talk to yourself in German as much as possible. Try describing what you see as you are travelling around, for instance. *Viel Glück! Good luck!*

At the back of the book

At the back of the book is a reference section which contains:

1 TALKING ABOUT YOURSELF

WHAT YOU WILL LEARN

▶ ways of saying hello
▶ introducing yourself and your family
▶ saying where you're from
▶ spelling out your name
▶ you will also be given information about addressing people when you meet them for the first time

BEFORE YOU BEGIN

Do read the general introduction to the course where you will find advice about how to study on your own and which study pattern to adopt. It is most important to find a pace that feels comfortable. Don't overdo things, it's better to work in short but regular spells than to force yourself through one long marathon session. Remember also to use the pause/stop and rewind buttons as much as you like. This will help reinforce the foreign sound and language patterns until they begin to sound quite familiar.

The Marienplatz, Munich

Pronunciation notes

ch

The sound for this unit is **ch**. This sound does not occur in the English language, except in some Scottish words such as 'loch'. It's quite a throaty sound which will be slightly coloured by the preceding sound: for example, **ich** (I) sounds a lot lighter than the very guttural **ach** (oh!). On the recording, you'll be practising the following words: **ich** (I) – **ach** (oh!) – **Tochter** (daughter).

Mrs Zarend introduces Mrs Rach and Mr Krause to each other

LISTEN FOR...

Frau	Mrs
Herr	Mr
guten Tag	good day

Frau Zarend	Frau Rach, Herr Krause.
Herr Krause	Guten Tag, Frau Rach.
Frau Rach	Guten Tag, Herr Krause.

Frau   Mrs. **Frau** is the title for both married and single women, so it can also be used as an equivalent to the English Ms. In other contexts, **Frau** can mean 'woman' or 'wife'. The use of **Fräulein** for Miss (*lit.* little woman) is becoming slightly dated.

Herr   Mr

guten Tag   (good day or hello) is the most common form of greeting, said on meeting or being introduced (as here), and often shortened to just **Tag**. Note that in German, you will find that many words begin with a capital letter. All nouns as well as proper names, names of countries (and of course the first word in a sentence) start with a capital letter.

 Frau Rach introduces herself and her daughter Jessica to Frau Mohn

LISTEN FOR...

ich bin	I am
meine Tochter	my daughter

Frau Rach	Ich bin Frau Rach, und das ist meine Tochter Jessica.
Frau Mohn	Hallo Jessica!
Jessica	Hallo!

ich bin   I am
das ist   that is, this is
meine Tochter   my daughter

To introduce your wife, you'd need to say **Das ist meine Frau**. If you wanted to introduce your husband, you would use the word **Mann**, which means both 'man' and 'husband': **das ist mein Mann**. And to introduce your son, you'd say **das ist mein Sohn**.

hallo   (hi, hello) is a lot more informal than **guten Tag**. In South Germany and Austria, you'll often hear **grüß Gott** (*lit.* may God greet you) instead, and in Switzerland **gruezi**.

The next part of the unit aims at reinforcing the language patterns you have come across in the conversations. All the necessary instructions are in the book. For some of the exercises you'll only need the book. However, the majority of the exercises will require both the book and the recording (they are marked with the symbol 🎧) Don't rush – there's always the pause button if things move too fast.

PRACTICE

1 **Herr** or **Frau**? On the recording, a number of people are being introduced. Which are the women and which are the men? Listen carefully and fill in the gaps below.

ANSWERS P. 16

_____ Mohn, _____ Krause, _____ Hoch,

_____ Bach, _____ Fromm, _____ Kranich,

_____ Fichte, _____ Thoma.

2 What's happening in these pictures? Study them and answer the questions below, in English.
   a. Who's called Hermann?
   b. Who introduces whom?
   c. What blunder is being made here?
   d. Is it a girl or a boy?

ANSWERS P. 16

3 Your turn to speak and practise introductions. Pretend that you are Herr Becker meeting Frau Krause. First, she will greet you and introduce her family. Then you will introduce your own family. Turn to the recording where Tom will prompt you. The sequence of this (and most other speaking exercises in this course) is as follows: Tom will say the sentence in English, then there will be a pause to give you a chance to press the pause button, think about what you are going to say in German, and then say it. After that, you should release the pause button and listen to the correct version on the recording. Then, Tom will give you the next prompt and the sequence continues as before.

You'll need phrases such as:
guten Tag / hallo / das ist / mein Mann / meine Tochter / mein Sohn

CONVERSATIONS 2

 Ruth introduces Mr Ramshaw to Frau Gallus

LISTEN FOR...

willkommen	welcome
aus London	from London

Ruth	Darf ich vorstellen, Herr Ramshaw aus London. Frau Gallus aus Kiel.
Frau Gallus	Guten Tag, Herr Ramshaw. Willkommen in Kiel.
Mr Ramshaw	Danke. Guten Tag, Frau Gallus.

darf ich vorstellen   may I introduce. There is no need to memorize this phrase for active usage at this stage, but it is useful to recognize it when you hear it.

aus London   from London

willkommen   welcome

danke   thank you

 Frau Bagan says good night and goodbye

LISTEN FOR...

gute Nacht	good night
auf Wiedersehen	goodbye
tschüs	cheerio

Ruth

Frau Bagan	Darf ich mich verabschieden, Frau Rach? Gute Nacht, Jessica.
Jessica	Gute Nacht.
Frau Bagan	Auf Wiedersehen, Frau Rach.
Frau Rach	Auf Wiedersehen.
Jessica	Tschüs.

darf ich mich verabschieden   may I say goodbye; again, no need to memorize this phrase at this stage but it's useful to be aware of its meaning.

gute Nacht   good night. Other useful terms are: **guten Abend**   good evening; **guten Morgen**   good morning. Note that in some cases we use **gute**, in others **guten**. At this early stage, it's sufficient to learn these expressions by heart. The details will be explained in a later unit.

auf Wiedersehen   (goodbye, see you again) is the standard form for saying goodbye.

tschüs   is a less formal way of saying goodbye used among friends and young people.

Talking about yourself   *Unit 1*

4 We have recorded four couples greeting each other. What time of the day is it? Listen to one couple at a time, stop the recording, tick the right box in the grid below, then go on. Replay the recording to double-check.

		day time	morning	evening	night
a.	first couple				
b.	second couple				
c.	third couple				
d.	fourth couple				

ANSWERS P. 16

5 Monsterwords. Each one represents a whole sentence. Mark the gaps between the words and rewrite the sentences in the spaces provided. Remember to use the appropriate capital and small letters.

DASISTHERRWILSONAUSLONDON _____

UNDDASISTFRAUVOLLMERTAUSBERLIN _____

GUTENMORGENHERRWILSON _____

WILLKOMMENINKIEL _____

ANSWERS P. 16 GUTENTAGFRAUVOLLMERT _____

6 Hello and goodbye. The jumbled up phrases below fall into two clear categories; sort them out and rewrite them under their correct headings.

darf ich vorstellen, guten Abend, auf Wiedersehen, guten Tag, tschüs, hallo, darf ich mich verabschieden, willkommen, gute Nacht, guten Morgen

greetings: _____

_____

goodbyes: _____

ANSWERS P. 16 _____

7 Your turn to speak. Turn to the recording. All you need to do this time is to respond to (i.e. repeat) the greetings that you'll hear.

CONVERSATION 3

> **Mr Marks tells Ruth that he's English but he lives in Munich (München)**

LISTEN FOR...

nein	no
ja	yes
Geschäftsreise	business trip
Urlaub	holiday

Ruth	Sind Sie aus München?
Mr Marks	Nein, ich bin Engländer.
Ruth	Aha! Sie sind aus England. Sind Sie aus London?
Mr Marks	Ja.
Ruth	Sind Sie auf Geschäftsreise oder sind Sie auf Urlaub?
Mr Marks	Nein, ich wohne hier.
Ruth	Arbeiten Sie hier?
Mr Marks	Ja.
Ruth	Und wo?
Mr Marks	Hier an der Universität.

sind Sie ...? are you ...? (**Sie sind** you are). More on questions in the notes below. Note that **Sie** meaning 'you' is the polite form of address and always spelt with a capital **S**.

München Munich

nein no

ich bin Engländer I am English (*lit.* I am Englishman). A woman would have said: **ich bin Engländerin**.

aus England from England

ja yes

auf Geschäftsreise on business (*lit.* on business trip)

oder or

auf Urlaub on holiday

ich wohne hier I live here

Arbeiten Sie hier? Do you work here? This is how you form basic questions. You take the usual word order in a German statement such as

Sie arbeiten hier (You work here) and change it round:

Arbeiten Sie hier? (*lit.* Work you here?).

Note that the English 'do' is not translated. Here's another example:

Sie wohnen hier (You live here) ▶ **Wohnen Sie hier?** (Do you live here?).

Useful question words are

wo where (Example: **Wo arbeiten Sie?** Where do you work?)

woher where from (Example: **Woher sind Sie?** Where are you from?)

hier here

an der Universität at the university

8 Who's on a business trip and who's on holiday? Listen to the recording and tick the right boxes in the grid below.

	Geschäftsreise	Urlaub
a. Matz		
b. Klingel		
c. Bagan		
d. Gallus		
e. Krause		

ANSWERS P. 16

9 A strange exchange. On the recording, Erich meets Dorit in Berlin and asks her some questions. You will find a transcript of the conversation below, however, the answers have got jumbled up. Put them back into their correct order and write them down next to the appropriate questions. Then listen to the recording to check the sequence.

Questions

Sind Sie aus Berlin? _____

Ah! Sind Sie Engländerin? _____

Sind Sie auf Geschäftsreise? _____

Und wo arbeiten Sie? _____

Answers
Ja, ich bin Engländerin.
Nein, ich bin aus England.
In Bristol an der Universität.
Nein, ich bin auf Urlaub.

10 Your turn to speak. Pretend you're Mr Miller. But before you start the recording, study the short passage below written by Mr Miller himself. It'll give you all the information you need. Keep your answers short.

Ich bin Paul Miller. Ich bin hier auf Geschäftsreise. Ich bin Engländer. Ich bin aus London, aber ich wohne in München. Ich arbeite an der Universität.

Munich

Little Anne learns the alphabet

Ruth	a, b, c, d	*Ruth*	o, p
Anne	a, b, c, d	*Anne*	o, p
Ruth	e, f, und g	*Ruth*	q, r, s, t
Anne	e, f, und g	*Anne*	q, r, s, t
Ruth	h, i, k, l	*Ruth*	u, v, w
Anne	h, i, k, l	*Anne*	u, v, w
Ruth	m, n, o, p	*Ruth*	x, y, z
Anne	n, m, o, p	*Anne*	... z
Ruth	m!	*Ruth*	x, y, z
Anne	m	*Anne*	x, y, z
Ruth	n!	*Ruth*	Jetzt kann ich das Abc.
Anne	n	*Anne*	Jetzt kann ich das Abc.

Jetzt kann ich das Abc.   Now I know (*lit.* can) the ABC. Note that Ruth left out the letter **j**. The umlauts **ä, ö, ü** will be practised in Unit 3.

Frau Bagan asks Jessica her name

> ## LISTEN FOR...
>
> **Wie heißt du?**   What's your name?

Frau Bagan	Wie heißt du?
Jessica	Jessica.
Frau Bagan	Jessica mit c oder mit k?
Jessica	Mit c. Großes j, e, s, s, i, c, a.

Wie heißt du?   What's your name? There are two ways of addressing someone in German: **Sie** and **du**. The familiar form **du** is used when talking to friends and children. **Sie** is used in all other cases when you need to be more formal. Should you wish to find out an adult's name, you'd have to ask:

Wie heißen Sie?   or **Wie ist Ihr Name?** (*lit.* How is your name?) What's your name?

Possible answers: **ich heiße Schmidt** or **mein Name ist Schmidt** my name is Schmidt.

Name   (sur)name

Vorname   first name

Little Anne

▶ *Ruth asks Jessica to spell a tricky word*

LISTEN FOR...

Straße   street
Gasse   alleyway, lane

Ruth	Jessica, wie schreibt man Straße?
Jessica	Großes s, t, r, a, scharfes s, e.
Ruth	Gut. Und wie schreibt man Gasse?
Jessica	Großes g, a, s, s, e.

Jessica

Wie schreibt man ...? How does one spell
(*lit.* write) ...? A very useful question to
memorize. And if you haven't quite
understood and would like somebody to repeat
something, you could ask: **Wie bitte?** What did you say? (*lit.* how please?)

Straße   street, road

scharfes s   (*lit.* sharp s) is the name for the **ß** symbol. It sounds exactly like **ss**
and is in fact replaced by **SS** when writing in capitals.

Gasse   alleyway, lane (for instance **Fischergasse** Fisherman's Lane)

A point to remember: when writing out a German address, the number should
always come after the name of the street, for example: **Goethestraße 8**. Here's an
example of an address written out in full:

> *Frau Rita Bach*
> *Seestraße 4*
> *D-48455 Bad Bentheim*

And this is how you should fill in a form – you'll need two more words:

PLZ   (short for **Postleitzahl**) postcode
Ort   place, town

Name	*Bach*
Vorname	*Rita*
Straße	*Seestraße 4*
PLZ Ort	*D-48455 Bad Bentheim*

PRACTICE

11 **Wie heißt du? Wie heißen Sie? Wie ist Ihr Name?** On the recording, a number of children and adults are being asked their names. The list below contains more names than you'll actually hear – mark off the ones that are being mentioned.

Felix, Stefan, Horst, Ernst, Urs, Florian, Hans, Marion, Katharina, Maria, Sandra, Gudrun, Helga, Maier, Müller, Schmitt, Becker, Häusler, Wietfeld

ANSWERS P. 16

12 Study the two cartoons and answer the questions – in English.

a. What's this conversation about? _____

ANSWERS P. 16

b. Does the woman live in Munich or Vienna? _____

13 And now for some German, Austrian and Swiss towns. Listen to the recording where Dorit and Erich are spelling them out for you. Write them down, try to read them aloud and compare your pronunciation with that of Dorit and Erich.

a. _____

b. _____

c. _____

d. _____

ANSWERS P. 16 e. _____

14

Instead of asking **Woher sind Sie?** (Where are you from?) people often ask **Woher kommen Sie?** (Where do you come from?). And another way of saying **ich bin aus England** would be **ich komme aus England**. You have already come across one country (**England**). Here are some more as introduced in the recording:

Deutschland	Germany	**Italien**	Italy
Österreich	Austria	**Portugal**	Portugal
die Schweiz	Switzerland	**Amerika**	America
Spanien	Spain	**die USA**	USA
die Türkei	Turkey	**Kanada**	Canada

ANSWERS P. 16

On the recording, Herr Gonzales is trying to introduce himself and three more people to Herr Maier. But things aren't going as smoothly as they might. Where do they all come from? Listen carefully and complete the name tags below.

Herr Gonzales

Frau Pamplona

Herr Klein

Frau Markgraf

15

Erich has offered to fill in a form for a lady. Listen to the lady's details on the recording, and complete the form below.

New word: **eins** one (1)

Name _____

Vorname _____

Straße _____

Ort _____

ANSWERS P. 16

16

Your turn to speak and give your own details. Let's pretend you are Julia Morse from Lewes in Sussex. Turn to the recording where Tom will prompt you. Be prepared to do some spelling.

You will find a grammar section in each unit. It will be as short and straightforward as possible. Its aim is to give you the basics of the language so that you will have firm ground to build on and understand how the language works. However, at this early stage, mistakes do not matter all that much as long as you can make yourself understood.

To some learners, grammar seems rather off-putting because of its rigid patterns and abstract terms. In this course, we have tried to use these as little as possible, but certain grammatical terms just cannot be avoided, such as 'noun', 'gender', 'article' etc. You will find explanations of these terms in the Grammar summary on p. 235.

The verb *sein* (to be)

This is one of the most important verbs. In Unit 1 you have already come across several forms. Like the English 'to be', **sein** is irregular. Here are all the forms of its present tense:

ich bin	I am
du bist	you are
er/sie/es ist	he/she/it is
wir sind	we are
ihr seid	you are
sie/Sie sind	they/you are

Note

... the different ways of saying 'you are'

du bist	to one friend or child
Sie sind	to one adult you don't know very well
ihr seid	to more than one friend or child
Sie sind	to more than one adult

Note

... the different meanings that **sie/Sie** can have. Here are three examples:

Ja, sie ist Engländerin.	Yes, she is English.
Wo sind sie?	Where are they?
Wo sind Sie?	Where are you?

Note

... the most important forms for active usage

Sie sind	you are
ich bin	I am
er/sie/es ist	he/she/it is

17 Translate

a. Ich bin Frau Rach.

_____

b. Das ist meine Tochter.

_____

c. Sie sind aus England.

_____

d. Sind sie auf Urlaub?

_____

e. Wie ist Ihr Name, bitte?

_____

f. Ich bin Engländer.

_____

ANSWERS P. 16

18 Fill in **bin**, **ist** or **sind**.

a. *Herr Horn*: Guten Abend. _____ Sie Herr Beck?

b. *Herr Beck*: Ja, ich _____ Herr Beck. Und Sie?

c. *Herr Horn*: Mein Name _____ Horn.

d. *Herr Beck*: _____ Sie von hier?

e. *Herr Horn*: Nein, ich _____ aus Berlin.

ANSWERS P. 16

19 Match up the German phrases with their correct English translations. Write them into the spaces provided.

a. This is my daughter.

_____

b. This is my wife.

_____

c. I am (an) English(woman).

_____

d. Are you on a business trip?

_____

e. Is that your husband?

_____

f. Where are you from?

_____

g. I am from Kiel.

_____

A. Das ist meine Frau.
B. Sind Sie auf Geschäftsreise?
C. Ich bin aus Kiel.
D. Ist das Ihr Mann?
E. Das ist meine Tochter.
F. Ich bin Engländerin.
G. Woher sind Sie?

ANSWERS P. 16

Flensburg harbour

KEY WORDS

Here are the most important words and phrases which you have either met in the conversations or which have been introduced in the notes. Make sure that you know them before you go onto the next unit. You could try and practise by reading them aloud.

Herr	Mr
Frau	Mrs; wife
Fräulein	Miss
guten Tag	hello; good day
guten Morgen	good morning
guten Abend	good evening
gute Nacht	good night
auf Wiedersehen	goodbye
tschüs	cheerio, bye (*colloquial*)
Das/Dies ist ...	This is ...
meine Frau	my wife
mein Mann	my husband
mein Sohn	my son

Wie heißen Sie?	What's your name?
Wie ist Ihr Name?	
Wie bitte?	What did you say?
Ich heiße ...	My name is ...
Mein Name ist ...	
Woher kommen Sie?	Where do you come from?
Ich komme aus London	I come from London
Sind Sie aus ...	Are you from ...
München?	Munich?
England?	England?
(Ja/Nein,) ich bin aus ...	(Yes/No,) I am from ...
London	London
Deutschland	Germany
Ich bin Engländer	I am English (if you're a man)
Ich bin Engländerin	I am English (if you're a woman)
Ich bin auf ...	I am on ...
Urlaub	holiday
Geschäftsreise	business
Wo wohnen Sie?	Where do you live?
Ich wohne ...	I live ...
hier	here
in Ulm	in Ulm
in London	in London
danke (schön)	thank you (very much)
bitte	please, you're welcome
jetzt	now

When meeting people ...

Handshakes

... are a matter of personal taste but still quite common in a social or business context and it would be rather rude to ignore them. Strictly speaking, the older person or the lady should hold out their hand first, but in practice it does not always happen like that. Don't worry if no hand is forthcoming – some people think handshakes are rather old-fashioned. Among closer acquaintances and friends the French 'peck' on the cheek (or rather, in the air) seems to be becoming increasingly popular.

First names

... are best avoided as an opening gambit, unless of course you are speaking to a child. On the whole, the use of first names is less common in German- than in English-speaking countries. To start with, it's best to stick to **Herr** and **Frau**. In formal situations, it is considered polite to use a title if appropriate: **Herr Doktor Maier**, **Frau Professor Müller**. And if you're not sure about the person's name or how to pronounce it, you can simply say: **Herr Doktor**, **Frau Professor**.

Common names

... can often be traced back to old trades or titles, as in English; for example **Müller** (miller), **Schmidt** (smith), **König** (king). Double names seem to be on the increase as more and more women are retaining their maiden names alongside their husband's when they marry. Christian names are becoming a lot more international; you'll come across **Natascha**, **Nathalie**, **Nicole**, **Tristan** or **Sascha** alongside the more traditional German names such as **Maria** (Mary), **Hans** (John, Jack) and **Frederike**.

Sie *or* du?

... it's advisable to stick to **Sie**, unless you are talking to a child. If people ask you to address them with **du** and by their first names it's usually meant as an offer of real friendship. Sometimes members of specific groups, such as mountaineers, sailors, actors or factory workers, call each other **du** straight away. And young people at college or university seem to have abandoned the use of **Sie** altogether.

AND FINALLY...

It's time to practise the most important structures in Unit 1. Before you turn to the recording, take another look at the key words.

20 Pretend you're Mr Kline from Rye in Sussex. You're on holiday with your son Max. Turn to the recording where you'll be asked a few questions about yourself. These structures will be useful: **guten Tag / ich bin / das ist / auf Urlaub / mein Sohn / aus Rye / in England**

Husum harbour

ANSWERS

EXERCISE 1
Herr Mohn, Frau Krause, Frau Hoch, Herr Bach, Herr Fromm, Herr Kranich, Frau Fichte, Frau Thoma.

EXERCISE 2
(a) the husband **(b)** Mr Herberti introduces his wife **(c)** Mrs Simsalabim introduces the little boy as her husband ('mein Mann') – she should have said: 'das ist mein Sohn' **(d)** a boy

EXERCISE 4
(a) morning **(b)** evening **(c)** daytime **(d)** night

EXERCISE 5
Das ist Herr Wilson aus London. Und das ist Frau Vollmert aus Berlin. Guten Morgen Herr Wilson. Willkommen in Kiel. Guten Tag Frau Vollmert.

EXERCISE 6
greetings: darf ich vorstellen; guten Abend; guten Tag; hallo; willkommen; guten Morgen; all others are goodbyes.

EXERCISE 8
Urlaub: **a, b, d.** Geschäftsreise: **c, e**

EXERCISE 11
Felix; Ernst; Florian; Urs; Katharina; Maria; Gudrun; Müller; Schmitt; Häusler; Wietfeld

EXERCISE 12
(a) The passenger on the left asks Mr Martin where he's from and he tells him he's from London. **(b)** She lives in Munich but works in Vienna.

EXERCISE 13
(a) Ulm **(b)** Salzburg **(c)** Leipzig **(d)** Basel **(e)** Wien

EXERCISE 14
Gonzales: Portugal; Pamplona: Italien; Klein: Österreich; Markgraf: Deutschland

EXERCISE 15
Name: Macke; Vorname: Anina; Straße: Marktgasse 1; Ort: Waldsee

EXERCISE 17
(a) I am Mrs Rach. **(b)** This (or That) is my daughter. **(c)** They (or You) are from England. **(d)** Are they on holiday? **(e)** What's your name, please? **(f)** I am English.

EXERCISE 18
(a) Sind **(b)** bin **(c)** ist **(d)** Sind **(e)** bin

EXERCISE 19
(a) E **(b)** A **(c)** F **(d)** B **(e)** D **(f)** G **(g)** C

2 YOURSELF AND OTHERS

WHAT YOU WILL LEARN

► providing basic information about yourself, your job and your family
► saying what languages you speak
► understanding and using the numbers from 1 to 20
► you will also be given some background information about Germany

BEFORE YOU BEGIN

As you make further progress in German, you'll meet quite a few 'friends' that will help you along the way: words that sound fairly similar in German and English and often share the same linguistic roots. You'll come across some of them in Unit 2; for example **Familie** = family, **Freund** = friend, **Monat** = month and **Jahr** = year. Some numbers will also sound fairly similar. Concentrate on these words first because they'll be easy to learn and help you to build up confidence and a good stock of basic vocabulary.

Pronunciation notes

r

If you wish to sound really genuine you'll need to practise the German **r**. It's a real giveaway, both for foreigners trying to speak German and for Germans trying to speak a foreign language. The German **r** tends to be somewhat guttural, except in a few dialects (such as Bavarian) where it is rolled rather dramatically. However, the **r** is hardly pronounced at all if it's right at the end of a word. Unit 2 will give you plenty of chances to become familiar with this very distinctive German sound. On the recording you'll start by practising the following words:

Frau (woman) – **drei** (three) – **Sprache** (language): here the **r** is clearly pronounced.
Schwester (sister) – **Kinder** (children) – **Zimmer** (room): here the **r** is hardly heard at all.
Bruder (brother) – **Lehrer** (teacher) – **Frankfurter** (Frankfurter): here, the first **r** is clearly pronounced, whereas the second **r** is more or less dropped.

äu/eu

You will find that both **äu** and **eu** are pronounced as 'oi' in the English word 'coin'. Examples are **Freund** (friend) and **Fräulein** (Miss).

CONVERSATIONS

 Ruth asks Frau Zarend about her family

LISTEN FOR...		Ruth	Haben Sie Familie?
Familie	family	Frau Zarend	Nein, ich habe einen Freund.
Freund	(boy) friend		

Haben Sie Familie? Have you got/do you have a family? (*lit*. have you (got) family?) Note that the 'a' is not translated.

ich habe einen Freund I have a boy friend; **Freund** can mean both boy friend and friend. Similarly, **eine Freundin** a (girl) friend.

 Ruth asks Herr Hansen about his family

LISTEN FOR...		Ruth	Haben Sie Familie?
seit vierzehn Jahren	for fourteen years	Herr Hansen	Ja, ich hab' Familie, bin seit vierzehn (14) Jahren verheiratet und hab' eine Tochter.
verheiratet	married		

(ich) bin seit vierzehn Jahren verheiratet I've been married for fourteen years. **Ich bin verheiratet** I am married. If you want to say you are single: **ich bin ledig** I am single.

seit vierzehn Jahren for (*lit*. since) fourteen years. The construction **seit** + present tense is used when you make a statement about past actions which are still continuing into the present. Here's another example: **ich lerne seit zwei Jahren Deutsch** I've been learning German for two years (and still am).

hab' instead of **habe**: in spoken German the **e** at the end of **habe** is frequently dropped.

Note the different endings for the German word for 'a' in the last two clips: **ich habe einen Freund** but **(ich) hab' eine Tochter**. At this stage, it's best to learn these phrases by heart. Their pattern will be explained later on. Similarly, **ich habe einen Bruder** I have a brother, but **ich habe eine Schwester** I have a sister.

 And how about Frau Mohn?

LISTEN FOR...		Ruth	Haben Sie Familie?
vier	four	Frau Mohn	Ja, ich habe zwei (2) Kinder. Aber ich bin seit vier (4) Monaten geschieden.
zwei	two		
geschieden	divorced		

zwei Kinder two children. Note also: **ich habe keine Kinder** I have no children.

aber ich bin seit vier Monaten geschieden but I have been divorced for four months now

PRACTICE

1 Taking notes. On the recording, three people are being asked about their respective families. Try to pick up the details and tick the appropriate boxes below.

	a. Frau Stein	b. Herr Matz	c. Frau Rümmele
verheiratet			
geschieden			
ledig			
Freund			
Freundin			
Kind/Kinder			

ANSWERS P. 32

2 A crossword puzzle

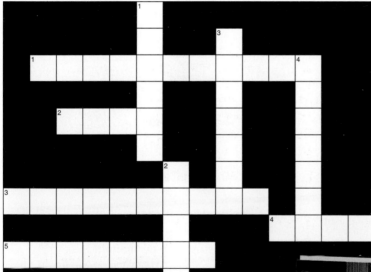

Down
1. man but not the husband
2. neither married nor divorced
3. it can have many members or just a few
4. close relative – female

Across
1. neither single nor divorced
2. a child but not a daughter
3. no longer married
4. wife, woman and Mrs in one
5. woman but not wife

ANSWERS P. 32

3 Your turn to speak and remember the various family words. Turn to the recording where Tom will prompt you.

What does Frau Hölk do for a living?

LISTEN FOR...

Beruf	profession
Verkäuferin	shop assistant

Ruth	Was sind Sie von Beruf?
Frau Hölk	Ich bin Verkäuferin.

Was sind Sie von Beruf? What's your job? (*lit.*What are you by profession?)

Verkäuferin (female) shop assistant. A male shop assistant would have said: **ich bin Verkäufer**. In German, nouns denoting occupations often add **-in** when describing a woman. For instance:

Student ▶ Studentin (student)
Sekretär ▶ Sekretärin (secretary)
Direktor ▶ Direktorin (director)
Schüler ▶ Schülerin (pupil)
Arbeiter ▶ Arbeiterin (worker)

Note also **ich bin arbeitslos** I am unemployed (*lit.* workless).

And here are three more occupations

LISTEN FOR...

Postbeamter	post office official
Bankkauffrau	bank clerk
Rentner	pensioner

Ruth	Was sind Sie von Beruf?
Herr Maier	Von Beruf bin ich Postbeamter.
	* * *
Ruth	Was sind Sie von Beruf?
Frau Zarend	Ich bin Bankkauffrau.
	* * *
Ruth	Was sind Sie von Beruf?
Herr Schmid	Ja, ich bin jetzt Rentner.

Postbeamter (male) post office official. **Beamter** is used for anyone employed by the state in a permanent pensionable position. A woman would have said: **ich bin Postbeamtin**. Note that Herr Maier has switched round the usual word order and started his sentence with **von Beruf** to place more emphasis on his job. This has also influenced the word order in the rest of the sentence. (More on word order on p. 239.)

Bankkauffrau (female) bank clerk; a male would be **Bankkaufmann**

Rentner (male) pensioner; a woman would have said **Rentnerin**.

ja is used here in much the same way as 'well' in English.

PRACTICE

4 Sex changes. Turn them into women. For example:
Student ▶ Studentin

Verkäufer ▶ _____

Bankkaufmann ▶ _____

Rentner ▶ _____

Schüler ▶ _____

Arbeiter ▶ _____

ANSWERS P. 32 Beamter ▶ _____

5 True or false? Study the German text and tick the correct statements below.

Mein Name ist Linda Gruber. Ich bin verheiratet und habe zwei Kinder. Von Beruf bin ich Postbeamtin, mein Mann ist Bankkaufmann. Ich arbeite in Bonn, mein Mann ist arbeitslos.

a. Linda is married ☐

divorced ☐

b. She works in a bank ☐

for the post office ☐

c. She has two children ☐

four children ☐

d. She works in Bonn and her husband is out of a job. ☐

ANSWERS P. 32 lives in Bonn and her husband works in Bonn too. ☐

6 Your turn to speak. This time you're pretending to be Linda Gruber from Exercise 5. Study the passage about her, then turn to the recording.

Talking languages

LISTEN FOR...

Lehrerin	teacher
sprechen	to speak
Sprachen	languages

Ruth	Was sind Sie von Beruf?
Frau Bagan	Ich bin Lehrerin. Ich gebe Englisch und Russisch.
	* * *
Ruth	Sprechen Sie Englisch?
Frau Mohn	Ja, ich spreche Englisch.
	* * *
Ruth	Sprechen Sie andere Sprachen?
Frau Gallus	Ja, Englisch und Spanisch.

Lehrerin   (female) teacher ; a male teacher would be **Lehrer**

ich gebe   here: I teach (*lit.* I give)

Russisch   Russian (**Rußland** Russia); *cf* **Deutsch** German (**Deutschland** Germany)

Here are some more countries and their languages:

China ▶ **Chinesisch** (Chinese)

Schweden ▶ **Schwedisch** (Swedish)

Italien ▶ **Italienisch** (Italian)

Portugal ▶ **Portugiesisch** (Portuguese)

Frankreich ▶ **Französisch** (French)

Spanien ▶ **Spanisch** (Spanish)

Amerika ▶ **Amerikanisch** (American English)

Japan ▶ **Japanisch** (Japanese)

Türkei ▶ **Türkisch** (Turkish)

sprechen   to speak
ich spreche I speak
Sie sprechen you speak (polite form).
Sprechen Sie Deutsch?   Do you speak German?
Ja, ein wenig. Yes, a little. More on verb endings in the grammar section.

andere Sprachen   other languages

7 Fill in the correct languages.

a. Ich komme aus England. Ich spreche _____

b. Ich komme aus Rußland. Ich spreche _____

c. Ich komme aus Deutschland. Ich spreche _____

ANSWERS P. 32 **d.** Ich komme aus China. Ich spreche _____

8 Missing letters. Write them in correctly and you'll get the name of a famous German town.

J A – A N I S C H

P – R T U G I E S I S C H

I – A L I E N I S C H

F R A N Z Ö – I S C H

S C H W E – I S C H

S P – N I S C H

A – E R I K A N I S C H

ANSWERS P. 32   MYSTERY WORD: _____

9 Your turn to speak. You're trying to outdo Dorit by speaking even more languages than she does. Tom will prompt you on the recording. Have your languages ready …

> ## At the railway station. A loudspeaker is being tested

LISTEN FOR...			
eins	1	sechs	6
zwo	2	sieben	7
drei	3	acht	8
vier	4	neun	9
fünf	5	zehn	10

zwei and **zwo** both mean 'two'; sometimes **zwo** is used in spoken German to make sure you don't confuse **zwei** and **drei**, especially when the sound is not very clear, for instance over the phone or a loudspeaker.

Note also **null** (nought).

> ## Frau Bagan asks Jessica her age and how long she's been living in London

LISTEN FOR...
alt   old

Frau Bagan	Wie alt bist du?
Jessica	Acht, fast neun.
Frau Bagan	Seit wann wohnst du in London?
Jessica	Seit fünf Jahren.

wie alt   how old; **ich bin acht (Jahre alt)** I am eight (years old)
fast   nearly
wohnst du ...?   do you live ...? This is the question form of **du wohnst** you live (see grammar section for further details on verb endings).
Seit wann wohnst du ...?   How long have you been living ...? (*lit.* Since when do you live ...?) Note again the use of the present tense after **seit** as in Conversations 1.

10 On the recording, a receptionist is checking a list of names against their respective room numbers. Write them down in the spaces provided.

New vocabulary:
Zimmernummer   room number

a. Müller	
b. Schmitt	
c. Wolf	
d. Haller	
e. Dron	

ANSWERS P. 32

11 Study the list of telephone numbers below. On the recording, Dorit will dial some of them – but not all. Tick off the numbers she's dialling.

Abel	12369	☐
Dron	11697	☐
Groß	12345	☐
Haller	73780	☐
Müller	22658	☐
Dittmar	22857	☐
Schmitt	34957	☐
Wolf	30859	☐

ANSWERS P. 32

12 And now it's your turn to call up a few numbers from the list provided in Exercise 11. Turn to the recording where Dorit will give you a name and wait for you to say the number – then you'll hear Erich repeat the number as you should have said it.

▶ *In the Hotel Erkenhof in Kiel, Frau Mohn is sorting out the morning papers and magazines for the various rooms*

Frau Mohn	Eine Kieler Nachrichten, Zimmernummer elf (11).
	Eine Kieler Nachrichten für Zimmernummer neunzehn (19).
	Einmal Die Zeit, Zimmer zwölf (12).
	Einmal Die Welt, Zimmer siebzehn (17).
	Und eine Frankfurter, Zimmer fünfzehn (15).

Kieler Nachrichten   a daily local paper in Kiel (**Nachrichten** news)
für   for
einmal   once (similarly **zweimal** twice, **dreimal** three times)
Die Zeit   a national weekly (**Zeit** time)
Die Welt   a national daily paper (**Welt** world)
Frankfurter   short for **Frankfurter Allgemeine Zeitung** or **FAZ**, a conservative national daily, not to be confused with the Frankfurter Rundschau, also a national daily, but rather more social-liberal in outlook.

Frankfurter Rundschau
60266 Frankfurt am Main
Telefon 069/21991
Telefax 069/2199-421
Anzeigenannahme Telefon 069

Frankfurter Allgemeine
THEMEN VOM TAGE

DIE ZEIT
WOCHENZEITUNG FÜR POLITIK · WIRTSCHAFT · HANDEL UND KULTUR

Neue Zürcher Zeitung
INTERNATIONALE AUSGABE

... and here are the numbers from 11 to 20:

11	elf	16	sechzehn (note that the **s** in **sechs** is dropped)
12	zwölf	17	siebzehn (note that the **en** in **sieben** is dropped)
13	dreizehn	18	achtzehn
14	vierzehn	19	neunzehn
15	fünfzehn	20	zwanzig

13 Which are the seven lucky numbers? Listen to the recording and make a ring round them.

11 12 13 14 15 16 17 18 19 20

ANSWERS P. 32

14 How long? (**Seit wann?**) How old? (**Wie alt?**) Herr Händle is being interviewed about his personal details. Listen to the recording and take notes.

a.   Hans has been married for ..... years.
b.   He has ..... children.
c.   His daughter is ..... years old.
d.   His son is ..... years old.
e.   His baby is ..... months old.
f.   He has been working for the post office for ..... years.

ANSWERS P. 32

g.   He has been living in Starnberg for ..... months now.

15 And now it's your turn to come up with some numbers. Of course, this is not a test of arithmetic; we simply want to give you a chance to practise some German numbers. Switch on the recording where Erich will prompt you. He might say, for example, **neun plus zehn** and then pause for you to say **neunzehn**. Check your answers with those of Dorit.

ANSWERS P. 32

GRAMMAR AND EXERCISES

The verb *haben* (to have)

Along with **sein** (to be), **haben** is the most important German verb. Both are irregular, just like 'to be' and 'to have' in English. This means that they don't quite follow the rules for regular verbs endings as set out below but come up with different forms that are best learnt by heart. Pay special attention to the **ich** and **Sie** forms of the verb **haben** which are the ones you will probably need most.

Below are all the forms of **haben** in the present tense:

ich habe	I have	
du hast	you have (*singular*)	
er	he	
sie } **hat**	she }	has
es	it	
wir haben	we have	
ihr habt	you have (*plural*)	
sie haben	they have	
Sie haben	you have (*polite form*)	

Regular verb endings

Luckily, most verb endings are regular and follow the basic pattern below. We'll use **wohnen** (to live) as an example:

ich wohne	I live	
du wohnst	you live (*singular*)	
er	he	
sie } **wohnt**	she }	lives
es	it	
wir wohnen	we live	
ihr wohnt	you live (*plural*)	
sie wohnen	they live	
Sie wohnen	you live (*polite form*)	

The rule is: take the main part of a verb (the stem) and add the appropriate endings as underlined above.

To get the main part or stem of a verb take the basic form you'll find in the dictionary (the infinitive), for example **wohnen**, and take off the ending **-en**. You're then left with the stem. Here's another example:

sagen	infinitive (to say)
sag-	stem
ich sage	I say
du sagst	you say (*singular*)
er	he
sie } **sagt**	she } says
es	it
wir sagen	we say
ihr sagt	you say (*plural*)
sie sagen	they say
Sie sagen	you say (*polite form*)

There are some minor variations of this pattern, but these are mostly because of awkward spelling or pronunciation.

16 Fill in the right forms of **haben** and translate the sentences into English.

> haben haben haben habe habe hast hat hat

a. H_____Sie Familie?

_____

b. Ja, ich h_____ einen Sohn.

_____

c. H_____ du eine Schwester?

_____

d. Nein, ich h_____ einen Bruder.

_____

e. H_____ Frau Maier ein Kind?

_____

f. Nein, sie h_____ zwei Kinder.

_____

g. H_____ Sie Kinder?

_____

h. Ja, wir h_____ drei Kinder.

ANSWERS P. 32

17 Write out all the forms of the verb **kommen** (to come) in the present tense, together with their translations. Follow the same pattern as set out with the verb **sagen**.

ich komme (I come) _____

du _____

_____

_____

_____

_____

_____

ANSWERS P. 32

18 Verbs galore. Choose them from the box below and write them in their appropriate places.

bin sind arbeiten gebe* kommt sprechen arbeite

a. Frau Bagan, _____ Sie Lehrerin?

b. Ja, ich _____ Lehrerin.

c. Ich _____ Englisch und Russisch.

d. Und _____ Sie auch Spanisch?

e. Ja, mein Mann _____ aus Spanien.

f. _____ Sie hier in Kiel?

g. Ja, ich _____ hier in Kiel.

* Remember **geben** normally means 'to give' but is used in this specific context as 'to teach'.

ANSWERS P. 32

KEY WORDS

Haben Sie Familie?	Have you got a family?
Ja, ich habe ...	Yes, I've got ...
eine Frau	a wife
einen Mann	a husband
eine Tochter	a daughter
einen Sohn	a son
einen Freund	a (boy) friend
eine Freundin	a (girl) friend
eine Schwester	a sister
einen Bruder	a brother
zwei/drei Kinder	two/three children
Nein, ich habe kein Kind	No, I haven't got a child
Ich bin ...	I am ...
verheiratet	married
ledig	single
geschieden	divorced
Wie alt bist du?	How old are you?
Ich bin acht (Jahre alt)	I am eight (years old)
Seit wann ...	How long ... (*lit.* Since when)
wohnen Sie hier?	have you been living here?
arbeiten Sie in Ulm?	have you been working in Ulm?
seit vierzehn Jahren	for fourteen years
seit vier Monaten	for four months
Was sind Sie von Beruf?	What's your job?
Ich bin ...	I am a ...
Verkäufer/in	shop assistant
Rentner/in	pensioner
Postbeamter/Postbeamtin	post office official
Bankkaufmann/Bankkauffrau	male/female bank clerk
Lehrer/in	teacher
Student/in	student
Schüler/in	pupil
Direktor/in	director
Sekretär/in	secretary
arbeitslos	out of work, unemployed
Sprechen Sie ...?	Do you speak ...?
Ja, ich spreche ...	Yes, I speak ...
Englisch	English
Deutsch	German
Französisch	French
Spanisch	Spanish
Japanisch	Japanese
Russisch	Russian
Chinesisch	Chinese
Italienisch	Italian

... and don't forget the Numbers 1–20 as set out in Conversations 4 and 5

GERMAN is the official language of the Federal Republic of Germany, Austria, Switzerland (together with French, Italian and Romansh), and the principality of **Liechtenstein**. Some German is also spoken in the **Elsaß** region (Alsace, in France) and in **Südtirol** (South Tyrol), a region in northern Italy.

The Federal Republic is the largest of the German-speaking countries with an area of 356,945 square kilometres and a population of 81 million (UK 244,000 square kilometres, 56 million inhabitants).

The Federal Republic is called 'Federal' because it consists of a federation of fifteen **Länder** (states). **Bayern** (Bavaria) is the largest in area, but **Nordrhein-Westfalen** (North Rhine-Westphalia) is the most populous. The **Ruhrgebiet** (an area east of Düsseldorf along the river **Ruhr**) is the largest single industrial region in Europe, producing a third of Germany's exports (mainly machinery).

There are several million foreigners living in the Federal Republic. Most of them are **Gastarbeiter** (immigrant workers, *lit.* 'guest workers') from Turkey, Italy, Spain, the former Yugoslavia and Greece, and more recently from Eastern Europe.

The Federal Republic has borders with nine countries: Poland, the Czech Republic, Austria, Switzerland, France, Belgium, Luxembourg, the Netherlands and Denmark.

AND FINALLY...

19 Read the following passage about Herr Motte and then turn to the recording and pretend to be Herr Motte. For this exercise, it will help to leave the book open.

Ich heiße Michael Motte. Ich bin verheiratet und habe einen Sohn. Er heißt Klaus und ist 19 Jahre alt. Klaus ist seit 3 Monaten Student an der Universität. Ich arbeite seit 13 Jahren bei Procter und Gamble. Wir wohnen seit 5 Jahren in Frankfurt.

ANSWERS

EXERCISE 1
(a) verheiratet; (zwei) Kinder (b) (vier) Kinder; geschieden; Freundin (c) ledig; Freund

EXERCISE 2
down: 1. Freund 2. ledig 3. Familie 4. Tochter;
across: 1. verheiratet 2. Sohn 3. geschieden 4. Frau 5. Freundin

EXERCISE 4
Verkäuferin; Bankkauffrau; Rentnerin; Schülerin; Arbeiterin; Beamtin

EXERCISE 5
(a) married (b) post office (c) two children (d) works in Bonn and her husband is out of a job

EXERCISE 7
(a) Englisch (b) Russisch (c) Deutsch (d) Chinesisch

EXERCISE 8
Japanisch; Portugiesisch; Italienisch; Französisch; Schwedisch; Spanisch; Amerikanisch; MYSTERY WORD: Potsdam

EXERCISE 10
(a) 3 (b) 2 (c) 7 (d) 9 (e) 4

EXERCISE 11
You should have ticked off: Abel; Haller; Dittmar; Schmitt

EXERCISE 13
11 – 12 – 14 – 15 – 17 – 19 – 20

EXERCISE 14
(a) 20 (b) 3 (c) 14 (d) 9 (e) 11 (f) 15 (g) 7

EXERCISE 16
(a) Haben Do you have a family? (b) habe Yes, I have a son. (c) Hast Do you have a sister? (d) habe No, I have a brother. (e) Hat Does Frau Meier have a/one child? (f) hat No, she has two children. (g) Haben Do you have (any) children? (h) haben Yes, we have three children.

EXERCISE 17
ich komme ▶ I come; du kommst ▶ you come; er/sie/es kommt ▶ he/she/it comes; wir kommen ▶ we come; ihr kommt ▶ you come; sie/Sie kommen ▶ they/you come

EXERCISE 18
(a) sind (b) bin (c) gebe (d) sprechen (e) kommt (f) Arbeiten (g) arbeite

3 GETTING INFORMATION

WHAT YOU WILL LEARN

▶ changing traveller's cheques
▶ basic telephone skills
▶ booking a room at a hotel
▶ you will also read about different types of accommodation and places where you can change your money

BEFORE YOU BEGIN

When learning new words and phrases, it will be helpful to make a distinction between active and passive knowledge. For example, you will need to be able to ask the telephone operator a few basic questions (active knowledge). You will need to understand what he or she is saying in return, but you are unlikely to have to use these phrases yourself (passive knowledge). So to economize on what you try to remember go for phrases you are most likely to need to say, and concentrate on those first. Then develop strategies for recognizing the others. Eventually and with lots more practice, some of the passive skills will no doubt turn into active ones without your even noticing it.

Pronunciation notes

ä
The easiest umlaut to pronounce is **ä**. It's the same sound as in the English word 'fair'.

ö
For the **ö** (and **ü**) sound you will need to purse your lips and pout. Try the following experiment: say a long German **e** first, as in the word **Lehrer** (teacher) and while you keep saying it start pursing your lips and you can actually hear the **e** turning into an **ö**.

ü
The same principle applies to the **ü**: start out with a long **i** sound, as in the German word **hier**, purse your lips while holding the tone loud and clear and you should be getting a perfect **ü**.

Words to practise those sounds in this unit will be: **Währung** (currency); **ich möchte** (I want); **danke schön** (thank you); **fünfzig** (fifty) and – a double challenge – **Frühstück** (breakfast).

▶ *At the bank, Ruth wants to cash some traveller's cheques*

LISTEN FOR...

Reiseschecks traveller's cheques
Währung currency
Kasse cash desk

Ruth	Guten Tag.
Frau Zarend	Guten Tag.
Ruth	Ich möchte gerne Reiseschecks einlösen, bitte.
Frau Zarend	Welche Währung haben Sie?
Ruth	D-Mark. Bitte sehr.
Frau Zarend	Danke. Gehen Sie bitte zur Kasse.
Ruth	Danke schön.

ich möchte gerne Reiseschecks einlösen I'd like to cash some traveller's cheques. (**ich möchte** I'd like to; **der Reisescheck** traveller's cheque; **einlösen** to cash.) The word order in a sentence with two verbs (here **möchte** and **einlösen**) will be explained on page 239.

Welche Währung haben Sie? Which currency do you have? (**die Währung** currency). Ruth has taken traveller's cheques in German marks (**D-Mark**) to save on bank charges.

gehen Sie bitte zur Kasse please go to the cash desk (**die Kasse** cash desk or till). Note that the word order in a request or an instruction is the same as in a question: **gehen Sie** (*lit.* go you).

bitte sehr is often said when handing something over (*cf* 'there you go' or 'here you are')

danke schön many thanks (**schön** normally means 'beautiful')

▶ *At the cash desk*

LISTEN FOR...

in kleinen Scheinen in small notes

Wie möchten Sie's? short for **Wie möchten Sie es?** How would you like it?
in kleinen Scheinen in small notes (**der Schein** note)
fünfzig (50), einhundert (100) ... Frau Kolb is handing out the money in 50 mark notes.
danke auch short for **ich danke auch** I thank (you) too (**auch** too)

Frau Kolb	Wie möchten Sie's?
Ruth	In kleinen Scheinen, bitte.
Frau Kolb	Fünfzig (50), einhundert (100), fünfzig (50), zwohundert (200), zwohundertzwo (202). Bitte sehr!
Ruth	Danke schön.
Frau Kolb	Danke auch. Auf Wiedersehen.

Here are the numbers as read out on the recording:
(ein)hundert (100); **zweihundert** (200); **dreihundert** (300); **vierhundert** (400); **fünfhundert** (500); **sechshundert** (600); **siebenhundert** (700); **achthundert** (800); **neunhundert** (900); **(ein) tausend** (1000)

PRACTICE

1

Zahlendiktat   Number dictation. On the recording Dorit will pronounce a series of numbers between 100 and 1000.
Write them down (in figures only).

_____

_____

ANSWERS P. 46

2

A busy day at the bank. What's being exchanged? Make a ring round the correct amounts and currencies. Remember to stop the recording to give yourself more time.

New words:
irisch   Irish
Pfund   pound

First customer: 100 US-Dollar; 100 englische Pfund; 1000 US-Dollar
Second customer: 300 US-Dollar; 500 US-Dollar; 300 englische Pfund
Third customer: 100 französische Franc; 1000 irische Pfund; 1000 französische Franc

ANSWERS P. 46

Fourth customer: 300 irische Pfund; 200 irische Pfund; 300 englische Pfund

3

Your turn to speak. Imagine you want to cash some traveller's cheques. You need to come up with a rather long phrase. On the recording Tom will help you put it together.

Telephone enquiries. A number in Kiel, please ...

LISTEN FOR...

26 28 28 21 30 27 22 23 21

Nummer number
Firma firm

Telefonistin	Auskunft Kiel, Platz 24. Guten Tag.
Ruth	Guten Tag. Eine Nummer in Kiel, bitte.
Telefonistin	Ja?
Ruth	Die Firma heißt Siemens.

die Telefonistin   (female) telephonist
die Auskunft   information; directory enquiries
Platz 24   position 24; each telephonist has his or her own 'position number' (**der Platz** place, position).
die Nummer   number (**Telefonnummer** or **Rufnummer** telephone number)
die Firma heißt ...   the firm is called ...

Note that there will be more on making phone calls in Unit 8.

105 Telefonbuch 1995/96 für den Bereich Freiburg im Breisgau.

Das Telefonbuch der Deutschen Telekom AG.

Deutsche Telekom
Von Mensch zu Mensch.

The numbers from 21–90

21	**einundzwanzig** (*lit.* 'one and twenty')
22	**zweiundzwanzig**
23	**dreiundzwanzig**
24	**vierundzwanzig**
25	**fünfundzwanzig**
26	**sechsundzwanzig**
27	**siebenundzwanzig**
28	**achtundzwanzig**
29	**neunundzwanzig**
30	**dreißig**
31	**einunddreißig**
32	**zweiunddreißig**
40	**vierzig**
50	**fünfzig**
60	**sechzig**
70	**siebzig**
80	**achtzig**
90	**neunzig**

4

Numberwork. Convert the written out numbers into figures, but do it in two stages. For example: **vierundzwanzig** ▶ 4 + 20 = 24

vierundzwanzig ▶ _____

achtundachtzig ▶ _____

dreiundsiebzig ▶ _____

sechsundfünfzig ▶ _____

neunundneunzig ▶ _____

siebenundsechzig ▶ _____

ANSWERS P. 46 fünfunddreißig ▶ _____

5

6 aus 49: Die Gewinnzahlen On the recording Dorit will tell you the winning numbers. Make your crosses on the six numbers mentioned on the form below.

ANSWERS P. 46

6

And now for another directory enquiry. Listen to the recording and fill in the missing words and numbers to complete the transcript below.

Telefonistin: Platz 36. Guten Tag.

               Guten Tag. (**a**) _____ in Wangen, bitte.

Telefonistin: Ja?

               (**b**) _____ Maier.

Telefonistin: Meier. Mit e, i?

ANSWERS P. 46   (**c**) _____

7

Your turn to speak and make a directory enquiry. You want to get the number of a Firma Kaiser in Frankfurt. Be prepared to spell it out! The following phrases will come in useful:

eine Nummer in ...

die Firma heißt ...

At the Hotel Erkenhof. Booking a family room

LISTEN FOR...

Familienzimmer	family room
für heute abend	for tonight
Dusche	shower
Bad	bath
Frühstück	breakfast
Was kostet das?	How much is it?

Frau Mohn	Guten Tag.
Ruth	Haben Sie für heute abend ein Familienzimmer frei?
Frau Mohn	Ja, das haben wir.
Ruth	Ist das mit Dusche oder mit Bad?
Frau Mohn	Das ist mit Dusche.
Ruth	Und was kostet das?
Frau Mohn	Das kostet einhundertfünfzig (150) D-Mark.
Ruth	Und ist das mit Frühstück?
Frau Mohn	Das ist mit Frühstück.

Halbinsel
WASSERBURG am Bodensee
LUFTKURORT

für heute abend   for tonight; similarly
für morgen abend for tomorrow night;
für wie lange? for how long?
für eine Woche for one week;
für eine Nacht for one night

frei   free, vacant; the opposite is
belegt occupied

ein Familienzimmer   a family room (in
a hotel) (**das Zimmer** room); note also
das Einzelzimmer single room;
das Doppelzimmer double room.

ja, das haben wir   yes, we do (have
one). The usual word order would be:
ja, wir haben das (i.e. **das Zimmer**), but
Frau Mohn wanted to emphasize **das**
and placed it at the beginning of the
sentence.
mit Dusche   with (a) shower
(**die Dusche** shower)

mit Bad   with (a) bath (**das Bad**
bath); similarly: **mit Balkon** with
(a) balcony (**der Balkon** balcony);
mit WC with (a) WC (**das WC** WC);
mit Telefon with (a) telephone (**das
Telefon** telephone). The opposite
would be:
ohne Bad/Dusche/Balkon/Telefon
without (a) bath/shower/balcony/
telephone.

Was kostet das?   How much is
it/that? What does it cost?

D-Mark   Note that in Germany,
you either say **D-Mark** or **Mark**, but
never **Deutschmark**.

mit Frühstück   with breakfast
(**das Frühstück** breakfast)

Restaurant – Pension
Zur
Fischerklause
Inh. Fam. Schmid
Uferstraße 17
88142 Wasserburg/
Bodensee
Tel. (08382) 887066,
Fax 89606

Lassen Sie sich verwöhnen und genießen
Sie erholsame Stunden direkt am See
in ruhiger Lage.

Moderne Zimmer. Dusche, Balkon und
WC. Telefon, TV, Frühstücksbuffet.
Parkplatz beim Haus.

8 Study the ad for the Fischerklause and then answer the questions below.

a. In which town is the Zur Fischerklause? _____

b. What's the road called? _____

c. Are the rooms modern in style or rather more traditional? _____

d. Have the rooms got a bath? _____

e. Have they got balconies? _____

ANSWERS P. 46

f. Can you get breakfast there? _____

9 On the recording you will hear Frau Kruse booking a room at the Hotel Stern. What kind of room is she booking? Make a ring round the appropriate words below.

Einzelzimmer – Doppelzimmer – Familienzimmer – Dusche – Bad – WC –
Telefon – Balkon

ANSWERS P. 46

10 And now it's Herr Lümmel's turn to book a room. Listen to the recording for details, then tick the correct statements below.

a. Herr Lümmel möchte das Zimmer für morgen abend. ☐

 Herr Lümmel möchte das Zimmer für heute abend. ☐

b. Er möchte ein Doppelzimmer. ☐

 Er möchte ein Einzelzimmer. ☐

c. Herr Lümmel möchte eine Woche bleiben. ☐

 Herr Lümmel möchte zwei Wochen bleiben. ☐

d. Eine Woche kostet 630 Mark. ☐

 Eine Woche kostet 360 Mark. ☐

e. Das Zimmer ist mit Frühstück. ☐

ANSWERS P. 46

 Das Zimmer ist ohne Frühstück. ☐

11 Study the selection of guesthouses and hotels in Wasserburg. Then answer the questions below.

Adresse	Telefon	Zimmer- Betten zahl		Gruppe	Zimmer mit Frühstück pro Person	Details
Haus des Gastes Fam. Schmid Auf der Halbinsel	887330 Fax 89795	6 x 2 2 x 1		E E	50, – 65, –	direkt am See, Zimmerservice
Gasthof-Pension Pfälzer Hof Fam. Augsten	887422 Fax 89765	1 x 3 2 x 2 6 x 2		E D E	47, – 37, – 47, –	Zimmer mit Telefon und Balkon, Terrasse
Pension-Restaurant Zur Fischerklause Fam. Schmid Uferstr. 17	887066 Fax 89606	6 x 2 1 x 1 1 x 1		E E E	65, – 75, – 75, –	Balkon, Telefon und TV im Zimmer
Gasthof Waldhorn Fam. Rauch Hengnau 21	89001	7 x 2 2 x 3		C C	32, 50 32, 50	
Gasthof-Café Wilhelmshöhe Fam. Malang Reutnerstr. 73	5446	6 x 2 1 x 1		E E	55, – 55, –	Balkon, Biergarten

Gruppe C: kaltes und warmes Wasser im Zimmer

Gruppe D: Privatbad oder Dusche im Zimmer

Gruppe E: Privatbad oder Dusche und WC im Zimmer

a. Which establishment offers the cheapest rooms?

_____

b. Is breakfast included in all cases?

_____

c. There are only two places with three-bed rooms. Which are they?

_____

d. If you wanted a room with a balcony, where would you go? (3 options)

_____

e. Does the Waldhorn have TV? _____

f. You want a room for one person with bath/shower, WC, balcony, TV, telephone. Which place would you choose and how much would you pay for one room?

_____

ANSWERS P. 46

_____

12 Read what kind of hotel room the following people would like and then see what the various hotels and guesthouses below have to offer. Where would each person be most happy? Write their names under the hotels.

Gisela Schmidt: Ich möchte ein Einzelzimmer mit Bad und Telefon.
Volker Nagel: Ich möchte ein Doppelzimmer mit Bad und WC, Telefon und TV.
Hanna Moser: Ein Einzelzimmer mit fließend warm und kalt Wasser.
Gerd Hanke: Ein Zimmer in einem Hotel mit Hausbar und Sauna.

Hotel Sonnenhof	**Pension König**	**Hotel Europa**	**Gasthof Bavaria**

_____ _____ _____ _____

ANSWERS P. 46

13 At the hotel reception. The conversation below got a little mixed up. The receptionist's sentences are in the right order, but the guest's responses aren't. Put them back in the right order and write them in the spaces provided. Then listen to the recording for the correct version.

Guest:
Ist das mit Frühstück?
Ein Doppelzimmer bitte.
Ja, für heute abend.
Für eine Nacht. Was kostet das?
Guten Abend. Haben Sie ein Zimmer frei?

Receptionist:	Guten Abend.
Guest:	_____
Receptionist:	Für heute abend?
Guest:	_____
Receptionist:	Möchten Sie ein Einzelzimmer oder ein Doppelzimmer?
Guest:	_____
Receptionist:	Für wie lange?
Guest:	_____
Receptionist:	Das kostet 65 Mark.
Guest:	_____
Receptionist:	Nein, das ist ohne Frühstück.

14 Your turn to speak and book a hotel room. Before you turn to the recording, take another good look at the phrases in Exercise 13. They'll come in very handy.

German nouns

All nouns in German are written with a capital initial letter, e.g. die **Frau** (the woman).

There are three categories of noun, called *genders* – masculine, feminine and neuter. You can tell the gender of a noun by the words for 'the' and 'a'.

masculine	der Mann	the man
	ein Mann	a man
feminine	die Frau	the woman
	eine Frau	a woman
neuter	das Kind	the child
	ein Kind	a child

Sometimes the gender is obvious, e.g. **der Vater** (the father) is masculine, and **die Mutter** (the mother) feminine. But in many cases the gender is arbitrary. It is for instance **die Bank**, **die Dusche**, **das Zimmer**, **das Hotel**, **der Tag**, **der Morgen**, etc. As from this unit, we will always include **der**, **die**, or **das** with a noun so that you know its gender. (In the vocabulary list at the back of the book they will be shown as *m*, *f*, or *n*.) Try to learn the genders of nouns as well as you can, but don't get too worried if you get them wrong – you'll still be understood.

However, you will find that learning **der**, **die**, **das** and **ein**, **eine**, **ein** is not the end of the story. Study the following sentences:

Der/Ein Schlüssel ist hier.   The/A key is here.
Ich habe den/einen Schlüssel.   I've got the/a key.

Note that in the second sentence **der** changes to **den** and **ein** to **einen**. This occurs when a masculine noun is the *direct object* in a sentence. (For definition of *object* see p. 236.) No change occurs when feminine and neuter nouns become direct objects, e.g.

Die/Eine Uhr ist hier .   The/A watch is here.
Ich habe die/eine Uhr.   I've got the/a watch.

Das/Ein Zimmer ist hier.   The/A room is here.
Ich habe das/ein Zimmer.   I've got the/a room.

When the noun becomes a direct object, grammar books call this the *accusative case*. There are four cases altogether in German. At this stage, just be aware that these cases involve changes in certain words (particularly 'the' and 'a' and nouns and adjectives) and we'll deal with them as they come up. You'll find a complete list for your reference in the Grammar summary on pp. 235–239.

15

Ein or **eine**? Write in the correct words for 'a'.

For example:

der Tag	*ein*	Tag

a. der Name	————	Name
b. die Tochter	————	Tochter
c. der Sohn	————	Sohn
d. der Abend	————	Abend
e. die Straße	————	Straße
f. der Morgen	————	Morgen
g. das Fräulein	————	Fräulein
h. die Frau	————	Frau
i. der Verkäufer	————	Verkäufer

ANSWERS P. 46

16

Fill in the gaps as in our example.

Example:

die Sprache	*eine*	Sprache

a. die Kasse	————	Kasse
b. ———— Nummer	eine	Nummer
c. das Telefon	————	Telefon
d. ———— Firma	eine	Firma
e. die Familie	————	Familie
f. das Kind	————	Kind
g. ———— Nacht	eine	Nacht
h. der Urlaub	————	Urlaub
i. das Jahr	————	Jahr

ANSWERS P. 46

17

Your turn to come up with the right articles and genders (**m**, **f** or **n**). You may need to check them in the vocabulary list at the back of the book.

Example:

die	Dusche
eine	Dusche (f)

a. ————	Bad
————	Bad (——)
b. ————	Lehrer
————	Lehrer (——)
c. ————	Mann
————	Mann (——)
d. ————	Engländerin
————	Engländerin (——)
e. ————	Telefon
————	Telefon (——)
f. ————	Balkon
————	Balkon (——)
g. ————	Morgen
————	Morgen (——)

ANSWERS P. 46

KEY WORDS

At the bank
To use yourself:

Ich möchte gerne Reiseschecks einlösen	I'd like to cash traveller's cheques

To understand:

Welche Währung haben Sie?	Which currency do you have?
Gehen Sie bitte zur Kasse!	Please go to the cashier's desk.

On the telephone
To use yourself:

(Ich möchte) eine Nummer in ... bitte	(I'd like) a number in ... please
Die Firma heißt ...	The firm is called ...

To understand:

die Auskunft	information; directory enquiries

At the hotel
To use yourself:

Haben Sie ein Zimmer frei?	Have you got a room (free)?
für heute abend	for tonight
für morgen abend	for tomorrow night
für eine Woche	for one week
ein Einzelzimmer/Doppelzimmer	a single/double room
ein Familienzimmer	a family room
mit Bad/Dusche/Balkon/WC	with (a) bath/shower/balcony/WC
mit oder ohne Frühstück	with or without breakfast
Was kostet das?	How much is that?

... and the numbers from 20 to 1000

Where to stay

A wide range of accommodation is available to suit most tastes and budgets. First there are of course hotels. Standards and prices vary enormously, but generally hotels are cheaper in rural areas and in the outskirts of cities. The local tourist office will usually be able to refer you to a hotel of your specification, or there will be a list of rooms with prices and telephone numbers on display outside the tourist office. At airports and large railway stations there is usually a counter with a sign **Zimmernachweis** (accommodation bureau) where you can book a room. If in doubt about standards and prices, look at the Michelin Guide or a similar guide.

Pubs, pensions, holiday flats

Rooms in a **Pension** (*pension*, guesthouse), a **Garni** (bed and breakfast) or a **Gasthof** (inn) tend to be cheaper than hotels, but again standards and prices vary considerably. Many of the country inns still have their own butcher's, and the food is often excellent. You'll also often find accommodation available in private houses, especially in holiday areas. Enquire at the local tourist office, or look for signs **Zimmer frei** (rooms available). But keep in mind that breakfast is usually not included in the price – if it is served at all. A **Ferienwohnung** (holiday flat) or **Ferienhaus** (holiday house) might suit you better – they are self-contained and you can do your own cooking. **Ferien auf dem Bauernhof** (farm holidays) are good value and great fun, especially for children. They are becoming more and more popular, so book well in advance. Details are available from the German, Swiss and Austrian Tourist Offices abroad, a regional tourist office (**Verkehrsbüro**) in the area you'd like to visit, or – if you can – read the advertisements in papers such as **Süddeutsche Zeitung**, **Die Zeit** or **Neue Zürcher Zeitung** (for Switzerland).

Camp sites, youth hostels and similar accommodation

Campingplätze (camp sites) tend to become rather crowded in the summer. The **ADAC** (German Automobile Association, the equivalent of the AA and RAC) issues a guide book for campers. **Jugendherbergen** (youth hostels) may be used by all young people under 24. In addition, adults over 24 may stay there, too – except in Bavaria – if there are still beds vacant after 7 p.m. In the peak season it is advisable to book in advance. To get a bed you need an International Youth Hostel Association membership card. YMCA hotels exist in many large towns, they are also mainly for young people. **Naturfreundehäuser** (Friends of Nature hostels) are located in scenically attractive regions. Some are hiking centres, or youth guesthouses, but it is also possible for others to stay overnight if they book. In the Bavarian, Swiss and Austrian Alps you will find that a **Berghütte** (mountain hut) will put you up if you're hiking or mountaineering and if they can fit you in.

Where to change money

Many hotel receptions will change your money for you. You will also find **Geldwechsel** (exchange) at all major railway stations and at airports. They tend to have longer opening hours than the banks, but their rates could be less favourable. Most banks are open Mondays to Fridays from 9.00 to 4.00. Slight variations are possible from region to region.

AND FINALLY...

18

You are ringing the Hotel Apollo to book a room. You want a double room with shower and WC for one night. You also want to know how much it will cost. You will hear one new phrase:

pro Nacht   per night

Turn to the recording where Tom will prompt you.

ANSWERS

Freiburg

EXERCISE 1

100; 400; 700; 300; 500; 200; 800; 1000; 900; 600

EXERCISE 2

First customer: 100 englische Pfund; *Second customer*: 300 US-Dollar; *Third customer*: 1000 französische Franc; *Fourth customer*: 200 irische Pfund

EXERCISE 4

24; 88; 73; 56; 99; 67; 35

EXERCISE 5

15; 24; 32; 39; 44; 48

EXERCISE 6

(a) Eine Nummer   (b) Die Firma heißt   (c) Nein, mit a, i.

EXERCISE 8

(a) Wasserburg   (b) Uferstraße   (c) modern   (d) no
(e) yes   (f) yes

EXERCISE 9

Doppelzimmer; Dusche; Telefon

EXERCISE 10

(a) heute abend   (b) Einzelzimmer   (c) eine Woche
(d) 630 Mark   (e) mit Frühstück

EXERCISE 11

(a) Waldhorn   (b) yes   (c) Waldhorn and Pfälzer Hof
(d) Zur Fischerklause or Wilhelmshöhe or Pfälzer Hof;
(e) no   (f) Fischerklause: 75 DM per person

EXERCISE 12

Gisela Schmidt: Hotel Sonnenhof; Volker Nagel: Gasthof Bavaria; Hanna Moser: Pension König; Gerd Hanke: Hotel Europa

EXERCISE 15

(a) ein   (b) eine   (c) ein   (d) ein   (e) eine   (f) ein   (g) ein
(h) eine   (i) ein

EXERCISE 16

(a) eine   (b) die   (c) ein   (d) die   (e) eine   (f) ein   (g) die
(h) ein   (i) ein

EXERCISE 17

(a) das – ein (n)   (b) der – ein (m)   (c) der – ein (m)
(d) die – eine (f)   (e) das – ein (n)   (f) der – ein (m)
(g) der – ein (m)

4 ORDERING BREAKFAST, DRINKS AND SNACKS

WHAT YOU WILL LEARN

▶ ordering breakfast
▶ getting yourself a drink, a snack and a dessert
▶ finding yourself a seat
▶ asking for the bill
▶ you will also be given some information about breakfast habits, pubs, cafés and where to buy snacks

BEFORE YOU BEGIN

German is famous for having long words. Luckily they can usually be disentangled quite easily, and make good sense once they are broken down into their various components. Here is just one example from the conversations in this unit: **Käsesahnetorte** = **Käse** (cheese) + **Sahne** (cream) + **Torte** (gateau or flan). Once you have recognized the words that make up the long word, it will also be much easier to pronounce. Try this one: **Sonnenblumenbrot**. It consists of **Sonne** (sun) + **Blume** (flower) + **Brot** (bread).

Pronunciation notes

Stress

Generally the first syllable is stressed, for example **Pfennig**, **Weißbrot** (white bread), **Wurstsalat** (sausage salad) and **Sonnenblumenbrot**.

However, there are exceptions, notably some words adopted from other languages such as **Moment** (moment), **Zitrone** (lemon) and **Marmelade** (jam). Certain German prefixes such as **ent-** and **be-** also remain unstressed. Examples are **entschuldigen** (to excuse) and **bezahlen** (to pay). Listen carefully to Tom who will pronounce all these words at the start of the unit.

▶ Ruth orders breakfast

Café Hauptwache

Frankfurt-Main ☎ 281026

Frau Pichler	Guten Morgen. Was wünschen Sie? Tee, Kaffee, Kakao, heiße Milch, kalte Milch, dazu ein weiches Ei?
Ruth	Ich möchte gerne ein Kännchen Tee, bitte.
Frau Pichler	Mit Zitrone oder mit Milch?
Ruth	Mit Zitrone, bitte.
Frau Pichler	Danke schön.

Was wünschen Sie?   What would you like (**wünschen** to wish, want)

der Tee   tea

der Kaffee   coffee; note that in South Germany the stress tends to be on the last syllable (as on the recording), otherwise it's on the first syllable.

der Kakao   cocoa

heiße Milch   hot milk, **kalte Milch** cold milk (**die Milch** milk); **heiß** (hot) and **kalt** (cold) are adjectives (see Grammar summary p. 239 for definition). If an adjective comes before a noun, its ending changes according to the gender of the noun. **Milch** is feminine, so **heiß** and **kalt** add an **-e**. (You'll find more on adjective endings in Unit 7 and a full list in the Grammar summary on p. 239.)

dazu ein weiches Ei   and a soft-boiled egg with it (**das Ei** egg, **weich** soft). Here we have a neuter noun (**das Ei**), so the adjective **weich** has to add **-es**.

ein Kännchen Tee   a small pot of tea; similarly **ein Kännchen Kaffee** a small pot of coffee. Note that the 'of' is not translated into German. Similarly **eine Tasse Kaffee** a cup of coffee; **ein Glas Tee** a glass of (hot) tea (**die Tasse** cup, **das Glas** glass). When a noun ends in **-chen** it means the object is small, e.g. **die Kanne** the pot – **das Kännchen** the small pot; **das Haus** the house – **das Häuschen** the small house. Words ending in **-chen** are always neuter. A similar ending is **-lein**; remember **das Fräulein** (*lit*. little woman).

mit Zitrone   with lemon   (**die Zitrone** lemon)

Even though many hotels have a **Frühstücksbar** or **Frühstücksbuffet** where you help yourself to your breakfast, the following words will still come in useful:

der Saft juice; **der Orangensaft** orange juice; **der Grapefruitsaft** grapefruit juice; **der Tomatensaft** tomato juice; **der Apfelsaft** apple juice; **der Toast** toast; **die Marmelade** but watch out! this usually means jam (rather than marmalade); **der Honig** honey; **der Käse** cheese; **die Wurst** sausage; **das Brot** bread; **die Butter** butter; **der Zucker** sugar; **das Salz** salt; **das Müsli** muesli

▶ At the baker's

LISTEN FOR...

Brötchen	roll
Weißbrot	white bread
Sonnenblumenbrot	sunflower bread

Ruth	Guten Tag.
Verkäuferin	Bitte?
Ruth	Ich möchte zwei Brötchen, bitte.
Verkäuferin	Ja. Sechsundachtzig Pfennig.
Ruth	Und ein französisches Weißbrot, bitte.
Verkäuferin	Zwei Mark und sechzig (2,60 DM).
Ruth	Und ein Sonnenblumenbrot, bitte.
Verkäuferin	Fünf Mark und achtzig (5,80 DM).

zwei Brötchen two rolls (**das Brötchen** roll)

ein französisches Weißbrot a French stick (**das Weißbrot** white bread); note also **ein Weißbrot** (as here) is a loaf of white bread.

zwei Mark und sechzig two marks sixty. Note that prices are written differently from the way they are spoken: 2,60 DM or even DM 2,60. **Sechsundachtzig Pfennig** would be written 0,86 DM (1 DM = 100 Pfennig). Quite often, the **Mark** and/or the **und** are dropped in spoken German, so you'll hear: **zwei Mark sechzig**, or even: **zwei sechzig** (2,60). Make sure you don't confuse that with zweiundsechzig – 62.

das Sonnenblumenbrot sunflower bread (**die Sonne** sun, **die Blume** flower). Another popular type of bread is **das Schwarzbrot** dark rye bread, black bread.

PRACTICE

1 Study the breakfast menu. Then listen to the recording and make a ring round the items that Erich is ordering for breakfast.

New words:
Eier eggs
Scheiben slices

ANSWERS P. 62

FRÜHSTÜCK
*
Glas Orangensaft oder Grapefruitsaft
Glas oder Kännchen Tee mit
Milch oder Zitrone
Tasse oder Kännchen Kaffee
*
zwei Brötchen, zwei Scheiben Brot
oder Toast mit Butter
*
Marmelade Honig
Wurst Käse

2 This time, it's the waitress who's telling you what's on the breakfast menu. Here is a transcript, but some words are missing – write them in the spaces provided.

Guten Morgen, was wünschen Sie zum **(a)** ______________ ? Wir haben Orangensaft, Apfelsaft, **(b)** ______________ , Tee, **(c)** ______________ , Kakao, heiße oder kalte **(d)** ______________ , Brötchen oder **(e)** ______________ , Weißbrot, Schwarzbrot, Eier, **(f)** ______________ , Marmelade, **(g)** ______________ , Käse und **(h)** ______________

ANSWERS P. 62

3 And here's the bill for a family breakfast at the café. How much are the individual items? Listen to the recording and write the prices down.

New word:
die Portion portion

a. ein Kännchen Tee ___ , ____ DM
b. eine Tasse Kaffee ___ , ____ DM
c. ein Kännchen Kakao ___ , ____ DM
d. fünf Scheiben Brot ___ , ____ DM
e. vier Brötchen ___ , ____ DM
f. drei Portionen Butter ___ , ____ DM
g. eine Portion Honig ___ , ____ DM
h. zwei Portionen Marmelade ___ , ____ DM

ANSWERS P. 62

4 An 'ear-sharpener'. Ruth is at another baker's. What does she buy and how much does it come to? Turn to the recording and listen ...

New vocabulary:

Was darf's sein? What would you like?

She buys ———————————— and she has to pay ——, —— DM

ANSWERS P. 62

5 Crossword puzzle. The numbers 1–4 will give you the name of an old German city, famous for its cathedral. And here's a clue: its English name is Cologne.

ANSWERS P. 62

MYSTERY WORD: ————————————————————

6 Your turn to speak and order some breakfast. Take another look at the breakfast menu in Exercise 1 of this unit and at Conversations 1. Tom will prompt you.

In the pub

LISTEN FOR...

ein großes	a large one
ein kleines	a small one
die Speisekarte	the menu

Frau Jahn	Grüß Gott. Sie wünschen bitte?
Ruth	Ein Bier bitte.
Frau Jahn	Ein großes oder ein kleines?
Ruth	Ein kleines.
Frau Jahn	Ja. Möchten Sie auch die Speisekarte?
Ruth	Ja, bitte. Gerne.
Frau Jahn	Mm.

ein großes oder ein kleines a large or a small one. Again the adjectives **groß** (large) and **klein** (small) have to add **-es** because **Bier** is a neuter noun: **das Bier**. A large beer is usually ½ litre and a small one ⅓ litre (1 litre = 1.76 pints). To order some wine, you can say **ein Glas Wein bitte** (a glass of wine please) or **eine Flasche Wein bitte** (a bottle of wine please); note that the 'of' is not translated into German (**der Wein** wine; **der Rotwein** red wine; **der Weißwein** white wine). A glass is usually ¼ litre (0,25 l) and a bottle ¾ litre (0, 75 l) or 1 litre.

auch also

die Speisekarte (or simply **die Karte**)   the menu; *cf* also **die Getränkekarte** the drinks menu; **das Getränk** the drink; **essen** to eat; **trinken** to drink

And now for the choice of snacks

LISTEN FOR...

Wurstsalate	sausage salads
belegte Brote	open sandwiches
Schinken	ham

Ruth	Und was haben Sie auf der kalten Karte?
Frau Jahn	Oh, da haben wir verschiedene Wurstsalate, russische Eier, belegte Brote mit Schinken, Salami und so weiter, und Rippchen ...

auf der kalten Karte   on the cold menu (cold snacks or dishes that can be ordered throughout the day)

verschiedene Wurstsalate   various sausage salads; these consist of thinly cut slices of sausage or cold meat served with a French dressing (**der Salat** salad; *cf* also **die Salatplatte** salad platter).

russische Eier   egg mayonnaise

belegte Brote   slices of bread topped with sausage, cold meat (**der Braten**), paté, or cheese. **Brote** is the plural of **Brot**, often used as here to mean open sandwiches (see grammar section p. 58).

der Schinken   ham;   **die Salami**   salami;   **die Rippchen**   spare ribs

und so weiter   and so on

▶ And finally – what's for dessert?

Kuchen	cake
Erdbeertorte	strawberry flan
Käsesahnetorte	rich cheesecake

Ruth	Haben Sie auch Kuchen?
Frau Jahn	Ja, zur Zeit haben wir Erdbeertorte aus frischen Erdbeeren und Käsesahnetorte, mit oder ohne Sahne.
Ruth	Dann nehme ich ein Kännchen Kaffee und eine Erdbeertorte.
Frau Jahn	Mit Sahne?
Ruth	Ohne Sahne, bitte.
Frau Jahn	Ohne Sahne. Sie sind für die schlanke Linie.

der Kuchen   cake

zur Zeit haben wir   at the moment we have. The usual word order would be: **wir** (*subject*) **haben** (*verb*) **zur Zeit** (*adverb*) ... However, if the sentence starts with an adverb, subject and verb change place.

dann nehme ich   then I'll have (*lit.* take) instead of **ich nehme dann**, another example of changed word order due to the adverb at the beginning of the sentence.

die Erdbeertorte   strawberry flan (**die Erdbeere** strawberry; **die Torte** gateau or flan); **eine Erdbeertorte** here means **ein Stück Erdbeertorte**, a piece of strawberry flan. Similarly **ein Stück Kuchen** a piece of cake.

aus frischen Erdbeeren   (made) with fresh strawberries

die Käsesahnetorte   cheesecake made with cream

die Sahne   cream (whipped or unwhipped). It is the whipped variety (**die Schlagsahne**) which is served with cakes.

Sie sind für die schlanke Linie   you're thinking of your figure (*lit.* you are for the slim line)

7

First the drinks: combine the three-word phrases below in different ways to put in at least six different orders (the maximum is eight). Write them down and then check them against the recording.

ein ⟶ Glas   Bier

eine   Flasche   Rotwein

kleines   Weißwein

großes

Example: **ein Glas Rotwein**

_____

_____

_____

_____

_____

8

A long order. Study the menu below, then turn to the recording and put a cross against the items that were actually ordered. After you've done that, listen a second time to compare the prices – several are shown wrongly on the menu below and will need to be corrected.

New vocabulary:

die Imbißkarte   snack menu
gemischt   mixed
der Nachtisch   dessert

Imbißkarte	
Currywurst mit Brötchen	6, 90
Grillwurst mit Brot	6, 30
Schweizer Wurstsalat	8, 00
Käsebrot garniert	7, 00
Wurstbrot garniert	7, 00
Bratenbrot	7, 00
Salatplatte mit Schinken und Ei	12, 00
Kalter Braten mit Brot und Butter	11, 30
Gemischte Käseplatte mit Brot und Butter	13, 80
Gemischte Schinkenplatte mit Brot und Butter	15, 00
Nachtisch	
Apfelkuchen	6, 20
Erdbeertorte mit Sahne	7, 80
Käsekuchen	5, 70

ANSWERS P. 62

Ordering breakfast, drinks and snacks *Unit 4*

9 Have a look at the menu in Exercise 8, and answer the following questions.

What would you order if you wanted

a. a savoury vegetarian snack? (2 options)

_____

_____

b. a dessert without fruit?

_____

c. a mixed salad with cold ham and a hard-boiled egg?

_____

d. a slice of bread topped with cold meat?

_____

e. a mixed cheese platter?

ANSWERS P. 62

_____

10 Make the right connections as in the example provided. Then listen to the recording for the right answers.

New vocabulary:
die Scheibe   the slice

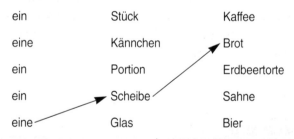

ein	Stück	Kaffee
eine	Kännchen	Brot
ein	Portion	Erdbeertorte
ein	Scheibe	Sahne
eine	Glas	Bier

11 Your turn to speak and order some snacks from the menu in Exercise 8. Keep your book open and remember to press the pause button to give yourself time to think.

klein ... aber fein

Schwennau Stube

Das kleine, gemütliche Restaurant direkt an der Flensburger Innenförde.

Restaurant _Schwennau Stube_ Glücksburg
Schwennaustr. 41 · Telefon (0 46 31) 26 70 · Fax 86 14

Auch den _Campingplatz Schwennau_ erreichen Sie
unter dieser Nummer. Sein Sie unser Gast.
Wir heißen Sie willkommen.

Finding a seat

LISTEN FOR...

frei	free
besetzt	occupied
entschuldigen Sie	excuse me

Ruth	Ist hier noch frei?
Mann	Nein, hier ist leider besetzt.
Ruth	Guten Tag. Ist hier noch frei?
Frau	Nein, hier ist leider besetzt.
Ruth	Entschuldigen Sie bitte. Ist hier noch frei?
Mann	Ja, natürlich. Nehmen Sie Platz!
Ruth	Vielen Dank.

Ist hier noch frei? Is this seat (still) free? It's perfectly acceptable in ordinary German pubs to share a table with a stranger (hence the large tables). However, to sit down at a table marked **Stammtisch** is a different matter; it's reserved for the regulars.

hier ist leider besetzt unfortunately this seat is taken (**leider** unfortunately; **besetzt** taken, occupied)

entschuldigen Sie bitte excuse me please. Note that the word order in a request is the same as in a question: you simply reverse subject and verb, so that **Sie entschuldigen** (you excuse) becomes **entschuldigen Sie**. There is another example of a request here: **nehmen Sie Platz** take a seat (**Sie nehmen** you take; **der Platz** place, seat)

natürlich naturally

vielen Dank many thanks

... and asking for the bill

LISTEN FOR...

bezahlen bitte	the bill please
zusammen	together
getrennt	separately

Ruth	Bezahlen bitte.
Bedienung	Ja, zusammen oder getrennt?
Ruth	Zusammen, bitte.
Bedienung	Ja, kleinen Moment bitte. Neunundvierzig Mark und dreißig (49,30 DM) bitte.
Ruth	Dreiundfünfzig (53). Stimmt so.
Bedienung	Ja, danke schön.

Ruth manages to catch the waitress's eye without calling her. The word for waitress is **Fräulein** but this is now less accepted. However, **Herr Ober** can still be used safely for calling the waiter.

bezahlen bitte the bill please. **Bezahlen** is literally to pay.

die Bedienung (*lit.* service) here means waitress, can also be a waiter.

Zusammen oder getrennt? Together or separately? *i.e.* one bill or separate bills?

stimmt so keep the change. **(Es) stimmt** normally means 'that's correct'.

12 Fill the gaps with the correct words from the following list. Then listen to the recording to check.

zusammen – entschuldigen – Platz – getrennt – frei – bezahlen – besetzt

a. Ist hier noch _____?

b. Nein, hier ist leider _____

c. _____ Sie bitte. Ist hier noch frei?

d. Ja, nehmen Sie doch _____

e. Herr Ober, _____ bitte.

f. Zusammen oder _____ ?

ANSWERS P. 62 **g.** _____ bitte.

13 A problem with the bill. On the recording, the waiter is making out the bill. But watch out, there are mistakes in the transcript below: each line has one error. Mark them – or even better, correct them.

a. eine Tasse Kakao .... 3, 70 DM

b. ein Glas Apfelsaft .... 2, 10 DM

c. ein kleines Bier .... 2, 50 DM

d. ein Wurstbrot .... 5, 90 DM

e. ein Salat .... 7, 50 DM

f. eine Grillwurst .... 4, 70 DM

ANSWERS P. 62 **g.** ein Erdbeerkuchen .... 6, 20 DM

14 Your turn to speak and practise the most useful phrases from Conversations 3. Turn to the recording where Tom will help you. You'll need some of the phrases below:

bezahlen bitte – getrennt – ist hier noch frei? – stimmt so – zusammen

Plural of nouns

The rules for forming the plural of German nouns are complex, but the following guidelines will help you recognize most of them. They do one of the following:

■ add **-e** (mostly masculine nouns; sometimes with an umlaut)

e.g.

der Tag   (the day)
  die Tage   (the days)
der Monat   (the month)
  die Monate   (the months)
der Sohn   (the son)
  die Söhne   (the sons)
das Jahr   (the year)
  die Jahre   (the years)

■ add **-er** (mostly neuter nouns; sometimes with an umlaut)

e.g.

das Kind   (the child)
  die Kinder   (the children)
das Buch   (the book)
  die Bücher   (the books)
der Mann   (the man)
  die Männer   (the men)

■ add **-en** or **-n** (mostly feminine nouns)

e.g.

die Frau   (the woman)
  die Frauen   (the women)
die Woche   (the week)
  die Wochen   (the weeks)

■ just add an umlaut

e.g.

die Mutter   (the mother)
  die Mütter   (the mothers)
der Vater   (the father)
  die Väter   (the fathers)
die Tochter   (the daughter)
  die Töchter   (the daughters)

■ don't change at all (most masculine and neuter nouns ending in **-el**, **-en**, **-er** and the diminutives **-chen** and **-lein**)

e.g

das Zimmer   (the room)
  die Zimmer   (the rooms)
das Mädchen   (the girl)
  die Mädchen   (the girls)
das Fräulein   (the young lady)
  die Fräulein   (the young ladies)

■ add **-s** (mostly words of foreign origin)

e.g.

das Auto   (the car)
  die Autos   (the cars)
das Radio   (the radio)
  die Radios   (the radios)

Note that the plural for 'the' is **die** with all three genders.

Good German dictionaries will always give you the plural of nouns. It's best to learn each noun with its plural form. If you find these forms difficult to remember, make a list of them as you learn new nouns.

15

Singular (e.g. **der Tag**) or plural (e.g. **die Tage**)? Sort them out and write them under the proper categories.

> die Mütter – die Wochen – das Zimmer – die Fräulein – das Jahr – der Tag – die Eier – der Salat – die Würste – das Brot – die Brüder – die Frau

Singular:

_____

_____

Plural:

_____

_____

ANSWERS P. 62

16

Complete the sentences below with the correct plural noun from the box.

> Tassen   Sprachen   Wochen   Kinder
> Berufe   Töchter   Brötchen

a. Sprechen sie auch andere _____ ?

b. Ich habe zwei _____ , ich bin Student und Verkäufer.

c. Zum Frühstück möchte ich gerne zwei _____ und zwei _____ Kaffee.

d. Ich habe vier _____ , zwei Söhne und zwei _____

e. Ich möchte gerne drei _____ bleiben.

ANSWERS P. 62

17

Convert the sentences below into the singular. Remember to change the verb form as well if necessary.

For example:

Die Frauen kommen nach New York.

▶ **Die Frau kommt nach New York.**

Ich bezahle für die Kinder.

▶ **Ich bezahle für das Kind.**

a. Die Töchter sind hier.

_____

b. Die Gläser kommen aus Paris.

_____

c. Die Kinder arbeiten.

_____

d. Ich bezahle die Biere.

_____

e. Ich nehme die Zimmer.

_____

ANSWERS P. 62

Albi Säfte
Apfelsaft klar oder trüb oder Multivitamin-Diät-Nektar

KEY WORDS

To use yourself:

Ist hier noch frei?	Is this seat free?
Haben Sie Kuchen/Torte?	Do you have any cake/gateau?
Was haben Sie auf der kalten Karte?	What have you got on the cold menu?
Die Karte bitte!	The menu please!
Ich möchte etwas zu essen/trinken	I'd like something to eat/drink
Dann nehme ich ...	I'll have ...
ein Glas Milch/Saft/Wein/Tee	a glass of milk/juice/wine/tea
eine Tasse Kaffee	a cup of coffee
ein Stück Kuchen/Torte	a piece of cake/gateau
ein Kännchen Tee	a pot of tea
ein großes/kleines Bier	a large/small beer
Mit/ohne ...	With/without ...
Milch	milk
Sahne	cream
Zitrone	lemon
Zucker	sugar
Herr Ober!	Waiter!
Zahlen bitte!	The bill please!
Stimmt so	Keep the change
Entschuldigen Sie bitte	Excuse me

To understand:

Möchten Sie ...	Would you like ...
Brot oder Brötchen?	some bread or some rolls?
Kuchen oder Torte?	some cake or some gateau?
ein weiches Ei?	a soft-boiled egg?
die Speisekarte?	the menu?
etwas zu essen/trinken?	something to eat/drink?
Wir haben ...	We've got ...
belegte Brote	open sandwiches
verschiedene Salate	various salads
Getrennt oder zusammen?	Separately or together?
Ja, hier ist noch frei	Yes, this seat is free
Nein, hier ist (leider) besetzt	No, (unfortunately) this seat is taken
Nehmen Sie Platz	Take a seat

And you often hear this at mealtimes (you may want to use it yourself):

Guten Appetit!	Enjoy your meal! Bon appetit!

Ordering breakfast, drinks and snacks   *Unit 4*

Snacks and drinks

Some snacks and drinks in Germany will be familiar to you – hamburgers, hot dogs, chips (**Pommes frites**), coke (**Cola**) – but many things are different.

Breakfast usually consists of rolls (or slices of bread or toast), butter and jam (**Marmelade**) or honey (**Honig**). You can also ask for a soft-boiled egg and assorted slices of sausage or cheese, but there are usually no cooked items like bacon or scrambled eggs. Breakfast is served in most snack bars, in cafés, pubs, hotels, and in the cafeterias of large department stores.

Coffee and tea The Continentals seem to prefer coffee to tea. You'll always be served 'real', i.e. ground coffee, even at the shabbiest kiosk, and it comes with a small jug of evaporated milk. You'll find it almost impossible to get fresh milk for your tea or coffee. Not many Continentals have milk with their tea – they prefer lemon or just have it black. A good (and cheap) cup of coffee can be bought in special quick-service coffee bars owned by the major coffee manufacturers. You just stand and sip your coffee – there's usually no food but you can often bring your own.

Snacks Best known is **Bratwurst** (a sausage for frying or grilling), served with **Pommes frites** or a roll plus mustard or ketchup. **Bratwurst** is sold in open stalls or kiosks in the streets (**Würstchenbude** or **Schnellimbiß**) or in snack bars (**Imbißstuben**). The **Bratwurst**, however, has many foreign rivals nowadays; there are Italian pizzas, French crêpes, Turkish kebabs, American pancakes, and, of course, hamburgers. But '**Fisch und

Pommes frites' don't seem to have caught on yet! In Austria and Bavaria, however, you may come across **Steckerlfisch**, i.e. grilled fish on a stick.

Drinks All kiosks and snack bars will serve alcohol as well as soft drinks. At least there'll be beer (bottled) and **Schnaps** or brandy. The best place to go for a drink though is a pub (colloquially called **Kneipe**) or a **Gaststätte**, which can be a combination of pub, restaurant and café, often very cosy. You can have a meal or just sit for hours with your **kleines Bier** – it's up to you. The choice of beers, wines, spirits and liqueurs is enormous. We can't list them all here, but you'll find some information about German wines in Unit 10. There are no licensing hours in Germany, Austria or Switzerland – many pubs are open all day and general closing time is between midnight and 1 a.m. although some bars and pubs are open even longer. Variations on the **Gaststätte** include **der Gasthof**, **die Wirtschaft** which is a more basic **Gaststätte**, and **das Lokal**, which is any premises where one can eat and drink (or just drink).

Torgifch Bier

Cafés Do not expect the equivalent of the British 'caf'; typical German (and Austrian and Swiss) cafés tend to be more upmarket with carpets, tablecloths, upholstered chairs, and, of course, a variety of the most delicious **Torten** and **Kuchen**. Cafés and patisseries (**Konditoreien**) can be quite expensive. Bakeries (**Bäckereien**) sometimes have a back room where you can have breakfast or a cup of coffee and a piece of cake for less money.

AND FINALLY...

18

You're at a **Gaststätte** ordering a drink and food. Some (but not all) of these expressions will come in handy:

ein kleines / großes Bier
Was haben Sie auf der kalten Karte?
Haben Sie Wurstbrote / Käsebrote / Salate?
Dann nehme ich ...
mit Butter / Brot / Sahne

The author, left, with friends

ANSWERS

EXERCISE 1
Glas Orangensaft; Kännchen Tee mit Milch; zwei Brötchen mit Butter, Honig und Käse

EXERCISE 2
(a) Frühstück   **(b)** Grapefruitsaft   **(c)** Kaffee   **(d)** Milch
(e) Toast   **(f)** Butter   **(g)** Honig   **(h)** Wurst

EXERCISE 3
(a) 6,00 DM   **(b)** 3,20 DM   **(c)** 4,50 DM   **(d)** 2,50 DM
(e) 2,80 DM   **(f)** 1,50 DM   **(g)** 0,80 DM   **(h)** 1,60 DM

EXERCISE 4
She buys 5 rolls and has to pay DM 1,95

EXERCISE 5
(a) Brötchen   **(b)** Tasse   **(c)** Marmelade   **(d)** Wurst   **(e)** Ei
(f) Käse   **(g)** Kännchen   MYSTERY WORD: Köln

EXERCISE 8
Currywurst mit Brötchen 6,80 DM; Schweizer Wurstsalat 8,00 DM; Käsebrot, garniert 7,10 DM; Salatplatte mit Schinken und Ei 12,00 DM; Gemischte Schinkenplatte mit Brot und Butter 15,40 DM; Apfelkuchen 6,20 DM

EXERCISE 9
(a) Käsebrot garniert or Gemischte Käseplatte mit Brot und Butter   **(b)** Käsekuchen   **(c)** Salatplatte mit Schinken und Ei
(d) Bratenbrot   **(e)** Gemischte Käseplatte mit Brot und Butter

EXERCISE 12
(a) frei   **(b)** besetzt   **(c)** Entschuldigen   **(d)** Platz
(e) bezahlen   **(f)** getrennt   **(g)** Zusammen

EXERCISE 13
(a) eine Tasse Kaffee 3,70 DM   **(b)** ein Glas Bier 2,10 DM
(c) ein großes Bier 2,50 DM   **(d)** ein Käsebrot 5,90 DM
(e) ein Salat 6,50 DM   **(f)** eine Grillwurst 4,20 DM
(g) ein Erdbeerkuchen 6,90 DM

EXERCISE 15
Singular: das Zimmer; das Jahr; der Tag; der Salat; das Brot; die Frau. *Plural*: die Mütter; die Wochen; die Fräulein; die Eier; die Würste; die Brüder

EXERCISE 16
(a) Sprachen   **(b)** Berufe   **(c)** Brötchen, Tassen
(d) Kinder, Töchter   **(e)** Wochen

EXERCISE 17
(a) Die Tochter ist hier.   **(b)** Das Glas kommt aus Paris.
(c) Das Kind arbeitet.   **(d)** Ich bezahle das Bier.
(e) Ich nehme das Zimmer.

5 DIRECTIONS

WHAT YOU WILL LEARN

▶ asking where a place is situated
▶ finding out how to get to your destination
▶ making sure you're on the right tracks
▶ you will also be reading about public transport and how to use it

BEFORE YOU BEGIN

Some people are good at giving directions, others aren't. No matter how competent they might be in other respects, they're hopeless at visualizing any given route and describing it clearly and succinctly. So if you can't follow somebody else's instructions in German, it's not necessarily just your fault. You'll simply have to pick up your courage once more and ask someone else. It's the same story when you're using public transport: if you want to make sure you're on the right tracks you will need to speak out and ask. And the key words to understand in this context are **einsteigen** (to get in), **aussteigen** (to get out) and **umsteigen** (to change).

Pronunciation notes

h

The **h** is always clearly pronounced at the beginning of a word, for example **H**and (hand) or **h**ier (here), or when a word beginning with **h** appears in a compound made up of more than one word, such as **H**auptbahn**h**of (main station). If an **h** comes in the middle of a word on the other hand, it is not pronounced and the preceding vowel is lengthened, as in **ste**h**en** (to stand) and **ge**h**en** (to go), or **fa**h**ren** (to travel) and **Le**h**rer** (teacher).

The nearest post office

LISTEN FOR...

Post	post office
um die Ecke	round the corner

Ruth	Und wo ist die nächste Post, bitte?
Frau Hölk	Die nächste Post ist g(e)rade hier um die Ecke.

wo ist ...?   where is ...?

die nächste Post   the nearest post office (**nächste** can mean both nearest and next)

die Post/das Postamt   post office

g(e)rade hier (also **gleich hier**)   right here, just here

um die Ecke   around the corner

Some more useful phrases: **Ist das weit?** Is that far?
zu Fuß on foot; **die Fußgängerzone** the pedestrian precinct

 And where's the nearest bank?

LISTEN FOR...

geradeaus	straight ahead
stehen	to stand

Ruth	Wo ist die nächste Bank, bitte?
Frau Mohn	Da gehen Sie bitte fünfhundert (500) Meter geradeaus, und die nächste rechts, und dann stehen Sie direkt vor der Deutschen Bank.

fünfhundert Meter   500 metres (about ⅓ mile);
1000 Meter = 1 Kilometer = 0.62 miles

geradeaus   straight on/ahead; you'll often hear **immer geradeaus** keep straight on (*lit.* always straight on)

die nächste (Straße) rechts   (take) the next (road/street) on the right. You will also hear **auf der rechten Seite** or **rechter Hand** on the right-hand side. The opposite is **links** or **auf der linken Seite** or **linker Hand** on the left.

direkt vor der Deutschen Bank   directly in front of the Deutsche Bank; note that it's **die Bank** (the bank) but **vor der Bank**. Further details in the grammar section of this unit.

And another important little query

LISTEN FOR...

Toilette toilet
Türe door

Jessica	Mama, wo ist denn die Toilette, bitte?
Ruth	G(e)radeaus, erste Türe links.

wo ist denn ...? where is ...? **denn** is just a filler word carrying little extra meaning.

die Toilette toilet; it can be **frei** vacant or **besetzt** occupied.

erste Türe links first door on the left (**die Türe** is South German for **die Tür** door).

The ordinal numbers are formed by adding **-te** to the numbers up to 19. There are only very few exceptions (marked with an asterisk). After 19, you will need to add **-ste**.

der/die/das	erste*	the first
	zweite	second
	dritte*	third
	vierte	fourth
	fünfte	fifth
	sechste	sixth
	siebte*	seventh
	achte	eighth
	neunte	ninth
	zehnte	tenth
	elfte	eleventh
	zwölfte	twelfth
	dreizehnte	thirteenth
	neunzehnte	nineteenth
	etc	
	zwanzigste	twentieth
	einundzwanzigste	twenty-first
	zweiundzwanzigste	twenty-second
	etc	
	dreißigste	thirtieth
	vierzigste	fortieth
	etc	

DAMEN   HERREN

PRACTICE

1 Treasure hunt. Identify the circles containing treasure by following the example below. But watch out, some are dummy circles. Here are the clues.

Example: **die erste Straße links, und dann die zweite rechts ▶ Restaurant Italia**

New word:
gleich immediately; **gleich hier** right here

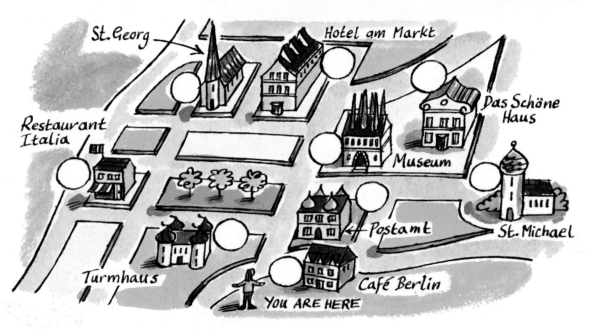

a. ... immer geradeaus und dann auf der rechten Seite
b. ... gleich hier rechts um die Ecke
c. ... geradeaus und dann die dritte Straße rechts
d. ... die zweite Straße rechts und dann immer geradeaus, und dann stehen Sie direkt davor
e. ... die vierte Straße links

ANSWERS P. 78

2 More directions. But this time, they are on the recording. You will hear four conversations. Listen carefully and tick the right answers.

a. The nearest bank is down
    ... the first on the right
    ... the first on the left
b. The nearest post office is
    ... straight ahead
    ... right here around the corner
c. For the Hotel Erkenhof
    ... take the second on the left and then keep straight on
    ... turn right and then take the third on the left

d. The Café am Markt is
    ... 100 metres straight ahead of you
    ... 200 metres straight ahead of you
e. The (hotel) room is straight on and then the
    ... fourth door on the left
    ... fifth door on the right

ANSWERS P. 78

Directions *Unit 5*

3 An incomplete transcript. Erich is asking Dorit for directions. Listen to the dialogue on the recording and fill in the missing words. Then translate Dorit's answers into English.

a. Entschuldigen Sie bitte. Wo ist das Hotel König?

Da gehen Sie fünfhundert Meter _____.

_____

b. Und wo ist die Gartenstraße?

Die Gartenstraße? Immer geradeaus, und dann auf der _____ Seite.

_____

c. Und wo ist denn hier die nächste Bank?

Gleich hier direkt um die _____

_____

d. Und die Post? Wo ist die Post, bitte?

Da gehen Sie bitte die _____ Straße _____ und dann stehen

Sie direkt vor der Post.

_____

e. Wo ist hier bitte das Bad?

Das Bad, das ist hier geradeaus und dann die _____ Tür _____

ANSWERS P. 78

_____

4 A puzzle to remind you of the main words in this unit so far. Translate the words into German. The mystery word formed from the lettered squares will give you a very popular holiday route in Germany.

1. where
2. corner
3. on the left
4. nearest/next
5. straight ahead
6. toilet
7. on the right
8. bank
9. street/road
10. directly

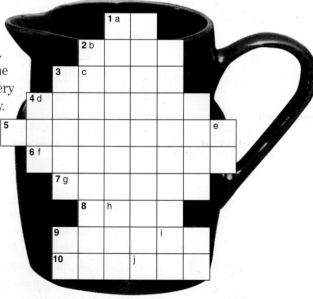

ANSWERS P. 78

MYSTERY WORD: _____

5 Your turn to speak and practise directions. Luckily the person you are asking for help is very sympathetic and gives you plenty of time to repeat the most important parts of his instructions. Turn to the recording where Tom will prompt you.

> **At the tram stop. Asking about destinations**

LISTEN FOR...	
fahren Sie	are you going
Endstation	last stop
andere Seite	other side
aussteigen	to get out
umsteigen	to change

Ruth	Fahren Sie nach Söflingen?
Fahrer	Ja, da ist Endstation.
Ruth	Gut. Danke schön.
	* * *
Ruth	Fahren Sie in Richtung Donauhalle?
Fahrer	Nein, gehen Sie bitte auf die andere Seite rüber.
	* * *
Ruth	Fahren Sie zum Hauptbahnhof?
Fahrer	Ich fahre nicht direkt zum Hauptbahnhof. Sie müssen eine Station vorher aussteigen und dann in die eins umsteigen.

Fahren Sie nach Söflingen? Are you going to Söflingen (a suburb of Ulm)? (**fahren** to go drive)

nach is the equivalent of 'to' with the name of a town or a country, e.g. **ich fahre nach London** I'm going to London; **ich fahre nach Kanada** I'm going to Canada. Note that you use **gehen** only if you are walking. If you go by bus (**der Bus**), train (**der Zug**) or car (**das Auto**) you'll need to say **fahren: ich fahre mit dem Bus nach Söflingen** I'm going by bus to Söflingen.

der Fahrer   driver

die Endstation   the last stop/terminus. The word for a normal stop is **die Haltestelle**.

in Richtung   in the direction of, towards (**die Richtung** direction). Note that 'the' is not translated. Here's another example: **ich fahre in Richtung Stadtzentrum** I am going/travelling towards the city centre.

Donauhalle   *lit*. Danube Hall, a large hall in Ulm.

auf die andere Seite rüber   over to the other side (**rüber** colloquial for over)

nicht direkt   not directly

zum Hauptbahnhof   to the main station (**der Hauptbahnhof** the main station). Note that 'to the' is translated as **zum** here which is a short form of **zu + dem**. Another example: **ich fahre zum Theater** I am going to the theatre; **zum** (or **zur** with feminine nouns) is used with buildings and streets. (Details in the grammar section of this unit.)

Sie müssen   you have to; you must

eine Station vorher   one stop before (that)

aussteigen   to get out; other important words are **einsteigen** to get on and **umsteigen** to change. Note also **alles aussteigen** all change.

in die eins umsteigen   short for **in die Linie eins umsteigen** change onto the number one (**die Linie** line, route)

6 Announcements on the tram. What do they tell you to do? Listen to the recordings and tick the correct translations.

New word:
das Rathaus town hall

First announcement:
a. Söflingen. Last stop. All change.
b. Change here for Söflingen.

Second announcement:
c. Town hall. Please change onto the number 2.
d. Town hall. Please change onto the number 3.

Third announcement:
e. Main station. For the theatre please change onto the number 1.

ANSWERS P. 78

f. Theatre. For the main station please change onto the number 2.

7 Read and understand. The extract below comes from a brochure issued by the Ulm tourist office. It tells you how to get to a nearby Baroque monastery (**Kloster Wiblingen**). Study it and answer the questions below in English.

> **Busverbindungen zum Kloster Wiblingen**
> Vom Hauptbahnhof Ulm Linie 3 Richtung Tannenplatz oder Linie 8 Richtung Wiblingen. Vom Rathaus Ulm Linie 4 Richtung Kuhberg, bei Haltestelle Ehinger Tor in Linie 3 oder 8 umsteigen.

a. Where can you catch buses numbers 3 and 8? _____

b. Which bus would you need to take first if you started off at the town hall?

_____

c. What will you need to do when you get to Ehinger Tor? _____

ANSWERS P. 78

_____

8 **zum – nach – in Richtung?** Turn to the recording to practise some of these directions in a speaking exercise. Tom will prompt you. Here are the words you will need:

Fahren Sie	zum	München
	nach	Stadtzentrum
	in Richtung	Hauptbahnhof
		Theater
		Starnberg

EinzelTicket

A **3.00** DM Erw.
Preisstufe 01/96

Nur gültig mit Entwerteraufdruck

Es gelten die Bestimmungen des Verbundtarifs Rhein-Ruhr

01 15888

Betriebe der Stadt
Mülheim an der Ruhr

▶ Where to get a ticket

LISTEN FOR...

Fahrschein	ticket
bei mir	from me
im Vorverkauf	in advance

Ruth	Und wo bekomme ich einen Fahrschein?
Fahrer	Den können Sie bei mir kaufen, oder im Vorverkauf, da sind die Fahrscheine billiger.
Ruth	Was kostet denn ein Fahrschein bei Ihnen?
Fahrer	Bei mir hier auf dem Wagen zwei Mark sechzig.
Ruth	Gut. Vielen Dank.

bekommen   to get. A note of caution: never translate 'become' as **bekommen**. It can lead to some very strange misunderstandings!

der Fahrschein (or **der Fahrausweis**)   ticket; *cf* also **die Fahrt** journey, trip

den (Fahrschein) können Sie bei mir kaufen   you can buy that (ticket) from me (**können** to be able to; **kaufen** to buy). Usual word order: **Sie können den Fahrschein bei mir kaufen** (more on word order on page 239).

im Vorverkauf   in advance, i.e. from the ticket machine (**der Fahrkartenautomat**)

da sind die Fahrscheine billiger   that way the tickets are cheaper (**billig** cheap)

bei Ihnen   from you

auf dem Wagen   on the (tram) car or bus; **der Wagen** is also another word for **das Auto** (motor car).

◆ How to get to Ulm-Jungingen

Ruth	Wie komme ich nach Ulm–Jungingen, bitte?
Frau Oswald	Also Ulm–Jungingen, das liegt ziemlich nördlich von Ulm. Es gibt eine ... es gibt keine gute Busverbindung dorthin. Da nehmen Sie bitte ein Taxi.

Jungingen   a village outside Ulm

ziemlich   rather

nördlich von   to the north of (**der Norden** north). And here are the other points of the compass:
südlich ▶ der Süden (south);
östlich ▶ der Osten (east);
westlich ▶ der Westen (west)

es gibt   there is (more on **es gibt** in the grammar section of Unit 10)

eine/keine gute Busverbindung.   a/no good bus connection or service. This is a good illustration of the use of **ein/kein**. First, Frau Oswald thinks there is a good bus service and starts to say: **es gibt eine gute Busverbindung**. But then she remembers that the bus service is no good and corrects herself: **es gibt keine gute Busverbindung**.

Other examples: **es gibt keine Sahne**   there is no cream. **Ich habe keinen Sohn** I have no son. **Ich habe kein Kind** I have no child.

Note that the endings for **kein** follow the same patterns as for **ein** and **eine**.

dorthin   (to) there, i.e. which goes there

das Taxi   taxi

9 Study the ticket printed below and answer the following questions.

a. Is the ticket valid for one trip or two trips?

_____

b. How much was it?

_____DM

c. In which town was it issued?

_____

_____

ANSWERS P. 78

10 Read and understand. You want to get to the Restaurant Fährhaus in Dommitzsch. Study the brochure below and decide whether the statements are true or false.

a. Torgau is 45 km from Leipzig.

b. Coming from Leipzig, you will need to take the B 87 first.

c. The B 87 will take you in the direction of Torgau.

d. After that, you'll need to take the A4 towards Meißen.

e. All in all, you will have covered 65 km in order to get from Leipzig to Dommitzsch.

ANSWERS P. 78

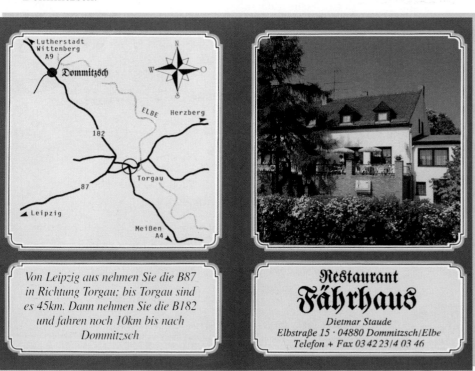

Von Leipzig aus nehmen Sie die B87 in Richtung Torgau; bis Torgau sind es 45km. Dann nehmen Sie die B182 und fahren noch 10km bis nach Dommitzsch

Restaurant
Fährhaus
Dietmar Staude
Elbstraße 15 · 04880 Dommitzsch/Elbe
Telefon + Fax 03 42 23/4 03 46

11 Informed guesswork. Match the German signs with their English equivalents. Only parts of the phrases will be known to you. The task is to try and deduce their meanings from the words you do know.

a **Vorsicht Kinder**

b **Hotel König wünscht Ihnen gute Fahrt**

c **Hotel König nächste Straße links**

e **Schöne Ferienbungalows erste Straße rechts**

f **Bitte nicht so schnell**

g **Selbsttanken**

i **Privatgrundstück Betreten verboten**

d **Nur P für Gäste**

h **Autowäsche**

A. Hotel König wishes you a good journey
B. Parking for guests only
C. Not so fast please
D. Carwash
E. Children welcome
F. Next turning on the left for Hotel König
G. Self service (fuel)
H. Private property. No trespassing
I. Take care, children
J. Nice holiday bungalows first right

j **Kinder willkommen**

ANSWERS P. 78

12 **Wie? Wo? Was?** Complete the questions below and then turn to the recording to check your version.

a. _____ ist die nächste Post bitte?

b. _____ komme ich nach Starnberg?

c. _____ liegt Ulm–Jungingen?

d. _____ bekomme ich einen Fahrschein?

e. _____ kostet ein Fahrschein?

f. _____ ist das Hotel Seewald bitte?

g. _____ komme ich zum Stadtzentrum?

13 Your turn to speak and practise some more questions. Tom will prompt you.

Prepositions

Prepositions are words such as 'on', 'at', 'to', and 'in'. You have already come across quite a few German prepositions on this course, for example **nach** and **zu** (to), **in** (in) and **vor** (in front of). Some more useful ones are: **durch** (through), **an** (at, by), **neben** (next to), **bis** (up to), **um** (round) and **auf** (on). If these prepositions are used, the words for 'the' (**der/die/das**) and 'a' (**ein/eine/ein**) might need to change, depending on their gender.

The changes required are far too detailed to be taken in all at once. The following explanation should therefore primarily act as a reference guide: something you can come back to again and again, rather than a set of rules to be learnt by heart immediately.

In Unit 3 we explained the change from **der** to **den** and **ein** to **einen**, which happens to masculine nouns when they become the direct object of a sentence and are then said to be in the accusative case. The same change from **der** to **den** and **ein** to **einen** also happens after certain prepositions, and here we say that these prepositions 'take' the accusative case. For example, after **durch** (through):

Gehen Sie durch den Bahnhof.   Go through the station.

Note again that there is no change for feminine or neuter nouns:
Gehen Sie durch die Fußgängerzone.   Go through the pedestrian precinct.
Gehen Sie durch das Hotel.   Go through the hotel.

Prepositions such as **durch** (through), **entlang** (along), **für** (for) and **um** (round) will always take the accusative case and thus affect all masculine nouns (but not feminine or neuter nouns).

However, not all prepositions take the accusative. Study the following sentences.
Ich komme aus dem/einem Bahnhof. (*masculine*)
I come out of the/a station.
Ich komme aus dem/einem Haus. (*neuter*)
I come out of the/a house.
Ich komme aus der/einer Post. (*feminine*)
I come out of the/a post office.

In this case, **der** and **das** (masculine and neuter) have changed to **dem**, **ein** has changed to **einem**, and **die/eine** (feminine) to **der/einer**. Articles and nouns such as those above are then said to be in the dative case. Prepositions such as **zu** (to), **von** (from), **bei** (at), **aus** (from, out of) and **mit** (with) always take the dative case.

There is also a third category of prepositions which can take both the dative and the accusative case, such as **auf** (on), **in** (in/into) and **vor** (before). The thinking behind it is quite simple: if the sentence expresses movements (with verbs such as **gehen** to go or **fahren** to travel), use the accusative; but if it expresses a stationary activity (as with **liegen** to lie or **sein** to be) use the dative.
For example:
Ich gehe in das Haus.   I go into the house.
(*movement ▶ accusative*)
But:
Ich bin in dem Haus.   I am in the house.
(*no movement ▶ dative*)

Ravensburg

You will find that certain prepositions tend to merge with the article:

an + dem = am

e.g. **Ich bin am Meer.** I am by the sea.

an + das = ans

e.g. **Sie gehen ans Meer.** They go to the sea.

in + dem = im

e.g. **Er ist im Hotel.** He is in the hotel.

in + das = ins

e.g. **Ich gehe ins Hotel.** I go into the hotel.

zu + dem = zum

e.g. **Du gehst zum Café.** You go to the café.

zu + der = zur

e.g. **Sie geht zur Bank.** She goes to the bank.

14 Write the shortened forms. Then translate the sentences into English.

Example: **Ich gehe zu der Bank.** ▶ **Ich gehe zur Bank.** I'm going to the bank.

a. Gehen Sie bitte zu der Karlstraße.

_____

_____

b. Das Café ist in dem Bahnhof.

_____

_____

c. Wie komme ich zu dem Hotel?

_____

_____

d. Ich gehe jetzt in das Theater.

_____

_____

e. Das Haus liegt direkt an dem Wasser.

_____

_____

ANSWERS P. 78

15 Find the German equivalents for the following sentences and write them into the spaces provided.

a. We are going into the city centre.

_____

b. I am going into town.

_____

c. I am in town.

_____

d. We are in the city centre.

_____

Ich fahre in die Stadt.

Ich bin in der Stadt.

Wir gehen ins Stadtzentrum.

Wir sind im Stadtzentrum.

ANSWERS P. 78

KEY WORDS

To use yourself:

Wo ist die nächste Bank?	Where is the nearest bank?
die Haltestelle?	the (tram/bus) stop?
die Fußgängerzone?	the pedestrian precinct?
Wo bekomme ich einen Fahrschein?	Where do I get a ticket?
Wie komme ich zum Theater?	How do I get to the theatre?
Fahren Sie zum Bahnhof?	Are you going to the station?
zum Stadtzentrum?	to the city centre?
nach Berlin?	to Berlin?
in Richtung Donauhalle?	in the direction of the Donauhalle?
Ist das weit?	Is that far?
immer geradeaus	(keep) straight on
und dann rechts	and then to the right
links	to the left
erste Tür rechts	first door on the right
zweite Straße links	second street on the left
um die Ecke	around the corner
zu Fuß	on foot

To understand:

Gehen Sie bitte auf die andere Seite	Please go to the other side
Da ist Endstation	That's the last stop
Sie können ...	You can ...
Sie müssen ...	You must ...
umsteigen	change
einsteigen	get on
aussteigen	get out
eine Station vorher	one stop before (that)
in die Linie eins	onto the number one
die Straßenbahn	tram
die U-Bahn	underground
der Bus	bus
der Wagen/das Auto	car
der Fahrschein/Fahrausweis	ticket
die Fahrt	trip
der Fahrer	driver
fahren	to travel, go (by bus/car/tram/train)
billig/billiger	cheap/cheaper

... and the ordinal numbers
on page 65

Getting around

If you want to find out about transport in a German town, it's best to go to the local tourist office (**Fremdenverkehrsamt** or **Verkehrsbüro**). Watch out for the **i** symbol (= **Information**). At many tourist offices you can also book theatre tickets and guided tours and generally find out what's going on. Some double as a travel agency (**Reisebüro**) and even sell rail or air tickets.

Means of transport

There are buses (**Busse**) practically everywhere. Their main terminal or bus station (**Busbahnhof**) tends to be near the railway station (**Bahnhof** or **Hauptbahnhof** – more information on trains in Unit 9). Information centres at the railway station (**Information**, **Auskunft**) will have bus timetables and provide you with the necessary information. Most larger towns and cities also have a tram network (**Straßenbahn**). In major cities you will usually find suburban trains (**S-Bahn**) and/or underground trains (**U-Bahn**).

Tickets and fares

The word for ticket is **Fahrschein**, **Karte**, or the more official-sounding **Fahrausweis**. You can buy a single ticket (**Einzelfahrschein**) or a ticket for several trips (**die Fahrt** = trip) which, depending on where you are, might be called either **Mehrfahrkarte**, **Streifenkarte** (because of its strips) or **Sammelkarte**. They might work out cheaper than the **Einzelfahrschein**. Many cities offer special tourist tickets or a **Tageskarte**, valid for one whole day. As a rule you can use the same type of ticket on buses, trams, the underground and/or **S-Bahn**.

On most buses and trams there is no conductor, just the driver. You will probably be able to buy a ticket from him or her when you get on, but it may be cheaper to buy one in advance from a ticket machine (**Fahrkartenautomat**) at the stop. There you will also find information on fares. The principle sounds simple: the further you travel, the more you pay. But in practice it's quite tricky because you are expected to work out your own fares, according to an elaborate map with fare stages (**Tarifzonen**). To foreigners (and many Germans) this can be a daunting task, so it's best to ask one of your fellow passengers for assistance.

Once you have your ticket and are on the bus or tram or underground, you must cancel your ticket, that is, have it stamped by a little machine called an **Entwerter** (canceller). The canceller is either inside the bus and/or somewhere in the **U-Bahn** or **S-Bahn** station or at the **Haltestelle** (bus/tram stop). The ticket is only valid if cancelled. There is no inspector on the bus or at the barrier, but there are spot checks and fines are quite hefty.

Stops

A stop is called **eine Haltestelle**. There are different symbols for the stops of the various means of transport. The next stop is usually announced by the driver or a taped message, which will also tell you what lines you need to change for. When you want to get off, press the button next to the **Ausstieg** (exit) – just make sure you don't confuse it with the **Notbremse** (emergency brake)!

AND FINALLY...

16 You want to get to the Schillertheater. You'll need to make sure you've understood all the information provided by the person answering your query: so be prepared to repeat the most important bits. Some – but not all – of the phrases below will come in useful.

Fahren Sie/wie komme ich/wo bekomme ich/wo ist/entschuldigen Sie/ wie bitte/danke/Haltestelle/Linie/Bahnhof/Stadtzentrum

Husum town centre

ANSWERS

EXERCISE 1

(a) Museum **(b)** Café Berlin **(c)** Das Schöne Haus **(d)** St. Michael **(e)** Hotel am Markt

EXERCISE 2

(a) the first on the right **(b)** just here around the corner **(c)** turn right and then take the third on the left **(d)** 100 metres straight ahead of you **(e)** fifth door on the right

EXERCISE 3

(a) geradeaus (You go straight on for 500 metres) **(b)** linken (Keep straight on and then it's on the left) **(c)** Ecke (Just here around the corner) **(d)** zweite Straße rechts (Take the second on the right and then you will be standing directly in front of the post office) **(e)** erste Tür links (The bathroom is straight ahead, and then the first door on the left)

EXERCISE 4

(a) wo **(b)** Ecke **(c)** links **(d)** nächste **(e)** geradeaus **(f)** Toilette **(g)** rechts **(h)** Bank **(i)** Straße **(j)** direkt
MYSTERY WORD: Weinstraße (famous route through a wine growing area)

EXERCISE 6

a; d; e

EXERCISE 7

(a) At the main station in Ulm and at the Ehinger Tor bus stop **(b)** number 4 **(c)** Change into the number 3 or 8

EXERCISE 9

(a) two **(b)** DM 2.00 **(c)** Leipzig

EXERCISE 10

true: a; b; c; the others are false

EXERCISE 11

(a) I **(b)** A **(c)** F **(d)** B **(e)** J **(f)** C **(g)** G **(h)** D **(i)** H **(j)** E

EXERCISE 14

(a) Gehen Sie bitte zur Karlstraße. (Please go to the Karlstraße.) **(b)** Das Café ist im Bahnhof. (The café is in the station.) **(c)** Wie komme ich zum Hotel? (How do I get to the hotel?) **(d)** Ich gehe jetzt ins Theater. (I am now going to the theatre.) **(e)** Das Haus liegt direkt am Wasser. (The house lies directly by the water.)

EXERCISE 15

(a) Wir gehen ins Stadtzentrum. **(b)** Ich gehe in die Stadt. **(c)** Ich bin in der Stadt. **(d)** Wir sind im Stadtzentrum.

6

TIME AND DATES

WHAT YOU WILL LEARN

▶ asking the time
▶ finding out about opening hours
▶ talking about holidays
▶ you will also read about opening times and holidays

BEFORE YOU BEGIN

Quite a few words and phrases in this unit should sound familiar to you, especially the numbers and figures. It's worth going back to Units 2 and 3 if you're not too sure about them. As far as times, dates, and the seasons are concerned, many words are quite similar to the English and should be relatively easy to remember. Try to incorporate the German phrases in your daily life by practising them as much as you can: look at your watch and tell yourself the time in German, have a go at saying today's date or the date of your birthday, or your friends' birthdays.

Pronunciation notes

v and f

In German, both **v** and **f** always get pronounced as **f**: it's exactly the same sound as in the English 'follow' or 'fall'. Examples you have already come across are **vielen Dank** (many thanks) and **vier** (four). Other examples from this unit are **Viertel** (quarter) and **von** (from).

w

The German **w** is always pronounced like the English 'v'. So the English word 'van' and the German word **Wagen** (waggon, car) start with the same sounds. Some more examples are **Wind** (wind) and **Wolle** (wool). Words containing both **v** and **w** seem the biggest challenge, for example **Volkswagen** (the German car manufacturer) and **wieviel** (how much).

Tom will practise all these words on the recording; there will also be additional exercises within Unit 6 focusing on **f**, **v** and **w**.

What's the time?

LISTEN FOR...

Wie spät ist es?	What's the time?
Uhr	o'clock

Ruth	Wie spät ist es bitte?
Frau Mohn	Es ist zwölf Uhr.
	* * *
Ruth	Wie spät ist es bitte?
Frau Bagan	Es ist fünf nach sechs.
	* * *
Ruth	Wie spät ist es bitte?
Jessica	Ehm ... Viertel nach zwei.
Ruth	Ah. Danke schön.

Wie spät ist es? What's the time? (**spät** late); so literally the question is 'How late is it?'

zwölf Uhr twelve o'clock (**die Uhr** clock)

fünf nach sechs five past six (*lit.* five after six)

Viertel nach zwei a quarter past two (**das Viertel** quarter)

Telling the time: the twelve-hour clock

The twelve-hour clock is very similar to the English*:
'past' is translated by **nach** (after) and 'to' is translated by **vor** (before)

Es ist ...		It is ...	
fünf	nach sechs	five	past six
zehn	nach sechs	ten	past six
Viertel	nach sechs	a quarter	past six
zwanzig	nach sechs	twenty	past six
halb sieben*		half	past six*
zwanzig	vor sieben	twenty	to seven
Viertel	vor sieben	a quarter	to seven
zehn	vor sieben	ten	to seven
fünf	vor sieben	five	to seven

* *Exception:* Times at the half-hour are the tricky ones. **Halb zehn** is half past nine and not – as you might expect from the English – half (past) ten. The thinking behind it is this: **halb zehn** is not yet full ten, you're only half way there, so it's only 9.30.

1 Match up the clocks and times.

a. neun Uhr

e. zwanzig vor drei

b. zehn nach sieben

f. Viertel vor acht

c. Viertel nach fünf

g. halb zwölf

ANSWERS P. 94

d. halb vier

h. fünf nach sechs

2 What's the time? Turn to the recording and practise asking the time. Repeat the answers in response to your question and compare them to the times on the clocks below. Tick the ones that are being mentioned. Don't forget to use your pause button to give yourself enough time.

ANSWERS P. 94

3 Your turn to speak. On the recording, you'll be asked to give a few times yourself.

Opening hours – At the museum in Ulm

LISTEN FOR...

Öffnungszeiten	opening hours
geöffnet	open
täglich	daily
außer samstags	except Saturdays

Ruth   Ist das Museum heute geöffnet?

Herr Schmid   Ja, die Öffnungszeiten des Städtischen Museums sind täglich von zehn bis siebzehn Uhr, und das Deutsche Brotmuseum hat täglich außer samstags geöffnet, von zehn bis zwölf (10.00–12.00) und dann von fünfzehn (15.00) bis siebzehn Uhr dreißig (17.30).

heute   today; *cf* also **morgen** tomorrow (not to be confused with **der Morgen** the morning or **morgens** in the morning).

geöffnet   open (*lit.* opened; **öffnen** to open); the opposite is **geschlossen** closed. Another useful question: **Wann ist das Museum geöffnet?** When is the museum open?

täglich   daily; other important expressions: **morgens** and **vormittags** (*lit.* before noon) in the morning; **nachmittags** in the afternoon (**der Nachmittag** afternoon); **abends** in the evening; **nachts** at night.

die Öffnungszeiten des Städtischen Museums   the opening times of the municipal museum; **des Städtischen Museums** is the genitive case which is one way to translate 'of' in German (see Grammar summary at the back of the book for details) (**das Museum** museum).

Note that quite a few museums are closed on Mondays, so it's always advisable to enquire. If you see a sign saying **Geschlossen** or **Heute Ruhetag** (*lit.* rest day) outside a **Gaststätte** you'll know that the place is shut for the day.

das Deutsche Brotmuseum   the German Bread Museum, a unique museum in Ulm that charts the history of breadmaking through the centuries.

von fünfzehn bis siebzehn Uhr dreißig Note that Herr Schmid is using the 24-hour clock (see next page) which sounds more official and is used for example in announcements, timetables and the speaking clock.

außer samstags   except on Saturdays (**der Samstag** Saturday), *cf* **der Sonntag** Sunday; **sonntags** on Sundays

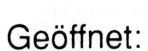

das Museum ist/hat geöffnet   the museum is open (both **ist** and **hat** are possible here)

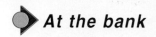 **At the bank**

Ruth	Wann sind Ihre Öffnungszeiten?
Frau Zarend	Montag, Dienstag und Freitag von acht Uhr dreißig (8.30 Uhr) bis sechzehn Uhr (16.00 Uhr). Mittwoch von acht Uhr dreißig (8.30 Uhr) bis dreizehn Uhr (13.00 Uhr) und Donnerstag von acht Uhr dreißig (8.30 Uhr) bis achtzehn Uhr (18.00 Uhr).

Here are the days of the week – they are all masculine:

Montag	Monday	**Donnerstag**	Thursday
Dienstag	Tuesday	**Freitag**	Friday
Mittwoch	Wednesday	**Samstag**	Saturday
	Sonntag Sunday		

 ## Telling the time – the 24-hour clock

Simply say **es ist** followed by the number of hours and the word **Uhr**:

Es ist	ein	Uhr	(1.00 Uhr)	It's	one o'clock	(i.e. 1 a.m.)
Es ist	sechs	Uhr	(6.00 Uhr)	It's	six o'clock	(i.e. 6 a.m.)
Es ist	dreizehn	Uhr	(13.00 Uhr)	It's	thirteen hundred hours	(i.e. 1 p.m.)
Es ist	achtzehn	Uhr	(18.00 Uhr)	It's	eighteen hundred hours	(i.e. 6 p.m.)
Es ist	vierundzwanzig	Uhr	(24.00 Uhr)	It's	24 hundred hours	(i.e. midnight)

Note that between hours you add the number of minutes after the word **Uhr** in *spoken* German, but when *written* in figures the word **Uhr** comes after the minutes: thus you'd *say* **siebzehn Uhr dreißig** but *write* **17.30 Uhr**, and you'd *say* **fünf Uhr fünfundzwanzig** but *write* **5.25 Uhr**.

Some further examples:

Es ist null	**Uhr**	**fünf**	(00.05 Uhr = 12.05 a.m. or five past midnight)
Es ist drei	**Uhr**	**fünfzehn**	(3.15 Uhr = 3.15 a.m.)
Es ist sechs	**Uhr**	**dreißig**	(6.30 Uhr = 6.30 a.m.)
Es ist siebzehn	**Uhr**	**fünfundvierzig**	(17.45 Uhr = 5.45 p.m.)

Two more words to do with time: **die Minute** minute; **die Sekunde** second. This is what you will hear on the speaking clock: **sieben Uhr vierundzwanzig Minuten dreizehn Sekunden** seven twenty-four and thirteen seconds.

4 Tongue twisters. Here are three sentences to read out aloud. Switch on the recording and Tom will tell you what to do.

a. Es ist Viertel vor vier.
b. Wir fahren mit dem Volkswagen vor das Theater.
c. Wieviel Fahrscheine haben wir hier?

5 Sharpen your ears. On the recording you will hear the four sets of words below read out. But the sequence is different. Which word in each pair is being read out first? Make a ring round it.

a. Fall – Wall
b. fein – Wein
c. voll – Wohl

ANSWERS P. 94
d. vier – wir

6 Match up the times in the three columns below as shown in the example given.

21.10	fünf nach vier	abends
06.20	fünf vor acht	nachmittags
19.55	zwanzig nach sechs	abends
00.45	halb zwei	nachts
16.05	zehn nach neun	nachmittags
13.30	Viertel vor eins	morgens

ANSWERS P. 94

7 The days of the week are usually abbreviated as below – write them out in full.

So _____   Mo _____

Di _____   Mi _____

Do _____   Fr _____

ANSWERS P. 94
Sa _____

Januar	Februar	März	April
4 11 18 25	1 8 15 22	1 8 15 22 29	5 **12** 19 26
5 12 19 26	2 9 16 23	2 9 16 23 30	6 13 20 27
6 13 20 27	3 10 17 24	3 10 17 24 31	7 14 21 28
7 14 21 28	4 11 18 25	4 11 18 25	1 8 15 22 29
1 8 15 22 29	5 12 19 26	5 12 19 26	2 **9** 16 23 30
2 9 16 23 30	6 13 20 27	6 13 20 27	3 10 17 24
3 10 17 24 31	**7 14 21 28**	**7 14 21 28**	**4 11 18 25**
53 1 2 3 4	5 6 7 8	9 10 11 12 13	13 14 15 16 17

8 Museums in Leipzig. Study the opening times and listen to the recording. Which one is the dialogue referring to?

ANSWER P. 94

> **Stadtgeschichtliches Museum (im Alten Rathaus)**
> Öffnungszeiten: Di-Fr 10.00-18.00 Uhr; Sa/So 10.00-16.00 Uhr
> Bibliothek zur Stadtgeschichte: Mo 14.00-18.00; Di-Do 10.00-13.00 Uhr Markt 1 Tel. 7 09 21
>
> **Buch- und Schriftmuseum (der Deutschen Bücherei)**
> Öffnungszeiten: Mo-Sa 9.00-16.00 Uhr
> Deutscher Platz (Westausgang Messegelände) Tel. 2 27 10
>
> **Naturkundemuseum (z.Z. geschlossen)**
> Öffnungszeiten: Di-Fr 9.00-18.00 Uhr; Sa 9.00-17.00 Uhr
> Lortzingstraße 3, 10 Minuten Fußweg in westlicher Richtung vom Bahnhof aus. Tel. 29 14 12 oder 28 31 29
>
> **Johann-Sebastian-Bach-Museum (im Bosehaus)**
> Nationale Forschung- und Gedenkstätten J.S. Bach: Bach-Archiv.
> Öffnungszeiten: Di-So 9.00-17.00 Uhr Thomaskirchhof 16
>
> **Ägyptisches Museum (der Leipziger Universität)**
> Öffnungszeiten: Di-Fr 14.00-18.00 Uhr; So 10.00-13.00 Uhr
> Schillerstraße 6. Tel. 28 21 66 oder 28 18 09

9 Take notes. On the recording, Erich is telling you about mass in Weingarten. Listen and take notes in English. Note that **Heilige Messe** (Holy Mass) is a Catholic mass, whilst **der evangelische Gottesdienst** is a Protestant service.

Heilige Messe is held _____ at _____ and on _____ at _____ and at _____ The **evangelische Gottesdienst** is held on _____ at _____ and on _____

ANSWERS P. 94

at _____

10 Read and understand. Here's a small extract from 'What's on in Hamburg'. It tells you the opening hours of some of the local museums. Study them, then read the statements below and tick off **R** (**richtig** right) or **F** (**falsch** wrong).

> KUNSTHALLE
> Glockengießerwall
> Di–So 10–17 Uhr
> Mo 10–19 Uhr
>
> MUSEUM RADE
> Naturpark Oberalster
> Sa, So 10–18 Uhr
>
> AUTO-MUSEUM HILLERS
> Kurt-Schumacher-Allee
> tägl. 10–18 Uhr
>
> POST-MUSEUM
> Stefansplatz 1
> Di, Fr 10–14 Uhr
> Do 10–16 Uhr

Internationales Keramik-Museum
Zweigmuseum der Neuen Sammlung
Weiden i. d. OPf

a. Die Kunsthalle hat täglich geöffnet.   R ☐   F ☐
b. Das Museum Rade hat die ganze Woche geöffnet.   R ☐   F ☐
c. Die Kunsthalle hat Mittwoch auch abends geöffnet.   R ☐   F ☐
d. Das Post-Museum ist am Samstag und Sonntag geschlossen. R ☐   F ☐
e. Das Auto-Museum hat am Montag Ruhetag.   R ☐   F ☐
f. Das Auto-Museum ist vormittags immer geöffnet.   R ☐   F ☐

11 Your turn to speak. You're at the tourist office trying to find out about various opening hours. Words to bear in mind are

Wann .../ist .../heute .../nachmittags .../geöffnet/geschlossen

Frau Bagan's holidays

LISTEN FOR...

Ferien	holidays
Ostern	Easter
Herbst	autumn
Weihnachten	Christmas

Ruth Wann haben Sie Ferien?

Frau Bagan Wir haben viermal im Jahr Ferien – große Ferien im Sommer sechs Wochen, zu Ostern zwei Wochen und im Herbst zwei Wochen und zu Weihnachten zwei Wochen.

große Ferien long (*lit.* big) holidays

im Sommer in the summer (**der Sommer**)

zu Ostern at Easter (**das Ostern**)

im Herbst in the autumn (**der Herbst**)

zu Weihnachten at Christmas (**das Weihnachten**, but it's mostly plural in greetings, etc.)

Wann haben Sie Ferien? When do you have your holidays? Another way of asking would be: **Wann sind Ihre Ferien?** When are your holidays? **(die) Ferien** (plural only) refer to school holidays as Frau Bagan is a teacher. Otherwise you'll need to use **(der) Urlaub.**

viermal im Jahr four times a year; **dreimal in der Woche** three times a week; **im** and **in der** are examples of the dative case (see Unit 5 grammar section).

Jessica's birthday

LISTEN FOR...

Geburtstag	birthday
Frühjahr	spring
März	March

Frau Bagan Wann hast du Geburtstag?
Jessica Im Frühjahr.
Frau Bagan Und wann genau?
Jessica Am sechzehnten März.

Wann hast du Geburtstag? When is your birthday? Another possibility (closer to the English) is **Wann ist dein Geburtstag?** (**der Geburtstag** birthday).

im Frühjahr in the spring; **das Frühjahr** and **der Frühling** both mean spring (**früh** early).

Und wann genau? And when exactly?

am sechzehnten März on the 16th of March; **am** (**an** + **dem**) is in the dative case. Note that 'of' is not translated.

am ersten März on the first of March

Dates

This is how you can give the date:

Written	Spoken
14. Mai 1985 or **14.5.85** **Heute ist der vierzehnte Mai.**	vierzehnter Mai neunzehnhundertfünfundachtzig vierzehnter fünfter fünfundachtzig Today is the 14th of May.

Note that the years are spoken as two blocks up to 1999 (**neunzehnhundert / neunundneunzig**), much as in English except that English usually omits the hundred while German always includes the **hundert**. For the years after 2000 (**zweitausend**) usage is parallel, so the year 2004 would be **das Jahr zweitausend(und)vier**.

The months of the year			
Januar	January	**Juli**	July
Februar	February	**August**	August
März	March	**September**	September
April	April	**Oktober**	October
Mai	May	**November**	November
Juni	June	**Dezember**	December
All the months are masculine			

Frau Vollmert's favourite holiday times

LISTEN FOR...

Urlaub   holiday

Ruth	Wann machen Sie Urlaub?
Frau Vollmert	Im nächsten Jahr mache ich zweimal Urlaub, im Frühjahr und im Herbst.
Ruth	Und was machen Sie da?
Frau Vollmert	Oh, im Frühjahr möchte ich gern nach Griechenland fahren, da ist es noch nicht so heiß. Ja, und im Herbst, das weiß ich noch nicht genau, aber wahrscheinlich auch nach Südeuropa. Vielleicht im September oder Oktober nach Spanien, da ist es dann nicht mehr so heiß.

Wann machen Sie Urlaub?   When do you go on (*lit.* make) holiday? Note that **der Urlaub** is always singular in German, just as 'leave' is in English.

Und was machen Sie da?   And what will you do (then)? (*lit.* What are you doing there?) Note that **machen** means both 'to do' and 'to make'. A note on the tenses: Germans frequently use the present tense when referring to the future, provided it's clear from the context which time they are talking about.

im Frühjahr möchte ich gern nach Griechenland fahren in the spring I'd like to go to Greece. Frau Vollmert could also have used the present tense if her plans had been definite: **im Frühjahr fahre ich nach Griechenland** in the spring I'm going to Greece.

da ist es noch nicht so heiß   it's not so hot there then; more on the use of **nicht** in the grammar section in this unit.

das weiß ich noch nicht genau   I don't know (that) yet exactly, i.e. I'm not sure yet.

wahrscheinlich   probably

da ist es dann nicht mehr so heiß   it's no longer so hot there then; **nicht mehr** means no longer or not any more, e.g. **ich bin nicht mehr müde** I'm no longer tired or not tired any more.

PRACTICE

12

On the recording you'll hear a short interview with Herr Schneider about his work and his holidays. Listen as often as you need and tick the right answers.

New phrase:
wie lange? how long?

a. Herr Schneider works
   every day
   four days a week

b. He works from
   Tuesday to Friday
   Monday to Thursday

c. He works
   eight hours a day
   six hours a day

d. He always takes his holidays in
   the spring
   the summer

e. He goes away in
   July
   June

f. He goes away for
   two weeks
   three weeks

ANSWERS P. 94

13

Guesswork. Greetings and congratulations. Pair the German phrases with their English equivalents. Not all words will be familiar but you should be able to guess the gist of their meaning. This will also be a good chance to use a dictionary.

Fröhliche Ostern!

Alles Gute zum Geburtstag!

Die besten Wünsche zum Neuen Jahr!

Friedliche Weihnachten und ein gutes Neues Jahr!

Herzliche Urlaubsgrüße!

Gratulationen zum goldenen Jubiläum!

Best wishes for your Birthday

Holiday greetings!

Happy Easter!

Best wishes for the New Year

Congratulations on your Golden Jubilee

ANSWERS P. 94 *A peaceful Christmas and a happy New Year*

14

Dates of birth: make a ring round the ones that are being mentioned on the recording.

7. Juli 1947 – 13. März 1955 – 27. April 1967 – 17. Juni 1984 – 1. Mai 1948 –

10. Oktober 1936 – 24. Dezember 1974 – 3. Januar 1931 – 12. April 1961

ANSWERS P. 94

Holidays – when and where to? On the recording, Katie and Urs are being interviewed about their holidays. Fill in the grid below – in German.

Ferien	Katie	Urs
Wie oft?		
Wie lange?		
Wann?		
Wohin?		

ANSWERS P. 94

16

Travel dates. Around Germany in a year. On the recording you'll hear Frau Vogel's itinerary. Jot down the weekdays and dates next to the cities in the list below, in English. We have given you one example.

Hamburg ___ *Friday Jan. 1st* _____

Bremen _____

Essen _____

Frankfurt am Main _____

Mannheim _____

Stuttgart _____

Dresden _____

Leipzig _____

ANSWERS P. 94 Berlin _____

17

Your turn to speak and find out about Dorit's holidays. But first she'll want to know about your own holiday plans. Use the present tense (*for example*: **im Sommer fahre ich nach ...**). Some of these phrases will come in useful:

Wann machen Sie Urlaub?

Wie lange?

Was machen Sie da?

zweimal / dreimal

im Frühjahr / Sommer / Herbst / Winter

ich fahre nach ...

UFERLOS
07563/2636

Disco-Party
vor Feiertagen

Biergarten am See
Langschläfer-Frühstück
und warme Küche
So u. an Feiertagen
ab 11.00 Uhr geöffnet

The use of *nicht* and *kein*

nicht (not)

The basic German word for 'not' is **nicht**. In simple sentences, **nicht** comes straight after the verb:

Es ist heiß.   It is hot.
Es ist nicht heiß.   It is not hot.

You don't need to translate the English 'do' in a negative sentence, all you need is the word **nicht**.

Ich wohne in Berlin.   I live in Berlin.
Ich wohne nicht in Berlin.   I don't live in Berlin.

In sentences with two verbs, **nicht** tends to come after the first verb:

Ich will nach Griechenland   I want to go to
  fahren.   Greece.
Ich will nicht nach   I do not want to go
  Griechenland fahren.   to Greece.

However, you need not get bogged down in the subtleties of the positioning of **nicht** at this stage. The most important thing is to recognize **nicht** as a negative and place it after the verb.

kein/keine/kein
(no, not a/any)

The simple translation of **kein** is 'no':

Ich habe kein Kind.   I have no child.
Ich habe kein Auto.   I have no car.

However, it also translates as 'not a' (in German you cannot say **nicht ein**). So 'I don't have' or 'I haven't got a child' translates as **ich habe kein Kind**, and 'I don't have' or 'I haven't got a car' as **ich habe kein Auto**.

As far as endings are concerned, **kein** behaves just like the indefinite article **ein** (see Grammar summary for details):

Ich habe einen Mann.   I have a husband.
Ich habe keinen Mann.   I have no husband.

Ich habe eine Frau.   I have a wife.
Ich habe keine Frau.   I have no wife.

Remember that **nicht** (not) negates a verb (or an adjective or adverb), whereas **kein** negates a noun. *For example:*

Ich gehe.   I walk.
Ich gehe nicht.   I don't walk.
Meine Frau ist hier.   My wife is here.
Meine Frau ist nicht hier.   My wife is not here.
but:
Ich habe eine Freundin.   I have a girl friend.
Ich habe keine Freundin.   I have no girl friend.

18 Turn the negative statements into positive statements following the pattern below. Then translate the sentences into English.
Example:

Der Wein ist nicht gut. ▶ *Der Wein ist gut.*
　　　　　　　　　　　　 ▶ *The wine is good.*

a. Wir möchten nicht nach Kanada fahren.

_____

_____

b. Die Bank ist heute nicht geöffnet.

_____

_____

c. Ich habe keinen Fahrschein.

_____

_____

d. Klaus möchte keinen Saft.

_____

_____

ANSWERS P. 94

19 Answer the questions below – first with 'yes', then with 'no'.

Example: **Gehen Sie zum Bahnhof?**
　　　　　 ▶ **Ja, ich gehe zum Bahnhof.**
　　　　　 ▶ *Nein, ich gehe nicht zum Bahnhof.*

a. Sind Sie aus Ulm?

　Ja, _____

　Nein, _____

b. Fahren Sie zur Donauhalle?

　Ja, _____

　Nein, _____

c. Arbeiten Sie in München?

　Ja, _____

　Nein, _____

d. Ist das Zimmer frei?

　Ja, _____

　Nein, _____

ANSWERS P. 94

20 Negate the sentences below.

Example: **Dies ist ein guter Wein.**
　　　　　 ▶ *Dies ist kein guter Wein.*

a. Ich habe ein Zimmer.

_____

b. Zum Theater gibt es eine gute U-Bahn-Verbindung.

_____

c. Wir haben ein Auto.

_____

d. Ich möchte ein Bier.

_____

e. Möchten Sie eine heiße Milch?

_____

ANSWERS P. 94

KEY WORDS

Times:

Wie spät ist es (bitte)?	What's the time (please)?
(Es ist) zehn Uhr	(It is) ten o'clock
fünf nach zehn	five past ten
zehn nach zehn	ten past ten
Viertel nach zehn	a quarter past ten
zwanzig nach zehn	twenty past ten
fünfundzwanzig nach zehn	twenty-five past ten
halb elf	half past ten
fünfundzwanzig vor elf	twenty-five to eleven
zwanzig vor elf	twenty to eleven
Viertel vor elf	a quarter to eleven
zehn vor elf	ten to eleven
fünf vor elf	five to eleven

SEPT.- NOV. '94
30. AUGUST - 3. DEZEMBER 1994
TIGER PALAST
INTERNATIONALE HERBST-REVUE

More formal phrases:

Es ist dreizehn Uhr elf	It is one eleven p.m. (*lit.* thirteen eleven)
zwei Uhr zwölf Minuten drei Sekunden	two twelve and three seconds
Wann ...	When ...
sind die Öffnungszeiten?	are the opening times?
hat/ist das Museum geöffnet?	is the museum open?
geschlossen?	closed?
machen Sie Urlaub?	are you going on holiday?

Ich mache im Sommer Urlaub	I'm going on holiday in the summer
Das weiß ich noch nicht	I don't know yet
täglich	daily, every day
zwei Wochen/drei Monate	two weeks/three months
zweimal im Jahr	twice a year
heute	today
im Frühjahr/Sommer/Herbst/Winter	in spring/summer/autumn/winter
von 13 (dreizehn) bis 14 (vierzehn) Uhr	from 1 to 2 p.m.
morgens/vormittags	in the morning
nachmittags	in the afternoon
abends	in the evening
nachts	at night
montags ist Ruhetag	closed on Mondays

The days of the week:

Montag	Monday
Dienstag	Tuesday
Mittwoch	Wednesday
Donnerstag	Thursday
Freitag	Friday
Samstag	Saturday
Sonntag	Sunday

The months of the year:

Januar	Juli
Februar	August
März	September
April	Oktober
Mai	November
Juni	Dezember

The date:

Heute ist Freitag, der erste Mai	Today is Friday the first of May
Ich habe am dritten Juni Geburtstag	My birthday is on June the third
1984 (neunzehnhundertvierundachtzig)	1984 (nineteen eighty-four)
1.11.95 (der erste elfte fünfundneunzig)	1/11/95 (the first day of the eleventh ninety-five)
Das Jahr 2004 (zweitausend(und)vier)	The year 2004 (two thousand and four)

Opening times and holidays

Here are some general guidelines on hours of business. Slight variations from region to region are possible.

Shops

They usually open between 8 and 9 a.m. (Some baker's and butcher's open even earlier.) Shops shut either at 6 or at 6.30 p.m. from Mondays to Fridays. Saturday closing times vary: in Germany shops shut at 1 or 2 p.m. except for the first Saturday of the month, when most town shops are open till 6 p.m. for the **langer Samstag** (*lit.* long Saturday). In Switzerland and Austria the bigger shops tend to be open until 4 or 5 p.m. each Saturday. Alternatively they might offer late-night shopping once a week. You'll find (especially in smaller towns and in the country) that shops are closed at lunchtime, and in some regions for one morning or afternoon a week, or even for a whole day.

Pubs

Their hours vary considerably, but in general they open at around 11 a.m. and stay open till midnight or beyond.

Public holidays

These are called **Feiertage**. Many public holidays have religious origins and names. Predominantly Catholic regions sometimes have a holiday which is a working day in a mainly Protestant area and vice versa. On some of these holidays there will be special events like processions, festivals, etc. You can ask the tourist offices for a list of forthcoming events, and most of the bigger towns and resorts publish a 'What's on in ...' booklet. The local newspapers will also list what's on.

School holidays

These are called **Schulferien**. In Germany, summer holidays are staggered from **Land** (state) to **Land** in order to avoid chaos on the roads and railways, starting in June and generally ending by early September.

Carnival in Ravensburg

AND FINALLY...

21 Here are some important birthdays Herr Rosen has jotted down. Turn to the recording where you'll be asked to repeat some of them in German.

Maria	8. Oktober	Rosemarie	20. Januar
Maximilian	1. April	Regina	3. Juni
Petra	25. März	Angelika	16. Januar
Andreas	7. Juli	Sylvia	31. August

ANSWERS

EXERCISE 1
(a) B (b) C (c) H (d) G (e) F (f) E (g) A (h) D

EXERCISE 2
a; d; c

EXERCISE 5
You should have made a ring round: (a) Fall (b) Wein
(c) Wohl (d) vier

EXERCISE 6
06.20–zwanzig nach sechs–morgens; 19.55–fünf vor
acht–abends; 00.45–Viertel vor eins–nachts; 16.05–fünf nach
vier–nachmittags; 13.30–halb zwei–nachmittags

EXERCISE 7
Sonntag; Dienstag; Donnerstag; Samstag; Montag; Mittwoch;
Freitag

EXERCISE 8
Ägyptisches Museum

EXERCISE 9
Heilige Messe is held daily at 7 and on Sunday at 8.30 and
10 o'clock; the evangelische Gottesdienst is held on
Saturday at 5 p.m. and Sunday morning at 9

EXERCISE 10
(a) R (b) F (c) F (d) R (e) F (f) R

EXERCISE 12
(a) four days a week (b) Tuesday to Friday
(c) eight hours (d) summer (e) June (f) three weeks

EXERCISE 13
Fröhliche Ostern – Happy Easter; Alles Gute zum Geburtstag
– Best wishes for your Birthday; Die besten Wünsche zum
Neuen Jahr – Best wishes for the New Year; Friedliche
Weihnachten und ein gutes Neues Jahr – A peaceful
Christmas and a happy New Year; Herzliche Urlaubsgrüße
– Holiday greetings; Gratulationen zum goldenen Jubiläum –
Congratulations on your Golden Jubilee

EXERCISE 14
7. Juli 1947 1. Mai 1948 3. Januar 1931 13. März 1955
10. Oktober 1936 12. April 1961

EXERCISE 15

	Katie	Urs
how often	einmal im Jahr	zweimal im Jahr
how long	5–6 Wochen	zweimal zwei Wochen
when	Herbst (Sept. oder Okt.)	Winter und Sommer
where to	USA	Schweden und Kanada

EXERCISE 16
Bremen: Wednesday Jan. 26th; Essen: Sunday Feb.
10th; Frankfurt am Main: Wednesday March 16th;
Mannheim: Saturday April 2nd; Stuttgart: Monday May
9th; Dresden: Tuesday June 21st; Leipzig: Thursday
July 28th; Berlin: Wednesday August 31st

EXERCISE 18
(a) Wir möchten nach Kanada fahren. We want to go to
Canada. (b) Die Bank ist heute geöffnet. The bank is open
today. (c) Ich habe einen Fahrschein. I have a ticket.
(d) Klaus möchte einen Saft. Klaus would like a juice.

EXERCISE 19
(a) Ja, ich bin aus Ulm. Nein, ich bin nicht aus Ulm.
(b) Ja, ich fahre zur Donauhalle. Nein, ich fahre nicht zur
Donauhalle. (c) Ja, ich arbeite in München. Nein, ich arbeite
nicht in München. (d) Ja, das Zimmer ist frei. Nein, das
Zimmer ist nicht frei.

EXERCISE 20
(a) Ich habe kein Zimmer. (b) Zum Theater gibt es keine gute
U-Bahn-Verbindung. (c) Wir haben kein Auto. (d) Ich
möchte kein Bier. (e) Möchten Sie keine heiße Milch?

7 SHOPPING

WHAT YOU WILL LEARN

▶ asking for stamps and picture postcards
▶ choosing souvenirs
▶ doing your daily shopping
▶ you will also read about various kinds of shops and markets

BEFORE YOU BEGIN

Given the number of supermarkets and other shops where you just help yourself, you'll probably get away with very few words when doing your actual shopping. However, you might have to make more of an effort when visiting the local markets, and they are definitely more fun to explore. Do bear in mind that measures are metric on the Continent, so it will be useful to have a rough idea of the quantities to expect.

Flensburg

Pronunciation notes

au, ei and ie

au

The **au** as in **verkaufen** (to sell) is pronounced like 'ow' in the English word 'how'. Another example in this unit is **auch** (also).

On the other hand, **äu** and **eu** sound very different being pronounced like the 'oi' in the English word 'coin' – have another look at the pronunciation notes in Unit 2 to refresh your memory.

ei

The **ei** such as in **Wein** is the same sound as the 'i' in the English word 'wine'. It might also be helpful to think of **Heidi**.

ie

Do not confuse the **ei** with the **ie**, which is the same sound as in 'beef'. Think of **Bier** (beer) to make it stick, or **vier** (four). Turn to the recording to listen to all these words. There will also be a chance to practise these sounds with the adjective list on the grammar pages.

Buying postcards

LISTEN FOR...	
verkaufen	to sell
Briefmarken	stamps

Ruth	Verkaufen Sie Postkarten von Kiel?
Frau Hölk	Ja, wir verkaufen Postkarten von Kiel.
Ruth	Und was kostet das Stück?
Frau Hölk	Das Stück kostet fünfzig Pfennig.
Ruth	Aha. Darf ich mal sehen?
Frau Hölk	Gerne.
Ruth	Gut. Dann nehme ich diese zwei hier.
Frau Hölk	Bitte schön.
Ruth	Und haben Sie auch Briefmarken?
Frau Hölk	Nein, leider nicht. Die bekommen Sie bei der Post.

verkaufen to sell (but **kaufen** to buy)

die Postkarte also **die Ansichtskarte** picture postcard

Was kostet das Stück? What does one (*lit.* the piece) cost? This is a useful phrase when finding out the price per item, also when you don't know the gender of the word or even the word itself; *cf* also **65 Pf das Stück** 65 pfennig each.

das Stück kostet ... each one costs ..., they cost ... each. Note also **das macht**, used when saying how much you owe, for example **das macht eine Mark** that comes to one mark, that'll be one mark.

Darf ich mal sehen? May I see? **Mal** is a filler word to make the question sound less abrupt. Note the word order in a question with two verbs: the first verb goes right to the front, and the second verb to the end of the sentence. Another example:

Möchten Sie mal sehen? Would you like to see?

gerne with pleasure

dann nehme ich diese zwei hier then I'll take these two (**nehmen** to take). Ruth could also have said: **dann kaufe ich diese zwei hier**. Note the word order: the sentence starts with **dann**, the verb remains in second place, sending the subject (here: **ich**) into third place.

die Briefmarke stamp; other useful words: **der Brief** letter; **das Paket** parcel; **mit Luftpost** by airmail

die (Briefmarken) bekommen Sie bei der Post those (stamps) you get at the post office; this is another example of the verb and subject being switched round because **die** has been placed at the beginning of the sentence for emphasis. Usual word order: **Sie bekommen die bei der Post.** A very useful question to ask: **Wo bekomme ich Briefmarken?** Where do I get stamps?

1 There's more than one way of saying things in German. Study the sentences below and decide what you could also say instead of the first sentence in each set. Mark it with an asterisk. Then check your answers on the recording.

Example:
Was macht das?
* Was kostet das?
   Wo bekomme ich das?

a. Verkaufen Sie Postkarten?
    Haben Sie Postkarten?
    Möchten Sie Postkarten?

b. Was kostet eine Postkarte?
    Was kostet eine Briefmarke?
    Was kostet das Stück?

c. Darf ich mal sehen?
    Darf ich eine Karte kaufen?
    Ich möchte gerne eine Karte sehen.

d. Dann nehme ich zwei Karten.
    Ich möchte gerne zwei Karten kaufen.
    Ich möchte gerne zwei Karten verkaufen.

e. Und wo bekomme ich Briefmarken?
    Und wo verkaufen Sie Briefmarken?
    Und wo gibt es Briefmarken?

2 Make up the questions to the answers below.

a. _____ ?

Ja, wir verkaufen Postkarten von Hamburg.

b. _____ ?

Das Stück kostet eine Mark.

c. _____ ?

Nein, wir haben keine Briefmarken.

d. _____ ?

ANSWERS P. 108

Briefmarken bekommen Sie bei der Post.

3 Your turn to speak and buy a postcard or two. The words below will be useful:

verkaufen	**Darf ich mal sehen?**
Postkarten	**Haben Sie auch ...?**
Briefmarken	**Dann nehme ich ...**
das Stück	

Looking for souvenirs

LISTEN FOR...

Aschenbecher	ashtrays
Weingläser	wineglasses

Ruth	Grüß Gott!
Verkäufer	Guten Tag!
Ruth	Haben Sie auch Souvenirs?
Verkäufer	Ja, wir haben Aschenbecher und Weingläser.
Ruth	Aha. Was kostet denn dieses Weinglas hier?
Verkäufer	Das kostet fünf Mark das kleine; und das größere fünf Mark neunzig.
Ruth	Hm. Und der Aschenbecher hier?
Verkäufer	Der Aschenbecher ist aus Zinn und kostet dreizehn Mark fünfzig. Gibt es auch in kleiner, da kostet er neun Mark fünfundzwanzig.
Ruth	Ach ja. Dann nehm' ich den kleinen Aschenbecher, bitte.

das Souvenir   souvenir

der Aschenbecher   ashtray

Weingläser plural of **das Weinglas**   wineglass

das kleine   the small one. Note that 'one' is not translated. If you were talking about the ashtray, you'd need to say *der* **kleine kostet ...** because it's **der Aschenbecher**, and if you were talking about the stamp (**die Briefmarke**) you'd have to say: *die* **kleine kostet ...** but both are translated as the small one costs ...

das größere   the larger one

aus Zinn   made of pewter; more examples:
aus Gold   made of gold;
aus Metall   made of metal

(den) gibt es auch in kleiner   there's also a smaller one; **den** (that) is emphasized and therefore comes at the beginning of the sentence.

dann nehm' ich den kleinen Aschenbecher   then I'll take the small ashtray. Note that **Aschenbecher** here is the (accusative) object of the sentence and not only has **der** changed to **den**, but the adjective **klein** to **kleinen**. (More on this in the grammar pages in this unit.)

4 Sharpen your ears. How often can you hear the following words and phrases in the conversation on the recording? Make a cross each time they come up.

ANSWERS P. 108

a. verkaufen   e. Weingläser

b. haben   f. Darf ich ... mal ... sehen?

c. Souvenirs   g. Was kostet ...?

d. Aschenbecher   h. Was kosten ...?

5 Which answer fits? Decide which of the responses below are possible – there's only one possibility in each set. Then listen to the right answers on the recording.

a. Haben Sie auch Souvenirs?
   Nein, leider nicht.
   Ja, wir haben Tomatensuppe mit Brot.

b. Und wo bekomme ich Souvenirs?
   Gleich hier um die Ecke.
   Kommen Sie aus Berlin?

c. Was kostet dieses Weinglas hier?
   Für meine Frau.
   Fünfzehn Mark.

6 Your turn to speak and hunt for souvenirs. Turn to the recording where Tom will help you along. The name of the souvenir shop is **Souvenirmarkt** (souvenir market).

SOUVENIRMARKT

◗ Buying food – At the market

LISTEN FOR...

Pfirsiche	peaches
Karotten	carrots
Kirschen	cherries
Zwiebeln	onions

Ruth	Ein Pfund Pfirsich(e), bitte!
Verkäufer	Wir haben da verschiedene Pfirsiche, griechische, italienische, kleine, große ...
Ruth	Griechische.
Verkäufer	Griechische ... so, ein Pfund Pfirsiche.
Ruth	Ein Pfund Karotten.
Verkäufer	Ein Pfund Karotten.
Ruth	Und ein Pfund Kirschen.
Verkäufer	Ein Pfund Kirschen ... da, ein Pfund Kirschen.
Ruth	Zwei Pfund Zwiebeln.
Verkäufer	Da hätten wir rote, weiße und normale Zwiebeln.
Ruth	Rote bitte.
Verkäufer	Rote.

ein Pfund Pfirsiche a pound of peaches (**das Pfund** pound, **der Pfirsich** peach). Note that 'of' is not translated with measures, just as in **ein Glas Wein, eine Tasse Kaffee.**

verschiedene Pfirsiche various peaches

griechische, italienische, kleine, große ... Greek, Italian, small, large (ones). Note the multitude of plurals and adjectives in this dialogue. All of them are in the accusative case.

die Karotte (also **die Möhre**) carrot
die Kirsche cherry
die Zwiebel onion; some more useful words for the market (**der Markt**): **die Birne** pear; **die Banane** banana; **die Traube** grape; **die Aprikose** apricot; **die Kartoffel** potato; **die Bohne** bean; **die Tomate** tomato; **der Kopfsalat** lettuce; **das Kilo** kilo(gram); **ein Kilo Äpfel** a kilo(gram) (about two pounds) of apples.

The colours

gelb	yellow	**grün**	green
orange	orange	**braun**	brown
rot	red	**schwarz**	black
blau	blue	**grau**	grey

da hätten wir we have (conditional tense); a politer way of saying **da haben wir.**
rote, weiße und normale Zwiebeln red, white and normal onions

Weights
1 Kilo (or **kg**) = **2 Pfund** = **1000 Gramm** (or **g**)
1 Pfund = **500 Gramm** (or **g**)   28 grams = 1 ounce
Note: one English pound is about 50 g less than the metric pound

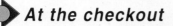

▶ *At the checkout*

Käseaufschnitt, zwei Mark neunundsechzig
(2,69);
Milch, eins neunundfünfzig (1,59);
sechs Flaschen Bier, fünf Mark neunundvierzig
(5,49);
(ein) halbes Pfund Kaffee, sechs Mark
neunundneunzig (6,99);
Salami, vierhundert Gramm, fünf neunundneunzig (5,99);
Butter, (ein) halbes Pfund, eine Mark neunundsiebzig (1,79);
Leberwurst, drei Mark neunundneunzig (3,99);
zwei Flaschen Wein vier neunundneunzig (4,99).
Macht zusammen achtunddreißig einundfünfzig (38,51).

Käseaufschnitt   assorted slices of cheese; similarly **Wurstaufschnitt** assorted slices of sausage

die Milch   (milk) is sold by the litre (**der Liter**, **ltr** or **l** for short) and half-litre; thus **ein Liter Milch** a litre of milk; **ein halber Liter Milch** half a litre of milk.

sechs Flaschen Bier   six bottles of beer (**die Flasche** bottle)

ein halbes Pfund Kaffee   half a pound of coffee (250 g)

vierhundert Gramm   400 grams. Smaller amounts of cheese and sausage can be bought by the gram or by the pound. You can say **ein halbes Pfund Käse** or **zweihundertfünfzig Gramm Käse**

die Leberwurst   liver sausage

macht zusammen ...   makes or comes to ... altogether

---

7 At the market, the stallholder is advertising his produce. But all is not well – the price tags below have got a bit mixed up. Sort them out while listening to the recording.

You'll hear a new phrase: **aus Omas Garten** from granny's garden

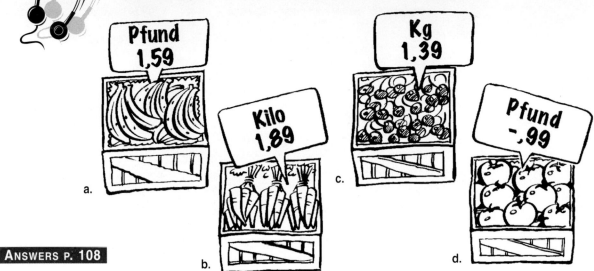

Pfund 1,59

a.

Kilo 1,89

b.

Kg 1,39

c.

Pfund –,99

d.

ANSWERS P. 108

8 This riddle is about one particular fruit. Try and guess which one it might be. Here is a transcript of the recording.

New vocabulary:
wie (here) as
der Schnee snow
der Klee clover
das Blut blood
schmeckt allen Kindern gut tastes good to all children

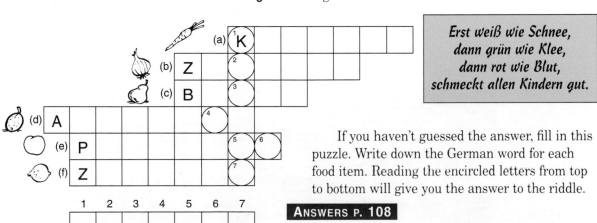

> *Erst weiß wie Schnee,*
> *dann grün wie Klee,*
> *dann rot wie Blut,*
> *schmeckt allen Kindern gut.*

(a) **K**
(b) **Z**
(c) **B**
(d) **A**
(e) **P**
(f) **Z**

If you haven't guessed the answer, fill in this puzzle. Write down the German word for each food item. Reading the encircled letters from top to bottom will give you the answer to the riddle.

ANSWERS P. 108

9 At the supermarket checkout. On the recording, the cashier is ringing up some more items and their prices. Study the new vocabulary, then turn on the recording and write down the prices next to the items. But watch out, the sequence is not the same as in the book.

New vocabulary:
das Mehl   flour
eine Tube Zahnpasta   a tube of toothpaste
eine Packung Taschentücher   a packet of paper handkerchiefs
die Seife   soap
die Eiernudeln   egg noodles
die Rindfleischsuppe   beef soup
das Öl   oil

 a. _____

 e. _____

 i. _____

 b. _____

 f. _____

 j. _____

 c. _____

 g. _____

 k. _____

 d. _____

 h. _____

 l. _____

ANSWERS P. 108

10 What fits together? Cross out the expressions that do not fit, write the correct expressions down and listen to the answers on the recording.

a. Käse: Tasse/Stück _____

b. Karotten: Pfund/Flasche _____

c. Wein: 100 g/Liter _____

d. Milch: Liter/Aufschnitt _____

e. Leberwurst: 1 l/250 g _____

f. Bier: Flasche/Tasse _____

g. Kirschen: Glas/Kilo _____

h. Zwiebeln: rote/Flasche _____

11 Your turn to do the shopping now – or rather, to delegate by telling a friend what you want. Tom will prompt you.

Here's a list of useful expressions (you won't need all of them):

Stück	Gramm	Milch	Wurstaufschnitt
Pfund	Packung	Taschentücher	Zucker
Flasche(n)	Kilo	Käseaufschnitt	Brötchen
Liter	Bier		

Adjectives

Adjectives are words such as **groß** (big, tall), **klein** (small), **grün** (green), **normal** (normal). They are used to describe things, for instance:

Der Apfel ist grün.	The apple is green.
Die Zitrone ist gelb.	The lemon is yellow.
Das Taxi ist schwarz.	The taxi is black.

In these sentences, where the adjective does not appear before a noun, the adjective never changes – it's the same for masculine, feminine and neuter nouns. And it doesn't change in the plural either:

Die Pfirsiche sind klein.	The peaches are small.

However, if adjectives come in front of the noun, their endings need to change, depending on

- the *article* in front: is it definite (**der** etc.) or indefinite (**ein** etc.)?
- the *gender* of the noun: is it masculine, feminine or neuter?
- its *case* (i.e. its function in the sentence): is it nominative (the subject), genitive, dative or accusative (the object)?
- the *number*: is it singular or plural?

Here are some examples:

Ich nehme das kleine Weinglas.
I'll take the small wineglass.
(**das Weinglas** ▶ definite article, neuter, accusative, singular)

Ich nehme ein kleines Weinglas.
I'll take a small wineglass.
(**ein Weinglas** ▶ indefinite article, neuter, accusative, singular)

Ich nehme den kleinen Aschenbecher.
I'll take the small ashtray.
(**den Aschenbecher** ▶ definite article, masculine, accusative, singular)

Wo sind die neuen Weingläser?
Where are the new wineglasses?
(**die Weingläser** ▶ definite article, neuter, accusative, plural)

The full set of endings is in the Grammar summary on page 243, mainly for reference as you could not be expected to learn them all at once.

However, it is very useful to expand your basic vocabulary at this stage and make sure you have a few more adjectives to play around with. Below is a list for you to learn; turn to the recording to practise their pronunciation. Erich will read each adjective in the left-hand column separately, and then pause for you to read the corresponding adjective on the right-hand side. After that you'll hear Dorit pronounce the same adjective for you.

alt	old	**neu**	new
billig	cheap	**teuer**	expensive
dunkel	dark	**hell**	light
süß	sweet	**sauer**	sour
früh	early	**spät**	late
kalt	cold	**heiß**	hot
schwer	heavy (in weight)	**leicht**	light (in weight)
	difficult		easy
voll	full	**leer**	empty
hart	hard	**weich**	soft
lang	long	**kurz**	short
gut	good	**schlecht**	bad

12 Transformations: change the phrases below following the same pattern as in the example provided. Then translate the sentences into English.

Example: **die weißen Zwiebeln**
► **die Zwiebeln sind weiß**
► The onions are white

a. die harten Pfirsiche ►

_____

_____

b. die billigen Würste ►

_____

_____

c. die kalten Getränke ►

_____

_____

d. die alten Weingläser ►

_____

_____

e. die kleinen Aschenbecher ►

_____

_____

f. die großen Kartoffeln ►

_____

_____

ANSWERS P. 108

13 Opposites: replace the adjectives with their opposites, paying particular attention to the adjective endings.

Examples: **eine harte Birne** ► **eine weiche Birne**
die kleinen Würste ► **die großen Würste**

a. kleine Damen

_____

b. der kalte Kaffee

_____

c. ein harter Apfel

_____

d. eine schwere Sprache

_____

e. die frühen Erdbeeren

_____

f. das kleine Auto

_____

g. lange Reisen

_____

ANSWERS P. 108

14 Criticisms: translate them into German.

a. The strawberries are old

_____

b. The wineglasses are expensive

_____

c. The apple is hard

_____

d. The grapes are bad

_____

e. The wine is sour

_____

f. The beer is warm

_____

ANSWERS P. 108

KEY WORDS

To use yourself:

Haben Sie/Verkaufen Sie (auch) ...	Do you (also) have/sell ...
Postkarten/Ansichtskarten?	postcards/picture postcards?
Souvenirs?	souvenirs?
Wo bekomme ich ...?	Where do I get ...?
Darf ich (mal) sehen?	May I see?
Was kostet das Stück?	How much are they each?
das Weinglas?	is the wineglass?
Dann nehme/kaufe ich ...	Then I'll take/have ...

ein (halbes) Pfund/Kilo ...	(half) a pound/kilogram of ...
Pfirsiche	peaches
Karotten (Möhren)	carrots
Kirschen	cherries
Zwiebeln	onions
Äpfel	apples
Birnen	pears
Trauben	grapes
Kartoffeln	potatoes
Tomaten	tomatoes

To understand:

Wir haben/verkaufen ...	We have/sell ...
große	large ones
kleine	small ones
normale	normal ones
griechische	Greek ones
italienische	Italian ones
gelbe/grüne/blaue	yellow/green/blue ones
Das Stück kostet ...	Each one costs ...
Der/Die/Das kleine kostet ...	The small one costs ...
(das) macht zusammen ...	(that) comes to/makes altogether

Weights and volumes:

1 ounce = 28 grams
1 (English) pound = 454 grams
1 kilogram = 2.2 pounds
1 gram = 0.035 ounces

Note that German weights and measures are
metric and a German pound (**ein Pfund**) is slightly
heavier than a British pound.

1 Pfund = 500 Gramm
1 Kilo = 2 Pfund
1 Liter = 1.7 pints

Shopping

Markets

Almost all towns, big or small, have one or two market days a week, often Wednesday or Saturday mornings. Some towns have a permanent market open throughout the week. You can buy fruit and vegetables, flowers, herbs, tea, eggs, cheese, meat, fish, poultry, bread, fresh pasta and other foreign specialities, and occasionally even wines and spirits. The choice is usually excellent. Quite a few of the stalls are run by local growers themselves, who will praise their own produce in eloquent terms – an excellent chance to witness regional dialects and (unlike in supermarkets) to practise German.

Supermarkets and other shops

In a supermarket you'll usually find a good selection of cheeses, sausage, bread and other foods, including fresh fruit and vegetables. Dried and tinned items as well as toiletries can be bought there, and the choice of wines, liqueurs and spirits (**Weine und Spirituosen**) can be (literally!) staggering. Prices vary considerably – generally speaking, the more self-service there is, the lower the prices. In some supermarkets you will see nothing but rows of boxes stacked on top of one another and filled with tins, bottles and packets: those are probably the cheapest. Some shops specialize in wines and spirits, but they are not open in the evening. However, most railway stations have kiosks (**Bahnhofskioske**) or small shops with 'emergency supplies' of food and drink.

Other useful shops are the **Metzgerei** (butcher's), **Bäckerei** (baker's), and the **Lebensmittelgeschäft** (general food store). If a shop is small and rather old-fashioned, it's lovingly called a **Tante-Emma-Laden** (*lit*. Auntie Emma's shop). Should you want to buy organic foods and vegetables, ask for the **Bioladen** (health food shop) or the more traditional **Reformhaus**.

The post office

This is called **die Post** or **das Postamt**. International calls can be made from any telephone box marked with a green **International** or **Ausland** sticker. You can also go to the post office and book your call at a counter marked **Ferngespräche** (long-distance calls). The advantage is that you don't have to feed the telephone with coins, but can pay afterwards.

15 You want to take advantage of some special offers at the greengrocer's. Study the advertisement below, then turn to the recording where Tom will prompt you.

Griechische Tafeltrauben
„Victoria", Klasse I, 1 kg Schale
2.99

Griechische Pfirsiche
Klasse I, 1 kg Schale
2.49

Französische Tafeläpfel „Ozark Gold"
Klasse I, 1 kg
2.99

Monatliche Tiefpreise im August

- **Deutsche Möhren**
  Klasse II, 1 kg Beutel **-.99**

- **Deutsche Speisefrühkartoffeln**
  „Arkula" oder „Karat", vorwiegend festkochend, Klasse I
  2,5 kg Beutel **2.49**

- **Deutscher Eisbergsalat**
  Klasse I, Kopf **1.99**

- **Deutscher Kopfsalat**
  Klasse I, Kopf **-.99**

- **Mexicanische Mango**
  Stück **1.99**

Belgische Tomaten
Klasse I, 1 kg
1.99

Frische aus deutschen Landen
Deutscher Porree
Klasse II, 1 kg
1.99

ANSWERS

EXERCISE 2
(a) Verkaufen Sie Postkarten von Hamburg? (b) Was kostet das Stück? (c) Haben Sie (auch) Briefmarken? (d) Und wo bekomme ich Briefmarken?

EXERCISE 4
(a) 2x (b) 2x (c) 2x (d) 2x (e) 2x (f) 2x (g) 1x (h) 1x

EXERCISE 7
(a) Kilo 1,89 (b) Pfund –,99 (c) Pfund 1,59 (d) kg 1,39

EXERCISE 8
(a) Karotte (b) Zwiebel (c) Birne (d) Aprikose (e) Pfirsich (f) Zitrone RIDDLE WORD: Kirsche

EXERCISE 9
(a) 2,99 (b) 1,47 (c) 3,69 (d) 1,48 (e) 1,99 (f) 2,10
(g) 2,79 (h) 2,19 (i) 1,79 (j) –,99 (k) –,79 (l) 3,99

EXERCISE 12
(a) Die Pfirsiche sind hart. (The peaches are hard.)
(b) Die Würste sind billig. (The sausages are cheap.)
(c) Die Getränke sind kalt. (The drinks are cold.)
(d) Die Weingläser sind alt. (The wineglasses are old.)
(e) Die Aschenbecher sind klein. (The ashtrays are small.)
(f) Die Kartoffeln sind groß. (The potatoes are big.)

EXERCISE 13
(a) große Damen (b) der heiße Kaffee (c) ein weicher Apfel
(d) eine leichte Sprache (e) die späten Erdbeeren
(f) das große Auto (g) kurze Reisen

EXERCISE 14
(a) Die Erdbeeren sind alt. (b) Die Weingläser sind teuer.
(c) Der Apfel ist hart. (d) Die Trauben sind schlecht.
(e) Der Wein ist sauer. (f) Das Bier ist warm.

WHAT YOU WILL LEARN

▶ how to buy clothes
▶ how to cope at the chemist's shop
▶ how to perfect your telephone skills
▶ you will also read more about doctors and hospitals, chemist's shops and drugstores

der Mantel
die Socken (pl.)
die Schuhe (pl.)
das Kleid

Moden

das Jackett
das Hemd
die Hose
der Pullover (Pulli)

BEFORE YOU BEGIN

There will be a lot of new vocabulary in this unit. However, you need not learn every single word by heart. Be selective: try to concentrate on your own personal needs and on words and skills you are most likely to want.

Pronunciation notes

Double consonants **ll**, **mm**, **tt**, **ss**, **nn** and **ck**

The vowels preceding these should always be short and stressed. Listen for the following words in this unit: **Modelle** (models), **Mittel** (means, *here*: remedy), **Tablette** (tablet), **besser** (better), **Nummer** (number) and **bitte** (please).

ck

The **ck** behaves just like a double consonant; listen for **Scheck** (cheque) and **schick** (chic, smart).

Try this tongue twister: **Mechthild und Eckhard machen schrecklich Krach.** (Mechthild and Eckhard make a terrible noise).

You'll practise all these words on the recording at the beginning of the unit.

▶ *Buying a skirt*

LISTEN FOR...

Rock	skirt
probieren	to try (on)
Größe	size

Verkäuferin	Guten Morgen.
Ruth	Guten Morgen.
Verkäuferin	Kann ich Ihnen helfen?
Ruth	Ja, bitte. Ich möchte gerne einen Rock.
Verkäuferin	Können Sie verschiedene Modelle probieren?
Ruth	Ja, gerne ...
Verkäuferin	Oh, das sieht ja schick aus. Der paßt sehr gut. Ja, sehr schön.
Ruth	Welche Größe ist das eigentlich?
Verkäuferin	Größe sechsunddreißig.
Ruth	Was kostet der denn?
Verkäuferin	Achtundsiebzig Mark.
Ruth	Eh – kann ich auch mit Scheck bezahlen?
Verkäuferin	Ja, selbstverständlich.

Kann ich Ihnen helfen? Can I help you? Note again the word order in a question with two verbs: the first verb comes at the beginning, the second verb goes right to the end of the sentence.

der Rock skirt (plural **die Röcke**)

Können Sie verschiedene Modelle probieren? Can you try various models? (**das Modell** model, style; **probieren** to try (on/out)). If you want to try something on, ask **Kann ich das probieren?** Can I try this on?

das sieht ja schick aus that looks smart (**schick** smart, stylish); **sehen ... aus = aussehen** (to look) is a separable verb which splits into two parts in certain cases (details in the grammar section of Unit 10).

der paßt sehr gut that (one) fits very well (**passen** to fit); **der Rock paßt gut** the skirt fits well or is a good fit; **der Rock paßt nicht** the skirt doesn't fit.

Wie paßt das? How does it fit?

Welche Größe ist das eigentlich? Which size is that actually? (**die Größe** size). Other useful phrases: **welche Farbe?** which colour? **welche Preislage?** what price range? Possible answer: **zirka 200 Mark** around 200 marks.

Kann ich auch mit Scheck bezahlen? Can I also pay by cheque? (**der Scheck** cheque; **der Euroscheck** Eurocheque). Note also **bar** in cash, e.g. **ich bezahle bar** I am paying in cash.

selbstverständlich of course

PRACTICE

1 On the recording Dorit wants to buy another skirt. Try to write a short version of the conversation by completing the speech bubbles in the pictures. Be as brief as possible.

Here are all the words that you'll need – but they've been jumbled up.

Euroscheck – ja – kostet – den – mit – gerne – Größe 38 – sehr – zirka – nehme – gut – 150 Mark – was – er – ja – ich – paßt – der

A Bitte schön? / Einen Rock bitte

B Welche Größe? / ____

C Welche Preislage? / ____

D Können Sie das Modell hier probieren? / ____

E Wie paßt der Rock? / ____

F Der kostet nur 135 DM / ____ ?

G Möchten Sie den Rock nehmen? / ____ !

H Und wie möchten Sie bezahlen? / ____

SUGGESTED ANSWERS P. 124

2 Study the advertisement below. One doesn't make sense. Can you spot it? Answer the questions below.

New words:
das Mädchen girl
das Hemd shirt

How much would you pay for ...

a. a ladies' T-shirt? _____

b. a girl's skirt _____

c. a man's shirt _____

d. a pair of children's shorts _____

ANSWERS P. 124

DAMEN SOMMER-RÖCKE 100% Baumwolle 49,-

Herren-Pullover für kleine Mädchen 100% Wolle 39,-

Modische Damen-T-shirts 25,-

Herren-Hemden Polyester + Baumwolle 29,-

Kinder-Jeans-shorts 15,-

MÄDCHEN-RÖCKE leichte Baumwollqualität 25,-

3 Your turn to speak. You are trying to buy a coat. Tom will prompt you. Here are some useful expressions:

ein(en) Mantel / Sommermantel / Wintermantel / grau / blau / zirka 200 Mark / er paßt (nicht/sehr) gut

At the chemist

LISTEN FOR...

Halsschmerzen	sore throat
Tablette	tablet
lutschen	to suck

Apotheker	Guten Tag, was darf es sein?
Ruth	Haben Sie ein Mittel gegen Halsschmerzen?
Apotheker	Ja, eh, dieses Präparat. Sie können vier- bis fünfmal täglich eine Tablette lutschen.
Ruth	Also nicht mehr als fünf Tabletten pro Tag.
Apotheker	Ja, zirka vier bis fünf Tabletten, und zwar lutschen, nicht schlucken.

der Apotheker chemist (male pharmacist); a female chemist is **eine Apothekerin** and the chemist's shop **die Apotheke**.

Was darf es sein? another idiomatic way of asking What would you like? (*lit.* What may it be?)

ein Mittel gegen Halsschmerzen something for a sore throat (*lit.* a means against throat pains) (**das Mittel** remedy; **der Hals** throat; **der Schmerz** pain)

dieses Präparat this preparation

täglich daily, here in the sense of 'per day' (also **pro Tag**).

nicht mehr als not more than

zirka vier bis fünf about four or five

lutschen to suck

und zwar that is, to be more precise

schlucken to swallow

Some useful phrases:
Wie geht es Ihnen? Wie geht es dir? or in a shorter form **Wie geht's?** How are you?
danke gut fine, thank you
es geht so-so
nicht so gut not so well

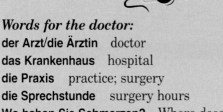

Words for the doctor:
der Arzt/die Ärztin doctor
das Krankenhaus hospital
die Praxis practice; surgery
die Sprechstunde surgery hours
Wo haben Sie Schmerzen? Where does it hurt? (*lit.* Where have you got pains?)
die Reisekrankheit travel sickness
die Krankheit sickness/disease
ich bin krank I am ill
ich habe Fieber I have a temperature
Gute Besserung! Get well soon!

Anything else?

LISTEN FOR...

Insektenstiche	insect bites
Lotion	lotion
Creme	cream

APOTHEKE
ROTH'S ALTE ENGLISCHE APOTHEKE

Apotheker	Sonst noch etwas?
Ruth	Ja. Haben Sie ein Mittel gegen Insektenstiche?
Apotheker	Ja, zum Einreiben – am besten ist die Lotio oder eine Creme.
Ruth	Haben Sie auch ein Spray?
Apotheker	Ein Spray haben wir auch.
Ruth	Hm. Aber Sie finden die Lotion besser?
Apotheker	Das Spray ist leider etwas teurer.
Ruth	Aha. Dann nehme ich lieber die Lotion.

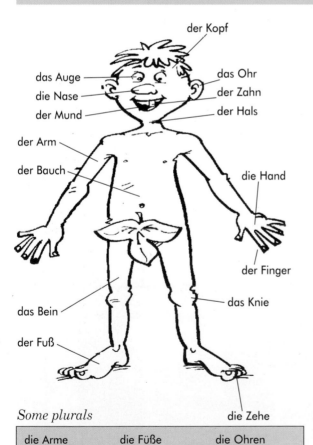

Some plurals

die Arme	die Füße	die Ohren
die Augen	die Hände	die Zähne
die Beine	die Knie	die Zehen
die Finger		

Sonst noch etwas?   Is there anything else?

der Insektenstich   insect bite

zum Einreiben   for rubbing in

am besten ist die Lotio   the best thing is the lotion (more on **am besten** in the grammar section of this unit)

die Lotio   Latin instead of **die Lotion** lotion.

die Creme   cream;

das Spray   spray

ein Spray haben wir auch   we also have a spray. Note the word order: the chemist wants to place special emphasis on **ein Spray** by placing it at the beginning of the sentence, the verb still taking second position and the **wir** being relegated to third place. Usual sentence order: **Wir haben auch ein Spray.**

Aber Sie finden die Lotion besser?   But you think (*lit.* find) the lotion is better?

etwas teurer   a little dearer (for more on comparatives see the grammar section in this unit).

dann nehme ich lieber ...   then I'd rather take ... (see grammar section of Unit 11).

4 Aches and pains. Listen to the conversation on the recording and make a ring round all the body parts that hurt.

New expression:
oh weh! oh dear!

ANSWERS P. 124

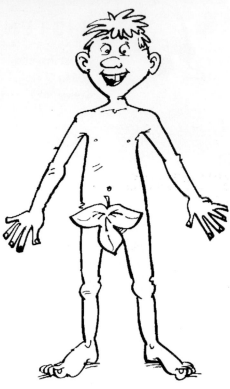

5 The medication – getting it right. Listen to the chemist's recommendations on the recording and tick the correct boxes.

a. The best thing is/are
    tablets
    a lotion
    a spray

b. You should take it/them
    three times a day
    twice a day
    once a day

c. You have to take it/them for about
    a week
    a month
    two weeks

d. and if you don't get better, you should
    come again
    see a doctor
    try another medicine

ANSWERS P. 124

6 Which answer fits?

a. Wie geht es Ihnen?
   Heute nicht.
   Nicht so gut.

b. Wo haben Sie Schmerzen?
   Für eine Woche.
   Im Hals.

c. Haben Sie Fieber?
   Ja, es ist heiß.
   Ja, schon seit Tagen.

d. Haben Sie auch Kopfschmerzen?
   Ja, seit einer Woche.
   Danke gut.

ANSWERS P. 124

7 Spot the body parts – there are
eight of them hidden in this puzzle – down and across. You will be looking for
the German equivalents of toes, arms, leg, eye, ears, finger(s), throat, stomach.
One word has been highlighted for you.

```
B A C X E D B M N Z P R S
P R T A Q W E V V E H J I
L P N U M R I P R H S D I
P L M G F R N S D E N V
O H R E N V B F I N G E
M A S T A A C K S L D J
T L B N S P Q V X C D W
X S Y T E P Q B A U C H S
```

ANSWERS P. 124

8 Your turn to suffer. You're off to the chemist with a variety of queries and
complaints. Tom will help you.

Unit 8   Getting what you want   115

Directory enquiries. A number in Kiel, please ...

LISTEN FOR...

Wie schreibt sich das?   How is that spelt?

Telefonistin	Guten Tag.
Ruth	Guten Tag. Eine Nummer in Kiel, bitte.
Telefonistin	Mhm?
Ruth	Die Firma heißt Thyssen.
Telefonistin	Wie heißt die?
Ruth	Thyssen.
Telefonistin	Wie schreibt sich das?
Ruth	T, h, y, s, s, e, n.
Telefonistin	Thyssen.

Wie heißt die?   What's it called?
Note that **die** stands for **die Firma**.

Wie schreibt sich das? or
Wie schreibt man das?   How is that spelt?
schreiben   literally means 'to write'

... and now for the number

LISTEN FOR...

Rufnummer	phone number
Ortsnetzkennzahl	area code

Telefonistin	
(recorded voice)	Die gewünschte Rufnummer lautet 682080. Ich wiederhole: 682080. Die Ortsnetzkennzahl lautet 0431. Die gewünschte Rufnummer lautet 682080. Die Ortsnetzkennzahl lautet 0431. Falls Sie weitere Auskünfte wünschen, bleiben Sie bitte am Telefon.

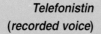

die gewünschte Rufnummer lautet ...   the (desired) number is ...

ich wiederhole   I repeat

die Ortsnetzkennzahl   the area code (**der Ort** town, location; **das Netz** net, network; **die Zahl** number)

falls Sie weitere Auskünfte wünschen   if you want further information

bleiben Sie bitte am Telefon   please hold the line (*lit.* stay on the phone please)

Other useful telephone words and phrases to recognize:

das **Telefon**	telephone
telefonieren	to telephone
der **Apparat**	telephone
der **Anruf**	phone call
anrufen	to telephone
die **Verbindung**	connection
der **Teilnehmer**	subscriber
die **Antwort**	reply

Einen Moment bitte, ich verbinde.   Just a moment, please, I'm connecting you.

Bleiben Sie bitte am Apparat.   Please hold the line.

Wer ist am Apparat?   Who's that? Who's speaking?

Die Verbindung ist schlecht.   It's a bad line.

Die Verbindung ist abgebrochen.   I/We have been cut off.

Kein Anschluß unter dieser Nummer.   The number you have called is not available.

Wie heißt der Teilnehmer?   What's the subscriber's name?

Keine Antwort unter dieser Nummer.   There's no reply.

Tip

By far the easiest way of phoning home is to buy a phone card (**die Telefonkarte**) at a post office and use it in the phone boxes marked **Telefonieren ohne Münzen** (telephone without coins). However, if you don't have one and don't want to worry about having enough change to feed the machine, you can go into the post office and look out for the counter marked **Ferngespräche** (long distance calls).

9

Another directory enquiry. A customer wants to know Dr. Schäuble's number. Listen to the recording and fill in the missing words and numbers to complete the transcript below.

New word:

der Kunde   customer

Telefonist:	Guten Tag.
Kunde:	Guten Tag. Ich **(a)** _____ eine **(b)** _____ in Konstanz, bitte.
Telefonist:	Ja. Wie heißt der Teilnehmer?
Kunde:	Das ist der **(c)** _____ Schäuble.
Telefonist:	Scheuble. Mit e, u?
Kunde:	**(d)** _____
Telefonist:	Die gewünschte Rufnummer lautet: **(e)** _____
	Ich wiederhole: **(f)** _____
	Die Ortsnetzkennzahl lautet: **(g)** _____
	Die gewünschte Rufnummer lautet: **(h)** _____
	Die Ortsnetzkennzahl lautet: **(i)** _____

ANSWERS P. 124

10   Important numbers. Study the extract from the phonebook and answer the following questions.

New words:

der Notruf   emergency call
die Polizei   police
das Fernamt   operator
die Feuerwehr   fire brigade

	Telefonauskunft	national	01188
		international	00118
	Fernamt	national	010
		international	0010
	Telegramm		01131

 Notruf   **Polizei** **110**   **Feuerwehr** **112**

a.   Which number would you ring if you were in Germany and wanted to find out a number in the UK? _____

b.   Which number would you ring in an emergency? _____

c.   Which number would you ring for help if you were in Germany and needed to be connected to a number outside Germany that you could not dial directly?

_____

d.   Which number would you ring if there was a fire? _____

e.   If you had a problem with getting through to a number inside Germany, which number would you ring for help? (There are two possible ways to approach the problem.)

_____

ANSWERS P. 124

11

What next? Tick the right reactions.

What are you meant to do if you hear these phrases?

a. Bleiben Sie bitte am Apparat.

ring off

hold the line

try again

b. Kein Anschluß unter dieser Nummer.

wait to be connected

speak your message on the answerphone

ring off and check the number with directory enquiries

c. Einen Moment bitte, ich verbinde.

ring again later

wait and hold the line

check the number with directory enquiries

d. Wie schreibt sich das?

wait to write down the number

spell out the word in question

repeat the subscriber's name and address

ANSWERS P. 124

12

Your turn to speak. Here's an extract with details of ear, nose and throat doctors available in the area. You want to go and see Dr. Cremer in Wangen, but unfortunately some crucial numbers, including the area code, have been blotted out. You are ringing directory enquiries to find the missing numbers. Dorit will play the part of the telephonist, and Erich will tell you what you should have said. Remember to write down the numbers.

Dr. Cremer's number _____

ANSWERS P. 124 His area code _____

Ärzte f. Hals-, Nasen-, Ohrenheilkunde

■ **Bad Waldsee (0 75 24)**
Haerie Dr.med. Biberacher Str. 45 .... Ⓒ 14 64

■ **Isny im Allgäu (0 75 62)**
Morgen Eckhard Dr.med. HNO-Arzt
Wassertorstr. 20 23

■ **Leutkirch im Allgäu (0 75 61)**
Krause M. Dr.med. 1 Memminger Str. 2 .... 60 88

■ **Ravensburg (07 51)**
Huber E. Dr.Med. Schussenstr. 5 .... Ⓒ 2 44 33
Mauch J.P. Dr.med. u. Panis R. Dr.med.
Elisabethenstr. 9 .... Ⓒ 39 89, 39 80

■ **Wangen im Allgäu**
Cremer A. Dr. Spatzenhalde 5/1 ....
Nenmann Horst Dr.med. Lindauer Str. 11/1 ....

■ **Weingarten, Württ. (07 51)**
Seitz H.M. Dr.med. Abt-Hyller-Str. 4/1 .... 4 36 37
Zwerger H. Dr.med. Abt-Hyller-Str. 2 .... Ⓒ 4 69 69

GRAMMAR AND EXERCISES

More on adjectives: comparison

So far you have come across

gut	besser	am besten
good	better	best

Here are some examples of how they are used:

Orangensaft ist gut	Orange juice is good
Milch ist besser	Milk is better
Wasser ist am besten	Water is best

In grammatical terms, **besser** (better) is called the comparative form and **am besten** (best) is called the superlative.

Like their English counterparts, **gut – besser – am besten** are irregular forms. However, most other adjectives follow one regular pattern with only minor variations. Here is an example of a regular pattern:

klein	kleiner	am kleinsten
small	smaller	smallest

Here are some more examples:

cheap	billig	billiger	am billigsten
beautiful	schön	schöner	am schönsten
short	kurz	kürzer*	am kürzesten***
long	lang	länger*	am längsten
big	groß	größer*	am größten
expensive	teuer	teurer**	am teuersten
young	jung	jünger*	am jüngsten

* note the umlaut in the comparative and superlative forms
** note that the **e** is dropped
*** note that an **e** is added

} for easier pronunciation

As with the basic adjective (see Grammar section in Unit 7), comparatives and superlatives change their endings when they come in front of the noun. For example:

der billigere Ring	the cheaper ring
die billigeren Ringe	the cheaper rings
but	
der Ring ist billiger	the ring is cheaper
die Ringe sind billiger	the rings are cheaper
das kleinste Kind	the smallest child
die kleinsten Kinder	the smallest children
but	
das Kind ist am kleinsten	the child is smallest
die Kinder sind am kleinsten	the children are smallest

Adverbs

If a word describes a verb, it is called an adverb. In English, you will recognize most adverbs because they are adjectives which have added –ly. In German, no change is required for an adjective to become an adverb.
For example:

Die Frau ist schön.
　The woman is beautiful (*adjective*).
Die Frau singt schön.
　The woman sings beautifully (*adverb*).

Er ist schöner.
　He is more beautiful (*adjective*).
Er singt schöner.
　He sings more beautifully (*adverb*).

Das Kind ist am schönsten.
　The child is (the) most beautiful (*adjective*).
Das Kind singt am schönsten.
　The child sings the most beautifully (*adverb*).

13 gut – besser – am besten?
Fill in the right words.

a. Diese Creme ist (*best*) _____

b. Die Lotion ist (*better*) _____

c. Frau Konradi ist (*good*) _____

d. Frau Hoffmann ist (*best*) _____

e. Was ist (*better*) _____ ,

Wein oder Wasser?

ANSWERS P. 124

14 Fill in the right forms from the list below.

> **kleinere** – **kleine** – **teuerste** – **am billigsten**
> – **schöner** – **längste** – **kleinste**

a. Das (*small*) _____ Kind

ist hier.

b. Hier ist das (*longest*) _____
Kleid.

c. Das (*most expensive*) _____

Restaurant ist beim Theater.

d. Das (*smaller*) _____ Hotel

ist (*more beautiful*) _____

e. Das (*smallest*) _____

Haus ist (*cheapest*) _____

ANSWERS P. 124

15 Translate into German.

a. This dress is cheaper.

_____

b. The coat is long.

_____

c. This skirt is shorter.

_____

d. The spray is most expensive.

_____

e. The garden is most beautiful.

_____

ANSWERS P. 124

KEY WORDS

Buying clothes and shoes

To understand:

Welche Größe ...?	Which size ...?
Welche Preislage ...?	What price range ...?
Wie paßt das?	How does it fit?

To use yourself:

Kann ich ...	Can/May I ...
das mal probieren?	try this on?
mit Scheck bezahlen?	pay by cheque?
Der/Die/Das paßt (nicht) gut	This is (not) a good fit

At the chemist

To understand:

Wo haben Sie Schmerzen?	Where does it hurt?
Am besten ist ...	The best thing is ...
die Lotion	the lotion
die Creme	the cream
das Spray	the spray
viermal täglich	four times a day
lutschen, nicht schlucken	suck (it), don't swallow (it)
zum Einreiben	for rubbing in

To use yourself:

Wie geht es Dir/Ihnen?	How are you?
Danke gut	Fine thank you
Es geht	so-so
Ich habe ...	I have ...
Haben Sie ein Mittel gegen ...	Have you got something for ...
Halsschmerzen?	a sore throat?
Kopfschmerzen?	a headache?
Zahnschmerzen?	a toothache?
Insektenstiche?	insect bites?
Fieber?	a temperature?
Ich bin gesund/krank	I am well/ill

On the phone

To understand:

Wie heißt der Teilnehmer/die Firma?	What's the subscriber's/firm's name?
Wie schreibt sich das?	How is that spelt?
die gewünschte Rufnummer	the number you want
die Ortsnetzkennzahl lautet	the area code is
Falls Sie weitere Auskünfte wünschen, bleiben Sie bitte am Telefon/am Apparat	Should you require any further information please hold the line

To use yourself:

Eine Nummer in ...	A number in ...
Die Firma heißt ...	The firm is called ...

More on health

Chemist's shops

At the chemist's (**die Apotheke**) drugs and medicines are dispensed. Some drugs require no doctor's prescription, others do. But you might find what is on prescription and what is isn't much different from the UK regulations. Drugs are generally cheaper on prescription, but you obviously have to see a doctor. You can also buy cosmetics and some health foods in an **Apotheke**.

Drugstores

A drugstore is called a **Drogerie** and will sell some medicines not on prescription, but has mainly toiletries, cosmetics, films, etc. More upmarket (and more expensive) than the **Drogerie** is the **Parfümerie**, where you can get mainly perfumes and cosmetics.

Doctors and hospitals

You are entitled to free medical treatment in EU member countries if you are insured under the National Health Service and can produce the necessary form from your DSS office in the UK. This you must take to the local DHSS (**Gesundheitsamt**) in Germany before seeing a doctor. A general practitioner is called a **Praktischer Arzt**. If he can't help you he'll refer you to a specialist (**Facharzt**) rather than sending you to hospital. In emergencies there is of course the hospital (**Krankenhaus**); the casualty department is called **Ambulanz**.

Augenarzt
Dr. med.
W. Maier-Janson

Sprechstunden: Mo–Fr 8.00–11.00
Mi–Do 14.00–16.00

TEMPERATURE CHART

°F	°C
98	36,7
99	37,2
100	37,8
102	38,9
104	40
106	41,1
108	42,2
110	43,3

A traditional health food shop

AND FINALLY...

16 Your turn to speak. You're trying to get hold of a Firma Kaiser in Berlin. Here's the address:

> *Firma Kaiser*
> *Westendstraße 10*
> *D–10584 Berlin*

Be prepared to spell the name of the firm. You will also be asked to give the street. And finally, jot down the numbers you're given. Tom will not need to prompt you as all the information you need is already provided.

Firma Kaiser. Rufnummer _____

Ortsnetzkennzahl _____

ANSWERS BELOW

ANSWERS

9 MAKING TRAVEL ARRANGEMENTS

WHAT YOU WILL LEARN

▶ understanding train announcements
▶ buying a ticket
▶ enquiring about connections
▶ you will also be given information on air travel and some general advice on travelling in German-speaking countries

Reisen mit der Bahn

Ein Ausflug in die Klassik: Naumburg/Weimar

Ein reizvoller Tagesausflug in Leipzigs schöne Umgebung.

BEFORE YOU BEGIN

It will be a lot easier to understand train announcements once you know what to expect and listen for. Luckily, these announcements are all highly predictable because they follow regular patterns; for example, shortly before the train arrives at the station, the announcement will identify the platform, the train, its city of origin, its destination and the towns passed en route. Try to find these patterns in the recordings and pinpoint important clues such as **Vorsicht am Gleis eins** (Caution on platform one). Of course, you will also need to make sure you have a good grasp of the time. So go back to Unit 6 if you need to refresh your memory ...

Pronunciation notes

z

Whenever you see a **z** anywhere in a German text, think of 'ts'. Except in a few very un-German words and names, the **z** is always pronounced as 'ts', the same sound as in the English words 'hats' or 'mats'. There will be plenty of chances to practise this sound in this unit with words such as **Zug** (train), **Flugzeug** (aeroplane), **zweiter Klasse** (second class), **zwölf Mark** (12 marks) and **Leipzig**.

> **An InterCity train is arriving at Ulm station**

LISTEN FOR...

Vorsicht   caution; take care
Gleis   platform
Abfahrt   departure

Lautsprecher   Bitte Vorsicht am Gleis eins. Es
fährt ein InterCity 518 Patrizier von
München nach Hamburg-Altona,
über Stuttgart, Heidelberg,
Mannheim, Bonn, Köln,
Düsseldorf, Dortmund, Osnabrück.
Planmäßige Abfahrt 8.59 Uhr.

die Vorsicht   caution

das Gleis   platform (*lit.* track)

es fährt ein   now arriving; **einfahren** (to come
in) is a separable verb; its two parts **ein +
fahren** are split if it's the only verb in the
sentence (more on this in the grammar section
in Unit 10)

InterCity Patrizier   the ICE (**InterCity Express**) is faster than the standard
InterCity or **IC**. The **EuroCity** (**EC**) connects various European cities, whilst
the **InterRegio** (**IR**) covers one region only

(der) Patrizier   Patrician – all expresses have names

München   German name for Munich

über   via

Altona   part of Hamburg with an important station

planmäßige Abfahrt   scheduled departure (**planmäßige Ankunft** scheduled arrival)

8.59 Uhr   remember that you say **acht Uhr neunundfünfzig** but you write **8.59 Uhr**.

> **Further connections**

LISTEN FOR...

Anschluß   connection
Eilzug   semi-fast train

Lautsprecher   Sie haben Anschluß zum Eilzug
nach Aalen über Langenau,
Niederstotzingen, Sontheim,
Giengen, Heidenheim. Planmäßige
Abfahrt 9.05 Uhr, Gleis 7.

der Anschluß   connection
der Eilzug   semi-fast stopping train (**der Zug** train); even 'semi-fast' is a bit
of a euphemism!

1

More trains are coming in. Listen to the recording and fill in the missing information.

New vocabulary: **hat Einfahrt** (another expression for **fährt ein**)   is arriving

a.   Bitte Vorsicht am Gleis _____. Es fährt ein _____

_____ 'Münchner Kindl' von _____ nach

_____ über Stuttgart, Mannheim, _____ , Fulda,

Kassel-Wilhelmshöhe, Göttingen, _____

Planmäßige Abfahrt _____ Uhr.

b.   Auf _____ _____ hat Einfahrt der _____ nach

_____ , über Ravensburg, Aulendorf, Biberach.

ANSWERS P. 138

Planmäßige Abfahrt _____ Uhr.

2

Another announcement. This time at **Hannover Hauptbahnhof** (Hanover's central station) where a train has just pulled in. Listen several times and tick the right answers below.

a. The train is
     an InterRegio
     an ICE

b. The number of the train is
     978
     897

c. The name of the train is
     Nymphenburg
     Burgnymphe

d. The train is travelling from
     Bremen to Munich
     Munich to Bremen

e. It stops in (cross out the towns that
    are not mentioned)
     Kassel-Wilhelmshöhe –
     Frankfurt – Heidelberg –
     Mannheim – Stuttgart – Ulm –
     Ravensburg – Augsburg

ANSWERS P. 138

3

Sie haben Anschluß ... You've just arrived in Stuttgart. Listen to a sequence of three announcements about connections to Heidelberg, Karlsruhe and Tübingen, and fill in the missing bits in the chart below.

category of train			
where to			
via	Vaihingen		Esslingen
	Mühlacker		Metzingen
	Pforzheim		Reutlingen
departs			
platform			

ANSWERS P. 138

Buying a ticket

LISTEN FOR...

einfach	single
Klasse	class

Deutsche Bahn DB

Beamtin	Guten Tag. Bitte schön?
Ruth	Nach Augsburg, einfach bitte.
Beamtin	Erster oder zweiter Klasse?
Ruth	Zweiter Klasse.
Beamtin	Zweiter Klasse – kostet zwölf Mark bitte.

einfach bitte   single, please; to ask for a return to Augsburg you would say **nach Augsburg hin und zurück** (*lit.* there and back) (**die Hinfahrt** outward journey; **die Rückfahrt** return journey). If you want to emphasize that you wish to buy one single ticket only, say **einmal einfach bitte**. For two single tickets to Augsburg you could say **nach Augsburg, zweimal einfach bitte**.

Erster oder zweiter Klasse   first or second class

Getting on the train

LISTEN FOR...

einsteigen	to get on
Türen schließen selbsttätig	(the) doors close automatically

Lautsprecher	Am Gleis zwei bitte einsteigen. Türen schließen selbsttätig. Vorsicht bei der Abfahrt.

am Gleis zwei bitte einsteigen   please board the train at platform two; **einsteigen** is another separable verb, so you'd need to say **ich steige ein** (I get on).

Türen schließen selbsttätig   (the) doors close automatically

Vorsicht bei der Abfahrt   stand clear, the train is about to leave (*lit.* caution during departure)

Zeichenerklärung / Key to Symbols		
ICE = InterCity Express (besonderer Fahrpreis / special fare)	**S** = *S-Bahn / urban train*
	RB = *RegionalBahn / regional train*
	ohne Buchstaben = *Nahverkehrszug / local train*
EC = *EuroCity*	🚌 = *Buslinie / bus service*
IC = *InterCity*	† = *an Sonn- und allg. Feiertagen / on Sundays and public holidays only*
IR = *InterRegio*	
SE = *Stadt Express / city express*	Ⓐ = *an Werktagen / on weekdays*
D = *Schnellzug / fast train*	*Montag–Sonntag / Monday to Sunday*
RE = *Regional Express / regional express*	🚃 = *Kurswagen / train with through coach*

4 Study the ticket below and answer the following questions.

Note: **Flugh.** short for **(der) Flughafen** airport
gültig valid

		Besondere Angaben		Ausgabestelle
DB **DR**				DER 2 RIEDSTADT 19.05.94 14 611251001 00

Klasse	Tarif				Ermäß.	Grund
2	*ICE* HIN- UND RUECKFAHRT					XX Erwachsene(r) XX Kind(er)

1. Geltungstag	Zur Hinfahrt gültig bis einschließlich	Zur Rückfahrt gültig bis einschließlich	Rückfahrt frühestens am	
22.05.94	21.06.94	21.06.94	22.05.94	Reserv. H: X R: 0

von Frankfurt(M)Flugh.   über   (ICE:F*UL)*Aulendorf

nach Ravensburg

877301725   MWST DB: **206,km0 15,0% = **26,87   ZA DM
87730172-80   XX **206,00 ⯀⯀⯀

a. Is it a first or second class ticket? _____

b. What kind of train is it for? _____

c. Is it a single or return? _____

d. What route is the ticket for? _____

_____

ANSWERS P. 138 e. How much is it? _____

5 Listen and understand. On the recording Dorit is buying a ticket at the station. Listen carefully and decide which of the statements below are **R** (**richtig** right) or **F** (**falsch** wrong).

a. Dorit kauft eine Fahrkarte nach Bremen.   **R** ☐   **F** ☐

b. Sie möchte erster Klasse fahren.   **R** ☐   **F** ☐

c. Die Fahrkarte ist für eine einfache Fahrt.   **R** ☐   **F** ☐

d. Dorit möchte den Eilzug nehmen.   **R** ☐   **F** ☐

ANSWERS P. 138 e. Die Fahrkarte kostet 75 Mark.   **R** ☐   **F** ☐

6 Your turn to speak. You are buying a ticket to Frankfurt (single, second class), and you want to go by ICE. Turn to the recording where Tom will help you to get the ticket.

At the travel agency in Kiel – connections to Berlin

LISTEN FOR...

mit der Bahn	by rail
ab	departs
Aufenthalt	stopover

Ruth	Guten Tag. Ich möchte gerne nach Berlin fahren.
Frau Gallus	Ja, mit dem Bus oder mit der Bahn?
Ruth	Mit der Bahn.
Frau Gallus	Und wann soll das sein?
Ruth	Morgen früh.
Frau Gallus	Morgen früh ... Ja, morgen früh 8.23 Uhr ab Kiel ...
Ruth	8.23 Uhr ab Kiel.
Frau Gallus	Ankunft Altona, 9.33 Uhr.
Ruth	9.33 Uhr, Altona.
Frau Gallus	Umsteigen ... und 10.08 Uhr ab Altona.
Ruth	10.08 Uhr ab Altona.
Frau Gallus	Und um 13.41 Uhr Ankunft Berlin.
Ruth	13.41 Berlin. Ich hab' also Aufenthalt in Hamburg?
Frau Gallus	Ja, 35 Minuten.
Ruth	Gut. Vielen Dank.

mit dem Bus oder mit der Bahn? by bus or by rail? (**die Bahn** railway, rail; **der Bus** bus); note that **mit** (with) takes the dative case. Here's another example: **das Auto** (car) but **mit dem Auto** with the car or by car.

Und wann soll das sein? And when would you like to go? (*lit.* and when shall that be?)

morgen früh (*lit.* tomorrow early) tomorrow morning. Don't confuse **morgen** = tomorrow with **morgen** = morning in **heute morgen** = this morning, **gestern morgen** = yesterday morning. The only day **morgen** can't come after is tomorrow = **morgen**, as this would give **morgen morgen** – hence **morgen früh**.

ab Kiel departs (from) Kiel (remember **die Abfahrt** departure)

Ankunft Altona arrives (*lit.* arrival) (in) Altona; or a shorter alternative: **an Altona** (short for **kommt an** arrives; from **ankommen** to arrive).

ich hab' also Aufenthalt so I'll have some time there (**der Aufenthalt** stay, here: stopover); another example: **ich habe eine Stunde Aufenthalt** I have a stopover of an hour (**die Stunde** hour).

heute morgen	this morning
heute nachmittag	this afternoon
heute abend	this evening
morgen früh	tomorrow morning
morgen nachmittag	tomorrow afternoon
morgen abend	tomorrow evening

7 Listen to Conversation 3 with your book closed and write down all the times you can hear. Then open your book and compare notes.

Kiel ab _____   Altona an _____

Altona ab _____   Berlin an _____

8 Study the excerpt from a timetable in Leipzig about connections to Vienna (**Wien**). Then answer the following questions, in English.

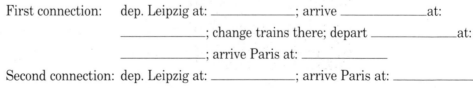

ab	Zug		Umsteigen	an	ab	Zug			an	Verkehrstage
6.13	E	4363	Zwickau(S)	7.28	7.43	IR	2066	⑰		täglich
			Regensburg Hbf	11.25	11.31	EC	23	✕	16.05	
8.33	IR	2603	⑰ Regensburg Hbf	13.25	13.31	EC	25		18.05	täglich
10.13	E	4367	Zwickau(S)	11.27	11.43	IR	2064	⑰		täglich
			Regensburg Hbf	15.25	15.31	EC	27		20.05	
12.13	E	4369	Zwickau(S)	13.27	13.43	IR	2062	⑰		täglich
			Regensburg Hbf	17.25	17.31	EC	29	✕	22.05	
22.07	IC	557	✕ Dresden Hbf	23.40	0.28	D	377			täglich
			Wien Süd	8.52	9.51	◐		2.Kl	10.13	
22.56	D	1907	🛏🍴 Regensburg Hbf	4.35	6.21	EN	225		10.58	täglich

a. Is there a direct train from Leipzig to Vienna? _____

b. How long do the faster trains to Vienna take? _____

c. Do all the trains run every day? _____

d. If you wanted to get into Vienna at approximately 6 p.m., which train would you need to take? _____

e. When does that train depart and where would you need to change?

_____

f. If you wanted to travel overnight but did not want to change trains at 4.30 in the morning, which train would you take? _____

ANSWERS P. 138
g. And where and when would you need to change? _____

9 Taking notes. On the recording Erich wants to take an overnight train from Leipzig to Paris. He is offered two connections. Jot down the details for both connections. Which one does he choose?

First connection: dep. Leipzig at: _____; arrive _____ at:

_____; change trains there; depart _____ at:

_____; arrive Paris at: _____

Second connection: dep. Leipzig at: _____; arrive Paris at: _____

ANSWERS P. 138
He chooses: _____

10 Your turn to speak. You're in Leipzig and want to enquire about connections to Dresden. This time, you want to take the bus. Some but not all of these phrases will be useful:

ich möchte gerne/mit dem Bus/mit der Bahn/morgen vormittag/morgen nachmittag/Abfahrt/ab/Ankunft/an

> **And the quickest way to Berlin?**

LISTEN FOR...

am schnellsten	quickest
Verbindung	connection, service
fliegen	to fly

Ruth	Wie komme ich am schnellsten nach Berlin?
Frau Lücking	Also, die schnellste Verbindung ist von Kiel nach Berlin zu fliegen, und zwar gibt es hier zwei tägliche Verbindungen von Kiel direkt nach Tempelhof. Die erste geht morgens um 7.25 Uhr, dann kommen Sie um 8.30 Uhr dort an. Und die zweite geht gegen Mittag um 11.25 Uhr, dann sind Sie um 12.30 Uhr in Berlin – wie gesagt, jeweils in Tempelhof.

More words to do with flying:

der Flug	flight
der Abflug	departure
der Hinflug/Rückflug	outward/return flight
die Flugzeit	flying time
der Flugschein ⎫ **das Flugticket** ⎭	air ticket
der Flughafen	airport
einen Flug buchen	to book a flight

Wie komme ich am schnellsten nach Berlin? What's the quickest way to get to Berlin?

die schnellste Verbindung ist ... zu fliegen the quickest way (*lit.* connection) is ... to fly

und zwar that is to say, to be precise

Tempelhof name of an airport in Berlin

gegen Mittag towards midday; **gegen** means 'approximately' in expressions of time. Here's another example: **gegen 10 Uhr** at about 10 o'clock.

wie gesagt as (I) said

jeweils in each case

> **How about weekend flights?**

LISTEN FOR...

Maschine	plane
am Wochenende	at the weekend

Ruth	Fliegt die Maschine auch am Wochenende?
Frau Lücking	Ja, am Wochenende haben wir nur die eine Maschine um 7.25 Uhr, die zweite gibt es nur von montags bis freitags.
Ruth	Aha, vielen Dank.
Frau Lücking	Ja, bitte, gern geschehen.

die Maschine plane (*lit.* machine); more colloquial than **das Flugzeug**

das Wochenende weekend

montags on Mondays

gern geschehen you're welcome

11 Which answer fits?

a. Wohin möchten Sie fliegen?
   Nach Berlin.
   Aus Berlin.

b. Wann möchten Sie fliegen?
   Gestern abend.
   Morgen abend.

c. Wie lange ist die Flugzeit?
   Zwei Stunden.
   Am Dienstag.

d. Wann ist der Abflug?
   Nach Rom.
   Um 13.45 Uhr.

ANSWERS P. 138

12 On the recording Erich is asking Dorit about flights to Rome. Complete the transcript below.

New vocabulary:

klar   clear; (*here*) of course

Dorit   Guten Tag. Kann ich Ihnen helfen?

Erich   Wie _____ nach Rom?

Dorit   Die schnellste Verbindung ist mit dem Flugzeug.

Erich   _____ Ja, klar.

Dorit   Wann möchten Sie denn dort sein?

Erich   _____

Dorit   Dann nehmen Sie am besten die Maschine um 17 Uhr. Dann sind Sie um

          17.45 Uhr in Rom.

ANSWERS P. 138

Erich   Gut, _____ um 17 Uhr.

13 Your turn to speak and enquire about flights. You want to fly to New York at the weekend. Turn to the recording where Tom will help you along.

Modal verbs
(müssen; können; wollen)

Verbs such as **müssen** (must; to have to), **können** (can; to be able to) or **wollen** (to want to) are called modal verbs. In most cases, they cannot be used on their own. There has to be another verb in the sentence, for instance **wir müssen jetzt gehen** (we must go now) or **Können Sie morgen kommen?** (Can you come tomorrow?)

As in English these verbs are irregular. Here are the four modal verbs you have met so far in the present tense:

müssen	
ich muß	I must
du mußt	you must
er/sie/es muß	he/she/it must
wir müssen	we must
ihr müßt	you must
sie/Sie müssen	they/you must

Wann muß ich abfahren?
> When do I have to leave? When must I leave?

Dann müssen Sie umsteigen.
> Then you have to change.

A note of advice: it is often better to translate **müssen** as 'to have to' rather than 'must', and in the negative it is the only possibility. Compare these two phrases:

Ich muß heute nach Berlin fliegen.
> I have to/I must fly to Berlin today.

Ich muß heute nicht nach Berlin fliegen.
> I don't have to fly to Berlin today.

It would be wrong to translate this phrase as:
I must not fly to Berlin today.

wollen	
ich will	I want to
du willst	you want to
er/sie/es will	he/she/it wants to
wir wollen	we want to
ihr wollt	you want to
sie/Sie wollen	they/you want to

An welchem Tag wollen Sie fahren?
> (On) which day do you want to go?

Ich will an einem Sonntag fahren.
> I want to go on a Sunday.

Note that a more restrained (and politer) way of saying 'I want to' than **ich will** is **ich möchte** (I'd like to). Here are all the forms:

ich möchte	**wir möchten**
du möchtest	**ihr möchtet**
er/sie/es möchte	**sie/Sie möchten**

können	
ich kann	I can
du kannst	you can
er/sie/es kann	he/she/it can
wir können	we can
ihr könnt	you can
sie/Sie können	they/you can

Können Sie mir sagen, wann der nächste Zug fährt?
> Can you tell me when the next train goes?

Kann ich Ihnen helfen?
> Can I help you?

Note that after all forms of **müssen**, **wollen** and **können** the second verb goes to the end of the sentence.

Occasionally you will also come across modal verbs used on their own, provided the meaning of the sentence is clear without the second verb. In most cases this would not be possible in English. For example:

Ich will zum Hauptbahnhof (fahren).
> I want to go to the station.

Ich muß ins Büro (gehen).
> I have to go to the office.

Ich möchte ein Eis (haben).
> I'd like to have an ice cream.

14 Muß or müssen? Fill in the correct forms and translate the sentences into English.

a. Ich _____ heute nach Kiel fahren.

_____

b. Wo _____ wir die Fahrkarten kaufen?

_____

c. Er _____ heute nicht arbeiten.

_____

d. Wir _____ diesen Wein probieren!

_____

e. _____ ich in Hamburg umsteigen?

_____

f. _____ wir mit dem Taxi fahren?

_____

ANSWERS P. 138

15 Ich will und ich kann ... Replace all the forms of **wollen** with the appropriate forms of **können**.

a. Mein Mann will mit dem Auto nach München fahren.

_____

b. Die Kinder wollen eine Pizza essen.

_____

c. Wollen Sie den ICE nehmen?

_____

d. Ich will heute nicht in die Firma.

_____

e. Wir wollen fliegen.

_____

ANSWERS P. 138

16 A letter. Here are the missing words to fill in.

> **möchte, muß, müssen, kannst, wollen**

New vocabulary: **am Bahnhof abholen**
to fetch from the station

Liebe Anna,

Vielen Dank für Deine Karte aus der Schweiz. Es (must) _____ dort sehr schön sein.

Ich (would like to) _____ Dir kurz schreiben, weil wir in einer Woche nach München kommen (want to) _____. Bis Freitag (have to) _____ wir aber noch arbeiten. (Can) _____ Du uns am Bahnhof abholen?

Viele Grüße, Jörg und Katrin

ANSWERS P. 138

KEY WORDS

Travelling by train

To use yourself:

die Fahrkarte	ticket
das Gleis	platform
Nach Augsburg ...	To Augsburg ...
einfach, bitte	single, please
hin und zurück, bitte	return, please
Einmal/Zweimal Augsburg einfach	One/Two single(s) to Augsburg
Erster/Zweiter Klasse, bitte	First/Second class, please
Wann fährt der nächste Zug nach ...?	When's the next train to ...?
Wie komme ich am schnellsten nach ...?	What's the quickest way to ...?
Ich möchte gerne ...	I'd like to ...
am Wochenende fahren	go at the weekend
am Sonntag reisen	travel on Sunday
(Wo) muß ich umsteigen?	(Where) do I have to change?

To understand:

Sie haben Anschluß (zum Zug) nach ...	There is a connection to ...
Planmäßige Abfahrt/Ankunft 12.05 Uhr	Scheduled departure/arrival 12.05
Ulm an/ab 19.40 Uhr	Arrives/departs Ulm 19.40
InterCity-Zuschlag	Intercity surcharge
Wann möchten Sie fahren?	When would you like to travel?
An welchem Tag und um wieviel Uhr?	On which day and at what time?
Vorsicht	caution
der Aufenthalt	stopover

Travelling by plane

Of course you can always get by in English at airports, but there are a few phrases you should know in German, such as:

der Flug	flight
der Abflug	departure
die Ankunft	arrival
das Flugticket/der Flugschein	air ticket
der Flughafen	airport
das Flugzeug/die Maschine	aeroplane/plane

To use yourself:

Wann ist der nächste Flug?	When's the next flight?
Wann fliegt die nächste Maschine?	When's the next plane?
Ich möchte gerne ...	I'd like to ...
am Wochenende fliegen	fly at the weekend
einen Flug buchen	book a flight
die Stunde	hour
heute morgen/nachmittag/abend	this morning/afternoon/evening
morgen früh/nachmittag/abend	tomorrow morning/afternoon/evening

Travelling in Germany

Travelling by rail

If you want to get quickly from one place to another in Germany, use the **InterRegio** (**IR**), the **InterCity** (**IC**) or, even faster, the **InterCity Express** (**ICE**) trains. The **Schnellzug** (**D**) and particularly **Eilzug** (**E**) are less fast in spite of their names, stopping quite often, while the **Nahverkehrszug** (local train) will stop at all the little stations.

It's considerably more expensive to travel first class, and there are special surcharges on **InterCity** trains and even higher ones on the **ICE** trains for both first and second class. They are, however, very comfortable and run quite frequently. Make sure you pay the surcharge before boarding the train, otherwise you might be liable to another surcharge on your surcharge. It is worth enquiring about special reductions (**Ermäßigungen**). Children, teenagers (**Junioren**) and older people (**Senioren**) can hope for reduced fares or special deals. In addition there are special schemes such as the **BahnCard**, a railpass valid for a whole year, giving you a 50% reduction on all fares. If you wish to travel through several European regions you might want to enquire about the **EURO DOMINO** system, a sort of individualized European network card valid for one month.

Travelling by car

If you're taking your car to Germany, don't forget your driving licence and the green card for the insurance. You should bear in mind that some people drive very fast indeed on German motorways. Within towns the speed limit is 50km/h (31 mph), on open roads 100 km/h (62 mph). The question of motorway tolls has been a very controversial issue.

Don't forget that traffic drives on the right. The most important traffic rule is **Rechts hat Vorfahrt** (traffic from the right has priority) *unless* otherwise regulated.

One game you might like to play when you're not in the driving seat is to guess where the cars you see come from by the first letters on the number plates. Large cities use one letter only:

F = Frankfurt
M = München (Munich)
B = Berlin
L = Leipzig
K = Köln (Cologne)

The exceptions are the old Hanseatic merchant towns which include the letter **H** (for **Hansestadt**) before the letter signifying the name of the town:

HH = Hansestadt Hamburg
HB = Hansestadt Bremen

Slightly smaller cities use two letters, particularly if the first letter has already been used for another place:

KI = Kiel   **UL = Ulm**
GI = Gießen   **RV = Ravensburg**

Smaller towns or rural districts use three letters (the maximum):

PLÖ = Plön
NMS = Neumünster

Priority road

End of priority road

Right of way on non-priority road

One-way street

No parking

No stopping

Give way to traffic on major roads

Traffic signals

Children

AND FINALLY...

17

You want to travel from Ulm to Lübeck so you'll need to buy the ticket and enquire about connections. Turn to the recording. As usual, Tom will prompt you.

And here's the relevant excerpt from the timetable just for interest – you won't really need it for the exercise.

Ulm Hbf → Lübeck Hbf [DB]

12.05	IC	612	☕	Mannheim Hbf	14.04	14.08	ICE	574	✕		täglich
				Hamburg Hbf	18.21	18.26	EC	188	☕	19.00	
13.05	ICE	591	✕	Augsburg Hbf	13.44	13.51	ICE	586	✕		täglich
				Hamburg Hbf	18.51	19.04	E	3074		19.47	
13.05	EC	112	✕	Heidelberg Hbf	14.52	15.16	IR	2574	🚌		täglich
				Lüneburg	21.44	21.56	E	4194		22.58	
13.54	ICE	894	✕	Hannover Hbf	18.38	18.43	ICE	784	✕		täglich
				Hamburg Hbf	19.56	20.04	E	3082		20.47	
15.00	IC	714	✕	Mainz Hbf	17.46	18.24	EC	26	✕		täglich
				Hamburg Hbf	0.11	0.34	E	3098		1.14	

ANSWERS

EXERCISE 1

(a) Bitte Vorsicht am Gleis *eins*. Es fährt ein *ICE 794* 'Münchner Kindl' von *München* nach *Hamburg*, über Stuttgart, Mannheim, *Frankfurt*, Fulda, Kassel-Wilhelmshöhe, Göttingen, *Hannover*.* Planmäßige Abfahrt *11.52* Uhr. **(b)** Auf Gleis *sieben* hat Einfahrt der Eilzug nach Ulm, über Ravensburg, Aulendorf, Biberach. Planmäßige Abfahrt *18.07* Uhr. *Note that Hanover is spelt with a double n (nn) in German.

EXERCISE 2

(a) ICE **(b)** 897 **(c)** Nymphenburg **(d)** Bremen to Munich **(e)** you should have crossed out Heidelberg and Ravensburg

EXERCISE 3

category of train	InterRegio	InterCity (Bacchus)	Eilzug
to	Karlsruhe	Heidelberg	Tübingen
departs	12.57 Uhr	13.11 Uhr	13.15 Uhr
platform	3	24	15

EXERCISE 4

(a) second class **(b)** ICE **(c)** return **(d)** from Frankfurt (airport) to Ravensburg **(e)** 206 DM

EXERCISE 5

richtig: a; d; e

EXERCISE 8

(a) no **(b)** 10 hours **(c)** yes **(d)** the IR 2603
(e) dep. Leipzig at 8.33; change at Regensburg into the EC 25 (arr. Vienna 18.05) **(f)** the IC 557 leaving Leipzig at 22.07 **(g)** change in Dresden at 23.40 and in Vienna South at 8.52 (arr. Vienna 10.13)

EXERCISE 9

First connection: dep. Leipzig at 17.16, arr. in Frankfurt at 23.15; change trains there; dep. Frankfurt 23.59; arr. Paris 4.57. Second connection: dep. Leipzig 19.55; arr. Paris 7.55. (He takes the second connection)

EXERCISE 11

(a) nach Berlin **(b)** morgen abend **(c)** zwei Stunden
(d) um 13.45 Uhr

EXERCISE 12

This is what Erich says: Wie komme ich am besten nach Rom? ... Mit dem Flugzeug. Ja, klar ... Freitag abend ... Gut, dann nehme ich den Flug um 17 Uhr.

EXERCISE 14

(a) muß (I have to go to Kiel today.) **(b)** müssen (Where do we have to get the tickets?) **(c)** muß (He doesn't have to work today.) **(d)** müssen (We must try this wine!)
(e) Muß (Do I have to change in Hamburg?)
(f) Müssen (Do we have to go by taxi?)

EXERCISE 15

(a) Mein Mann kann mit dem Auto nach München fahren.
(b) Die Kinder können eine Pizza essen. **(c)** Können Sie den ICE nehmen? **(d)** Ich kann heute nicht in die Firma.
(e) Wir können fliegen.

EXERCISE 16

muß; möchte; wollen; müssen; Kannst

10 ORDERING A MEAL

WHAT YOU WILL LEARN

▶ enquiring about different types of restaurant
▶ asking about local specialities
▶ ordering a meal and choosing a wine
▶ you will also read about national specialities, mealtimes and different wine regions in Germany

BEFORE YOU BEGIN

This unit will give you a chance to combine skills you've already acquired, such as understanding directions, enquiring about opening hours, making use of food vocabulary and placing an order. Although menus can look quite daunting at first sight, they can be broken down quite easily into basic categories such as **Fleisch** (meat), **Fisch** (fish), **Gemüse** (vegetables) and **Suppen** (soups). In some of the menus and advertisements you will also notice the continuing use of the old-fashioned Gothic script.

Pronunciation notes

st and sp

These two sounds are usually pronounced like the 'st' in the English word 'must' and the 'sp' in the English word 'grasp'. Here are two examples: **Gast** (guest) and **kosten** (to cost).

However, there is one big exception: if a word *starts* with **st** or **sp**, the **s** has to be pronounced like the 'sh' in 'short'. Examples from previous units are **sprechen** (to speak), **Straße** (street) and **Speisekarte** (menu). The same rule applies to words which are made up of a couple of short words stuck together, such as **Insektenstich** or **Hauptstraße**. You'll get another chance to practise these sounds in Exercise 9 of this unit.

Finding a meal at a reasonable price

LISTEN FOR...

preiswert   good value

Ruth	Wo kann man hier preiswert essen, bitte?
Frau Mohn	Gleich in der Nähe ist eine Pizzeria. Dort können Sie preiswert und gut essen.

Wo kann man hier preiswert essen?   Where can I get a meal at a reasonable price around here? (*lit.* Where can one eat for good value here?) Similarly:
Wo kann man hier schnell essen?   Where can one get a quick meal around here?
Wo kann man hier griechisch/vegetarisch essen?   Where can one get Greek/ vegetarian food around here?

gleich in der Nähe   right near here
(*lit.* right in the proximity)

die Pizzeria   pizzeria (**die Pizza** pizza)

Any other places for a cheap meal?

LISTEN FOR...

günstig	reasonable
Selbstbedienung	self-service
überall	everywhere

Ruth	Und wo kann man hier billig essen?
Frau Oswald	Also sehr günstig und zwar mit Selbstbedienung das McDonald's. (Das) gibt es ja überall in Europa, und das ist in der Nähe vom Hauptbahnhof.

günstig   reasonable

mit Selbstbedienung   (sometimes shortened to **SB**) with self-service.
Another useful term: **zum Mitnehmen** to take away.

überall in Europa   everywhere in Europe, all over Europe

in der Nähe vom Hauptbahnhof   near the main station (*lit.* in the proximity of the main station); **vom = von dem**

Where to eat well in Kiel

Ruth	Wo kann man hier in Kiel gut essen?
Frau Gallus	Möchten Sie deutsche Spezialitäten oder andere?
Ruth	Deutsche Spezialitäten.
Frau Gallus	Ja, dann bei uns gleich um die Ecke, im Friesenhof bekommen Sie schönen Fisch, kalte Platten mit Wurst und Käse, schönen Schinken, und ein gutes Bier.

deutsche Spezialitäten oder andere? German specialities or others? (**die Spezialität** the speciality)

(der) Friesenhof name of a restaurant

schönen Fisch nice fish (**der Fisch** fish). Note that all the items listed by Frau Gallus are in the accusative case; they are the object of the sentence (see grammar section in Unit 5).

kalte Platten mit Wurst und Käse cold dishes with (various types of) sausage and cheese (**die Platte** dish)

schönen Schinken nice ham (**der Schinken** ham)

1 An excerpt from a guidebook about good restaurants in Kiel. Read it and answer the questions below, in English.

New words: **die Küche** cuisine   **der Wintergarten** conservatory

> Das **‚Jever Böön'** ist ein gemütliches Restaurant in der Fußgängerzone. Man kann dort auch schon unter zehn Mark essen. Es gibt norddeutsche Spezialitäten, aber auch Vegetarisches (Tgl. 10–24 Uhr, So geschl.). Das **‚September'** ist ein elegantes Abendrestaurant mit leichter deutscher Küche, Wintergarten (Tgl. 17–24 Uhr, So geschl.). Im **‚Le Buffet'** gibt es kalte Platten und Salate (Tgl. 9–19 Uhr), und im **‚Hofrestaurant'** kann man vor allem Fischspezialitäten essen (Mo–Fr 10–19.30, Sa 10–18 Uhr und So 11–18 Uhr).

a. Where would you go for elegant surroundings and light German cuisine?

_____

b. Which restaurant serves North German specialities? _____

c. What if you wanted to eat fish specialities? _____

d. Spot the restaurant with a conservatory. _____

e. Which restaurants are open on a Sunday?

_____

f. And which ones open before noon?

ANSWERS P. 154

_____

Schloßkeller Freiberg
Historische Tanz- und Speisegaststätte
Familie Richter
Schloßplatz 4 • 09599 Freiberg • Tel. (0 37 31) 2 38 04
Täglich ab 11.00 Uhr geöffnet.
Freitag und Samstag Tanz.
Wir freuen uns auf Ihren Besuch!

Café Cather
das Café mit Tradition
mit eigener Konditorei
* Frühstück * Mittagsimbiß * Abendimbiß
* Diverse Kuchen-, Torten- und Kaffee-spezialitäten, "Bombe nach Liegnitzer Art"
* Außer-Haus-Verkauf - sonntags auch Brötchen
Katharinenstr. 15, 04109 Leipzig, Tel. 200243
Öffnungszeiten: Mo-Fr: 7.30 bis 20.00 Uhr
Sa/So: 9.00 bis 20.00 Uhr

Gotische Weinstube
St. Nicolai

Inh. Wolfram Krumbiegel

Kesselgasse 24
09599 Freiberg
Tel. 03731/47003

Mittagstisch mit typisch sächsischer Küche sowie Wild- und Fischgerichten
Spezialität: Hausgemachter Zwiebelkuchen
Meißner Weine in reicher Auswahl
Öffnungszeit:
Mo. 17 – 23 Uhr
Di. – So. 11 – 14 und 17 – 24 Uhr
Mi. Ruhetag

Weinstube »Küferstüble«
Bes. Josef Stader
Spiegelberg 17. Nähe Hochwart
Telefon 07534 / 73 51
Erlesene Weine und gutes Vesper.
Geöffnet: Dienstag bis Samstag ab 17 Uhr. Sonntag ab 15 Uhr. Montag Ruhetag.

Dafer-Stube
Reichenau-Waldsiedlung
Telefon 07531 / 7 84 21
Jeden Dienstag Spanferkel.
Grill-Spezialitäten, Fische vom Holzfeuer. Donnerstag Ruhetag.

ANSWERS P. 154

2 Three more food recommendations, this time on the recording. Each one refers to one of the eating establishments on the previous page. Which one?

New word:
sächsisch   Saxon

Recommendation No.1   Recommendation No.2   Recommendation No.3

_____   _____   _____

3 A selection of restaurants from a tourist information leaflet about Ulm. Read it through, then choose the right restaurants for the people below.

New vocabulary:
Hausmannskost   plain home cooking
für den eiligen Gast   for the customer in a hurry
das Wild   game
schwäbisch   Swabian (from an area around Ulm in South Germany)

No.	Name des Lokals	Öffnungszeiten	Ruhetag	Spezialitäten
1	**Adler**	10.00–24.00	Sonntag	Hausmannskost
2	**Bei Niko**	11.00–24.00	–	Griechische Spezialitäten
3	**Braustüble**	10.00–24.00	Montag	Schwäbische und spanische Spezialitäten
4	**Fischhaus Heilbronner**	9.00–18.00	Sonntag	Fisch und Wild
5	**McDonald's**	9.00–23.00	–	Big Mäc
6	**Hertie SB Restaurant**	10.30–18.30	Sonntag	für den eiligen Gast
7	**Schlössle**	10.00–24.00	Sonntag	Schweizer Spezialitäten

ANSWERS P. 154

4 Your chance to practise the phrases to help you find cheap, fast and good places to eat. On the recording, Tom will prompt you …

▶ The speciality of the day

Ruth	Was ist die Spezialität des Tages?
Bedienung	Gulasch mit Nudeln.
Ruth	Und was kostet das?
Bedienung	Sieben Mark und achtzig.
Ruth	Gut, dann nehme ich das Gulasch. Und für die Kleine, Bockwurst mit Pommes frites und Ketchup.
Bedienung	Und zu trinken?
Ruth	Zu trinken ... 'ne Cola und für mich 'ne Flasche Mineralwasser.

die Spezialität des Tages   speciality of the day, today's special; sometimes also called **Stammgericht** or **Tagesgericht** (dish of the day). Similarly **Spezialität des Hauses**   speciality of the house, chef's special (**des Tages** and **des Hauses** are both genitives conveying the idea 'of the').

das Gulasch   goulash

Nudeln   noodles, pasta; particularly popular in South Germany are the Swabian **Spätzle**, made with egg dough.
für die Kleine   for the little girl; quite often, there will be **der Kinderteller** children's dish/portion

die Bockwurst   long sausage, something like an oversize frankfurter
Pommes frites   (chips, French fries) oftened shortened to **Pommes** and pronounced as though it were a German word with two syllables. Note that to order one portion say **einmal Bockwurst mit Pommes** or **zweimal Bockwurst mit Pommes**   if you want two portions.

'ne Cola   short for **eine Cola**; the word for 'a' is often abbreviated in informal speech. Unfortunately, it is the **ei** of **eine** that disappears and the variable ending, the hard part, which remains!

Spezialitäten des Hauses

5 Listen and understand. On the recording Dorit orders food and drink in a restaurant. Listen to the conversation, then put a cross against the right statements below.

a. Die Spezialität des Tages ist ...
   Rumpsteak
   Wurst
   Fisch

b. Dazu gibt es ... (two are mentioned)
   grüne Bohnen
   Kartoffeln
   Salat

c. Dorit möchte ...
   die Wurst
   das Rumpsteak

d. Dazu trinkt sie ...
   ein dunkles Bier
   ein helles Bier

e. Sie möchte ...
   ein großes Bier
   ein kleines Bier

ANSWERS P. 154

Für Kenner und Liebhaber guter Biere

Alt-Rechenberger-Dunkel

die erzgebirgische Schwarzbierspezialität frisch vom Faß

Braurecht · seit 1558

Rechenberger

nach alter Brauart

6 Proofreading. We have recorded a brief conversation in a restaurant and printed the transcript below. But several errors have crept in – mark them and make the necessary changes.

Gast	Was ist die Spezialität des Abends?
Ober	Gulaschsuppe mit Nudeln und Bohnensalat.
Gast	Und was kostet das?
Ober	Elf Mark achtzig.
Gast	Haben Sie auch Fischsuppe?
Ober	Heute leider nicht. Das gibt es am Mittwoch wieder.
Gast	Dann nehme ich eine heiße Platte.
Ober	Und was möchten Sie trinken?
Gast	Eine Flasche Mineralwasser.

ANSWERS P. 154

BACCHUS
ofengemütlich-ursächsisch

Tägl. geöffnet ab 17.30 Uhr
warme Küche   bis 2.00 Uhr

Ur-Krostitzer

Fregestr. 6, 04105 Leipzig
☎ 03 41 / 28 76 17

Menu

Try reading this menu out loud before you listen to Erich and Dorit reading it on the recording. And remember, if you're not that interested in food, it's perfectly OK to skip this page and the exercises that go with it.

—— *Vorspeisen* ——

Gebackener Camembert mit Preiselbeeren und Toast	5,00 DM
Schnecken mit Kräuterbutter	8,00 DM
Omelett mit Pilzen	4,50 DM
Gemischte Salatplatte mit Schafskäse	6,00 DM

—— *Wild* ——

Wildsuppe mit Brot	7,00 DM
Wildschweingulasch mit Rotkraut und Kartoffelklößen	15,50 DM

—— *Hauptgerichte* ——

Schweineschnitzel mit Kartoffelsalat	10,50 DM
Kalbsteak mit Pfirsichen und Käse überbacken, Kroketten	16,00 DM
½ Brathähnchen mit Bratkartoffeln und Salat	9,00 DM
Putenbrust mit Käse-Schinkenfüllung und Salzkartoffeln	12,00 DM
Rinderbraten mit Champignons und Reis	13,00 DM

—— *Fischgerichte* ——

Forelle Müllerin mit frischem Gemüse und Salat	11,50 DM
Fischfilet mit Pommes frites und Buttererbsen	10,00 DM

—— *Nachspeisen* ——

Eisbecher mit Himbeeren und Sahne	6,50 DM
Frische Walderdbeeren mit Sahne	5,00 DM
Schwarzwälder Kirscheis-Spezialität	5,50 DM

New words:

		überbacken mit	with a baked topping of	**der Champignon**	(type of) mushroom
gebacken	baked	**das Brathähnchen**	roasted chicken	**das Wildschwein**	wild boar
die Preiselbeere	cranberry			**der Kartoffelkloß**	potato dumpling
die Schnecke	snail	**der Rinderbraten**	roast beef		
das Omelett	omelette	**die Forelle**	trout	**das Kalb**	veal
der Pilz	mushroom	**der Becher**	cup	**die Bratkartoffel**	fried potato
das Schaf	sheep	**die Vorspeise**	starter	**die Putenbrust**	turkey breast
das Kraut	cabbage	**das Hauptgericht**	main dish	**der Reis**	rice
das Schwein	pork	**das Fischgericht**	fish dish	**das Gemüse**	vegetable(s)
die Krokette	croquette	**die Nachspeise**	dessert	**der Wald**	forest

7 Study the menu on the left-hand page and answer the following questions.
Write out the items in German with a rough English translation.

What would you order if you wanted

a. a cold starter? _____

b. a soup to start with? _____

c. poultry as a main dish? (2 options) _____

_____

d. something that will remind you of fish and chips? _____

_____

ANSWERS P. 154 **e.** a dessert, but not an ice cream? _____

8 Slot the words below into their correct categories.

**Brot – Käse – Salami – Putensteak – Wildschweingulasch – Rotkraut – Kalbschnitzel –
Kartoffelsalat – Buttererbsen – Walderdbeeren – Klöße – gebackene Forelle**

	Fleisch	*kein Fleisch*
kalt		
warm		

ANSWERS P. 154

9 Pronunciation practice. Study the list of words below and make a ring round
those sounds that you think will be pronounced as 'shp' or 'sht', then turn to
the recording where Dorit will read the words out for you to repeat.

**Spezialitäten – Stück – kosten – Hauptstraße – Straße – Selbstbedienung – ist –
Speisekarte – Wurst – sprechen – Stunde – Spanien – Insektenstich – Stuttgart –
Sprache – Restaurant.**

10 Your turn to order something from
the menu on the opposite page.
The waitress is coming to take
your order. Turn to the
recording, where Tom will
prompt you …

Vom Bauern unserer Heimat

Qualitätsfleisch
Schwarzwald/Bodensee

Choosing the right wine

LISTEN FOR...

empfehlen	to recommend
süßlich	sweetish
herb	very dry

① **RHEINPFALZ**
② 1987
③ Winzerdorfer Rebberg
④ Riesling, Halbtrocken ⑤
⑥ Qualitätswein b. A.
⑦ A.P.Nr. 516 98788
⑧ Erzeugerabfüllung Winzer Bacchus, Winzerdorf

Ruth Ich hätte gerne einen Wein, bitte. Was können Sie mir da empfehlen?

Bedienung Ja, da haben wir einmal den Kröver Nacktarsch, der ist sehr süß, ist ein Moselwein. Und dann haben wir den Ihringer Vulkanfelsen, das ist auch ein süßlicher Wein. Die anderen sind alles Württemberger Weine, und die Württemberger sind sehr herb.

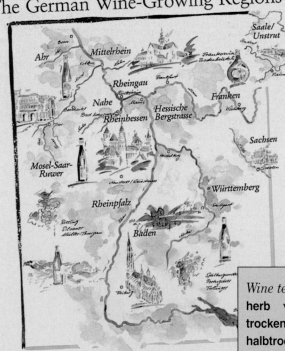

The German Wine-Growing Regions

Was können Sie (mir) empfehlen? What can you recommend (me)?

Kröver Nacktarsch some wines have rather eccentric, even rude names, like this 'bare bottom' from Kröv (the label shows a boy being spanked for pilfering wine).

der Moselwein Moselle wine

Ihringer Vulkanfelsen Another sweetish wine

Württemberger Weine wines from Württemberg, southern part of the South German federal state Baden-Württemberg around Stuttgart.

süßlich sweetish

die anderen the others

Wine terms
herb	very dry	**lieblich, süßlich**	sweetish
trocken	dry	**kräftig**	full-bodied
halbtrocken	medium dry	**fruchtig**	fruity

11 The wine list. Study the wine list and give the wines the appropriate English descriptions from the list below. You won't need all of them.

very dry; dry; medium dry; full-bodied but mild; mild; elegant with a touch of sweetness; rich and sweet; aromatic; light; refreshing

WEINE		
Thörnicher Ritsch Kabinett (trocken)	0,75 l ·	16,00
Huxelrebe Spätlese (lieblich elegant)	0,75 l	18,00
1991 Dornfelder Rotwein (mild)	1 l	16,00
1993 Müller Thurgau (halbtrocken)	1 l	16,00
1990 Spätburgunder (kräftig mild)	0,75 l	16,00

ANSWERS P. 154

12 Dear Paul. Here's a postcard Thomas wrote to his friend Paul while sitting in a famous wine cellar in Leipzig (see photo and advertisement on p. 141). Read it and answer the questions below, in English.

> *Lieber Paul,*
> *ich sitze in Auerbachs Keller in Leipzig und trinke gerade eine gute Flasche Wein – meine zweite! Ich bin schon seit heute mittag hier: am Sonntag kann man essen, so viel man will. Bald muß ich wieder nach New York zurück. Ich möchte die Karte heute noch zur Post bringen. Ich hoffe, ich finde den Weg aus dem Keller zum Hotel ...*
> *Viele Grüße*
> *Dein Thomas*

a. How much wine has Thomas drunk so far? _____

b. Since when has he been sitting in the cellar? _____

c. What's the special attraction about Sundays in this establishment?

_____

d. Why does he want to post the postcard today? _____

ANSWERS P. 154 **e.** What is he slightly worried about? _____

13 And now your turn to choose a wine on the recording. You will need some phrases such as:

ich möchte ... einen guten Rotwein/Weißwein
Was können Sie mir empfehlen?
Ist der (Wein) lieblich/herb/trocken?

Translating 'there is' and 'there are'

Both 'there is' (singular) and 'there are' (plural) can be translated into German by **es gibt**.

Singular
Es gibt ein Theater in Ulm.
There is a theatre in Ulm.
Gibt es hier eine Bank?
Is there a bank here?

Plural
Es gibt zwei Weinlokale in der Nähe.
There are two wine bars nearby.
Gibt es in Ulm griechische Restaurants?
Are there any Greek restaurants in Ulm?

Often you'll find **es gibt** followed by **zu** (+ verb) or **zum** (+ noun):
Was gibt es zu trinken?
What is there to drink?
Was gibt es zum Mittagessen?
What is there for lunch?

Sometimes **es gibt** is best translated idiomatically:
Das gibt es nicht.
That doesn't exist.
Das gibt es überall in Europa.
You'll find that/those all over Europe.
Wo gibt es denn so was?
Would you believe it?

Separable verbs

Verbs such as **einsteigen** (to get in) and **abfahren** (to leave, depart) are separable. They can be split into two parts:

prefix	verb
ein	steigen
ab	fahren

If the separable verb is the first (and often only) verb in the sentence, it splits up. The stem takes up its usual position and the prefix goes right to the end. For example:

Ich steige jetzt ein.   I am now getting in.
Ich fahre um 17.00 Uhr ab.   I am leaving at 5 p.m.

If there are two verbs in the sentence, the separable verb does not split up and behaves just like any other verb. For example:
Ich möchte jetzt einsteigen.   I'd like to get in now.
Ich will um 17.00 Uhr abfahren.   I want to leave at 5 p.m.

Word building

Nouns such as **Mineralwasser**, **Wintergarten** and **Salatplatte** are made up of more than one noun. Each constituent noun can also stand separately: **das Mineral, das Wasser; der Winter, der Garten; der Salat, die Platte.** The gender is always that of the last noun in the word.

For example: **der Flug + das Ticket ▶ das Flugticket**
der Fußgänger + die Zone ▶ die Fußgängerzone

Brauerei Clemens Härle
88299 Leutkirch im Allgäu

Löwenbräu Meckatz
88178 Heimenkirch-Meckatz

Edelweißbrauerei O. Farny
88228 Wangen im Allgäu

WLZ Raiffeisen AG Hopfen-
handel, 88069 Tettnang

Kronenbrauerei Tettnang
88069 Tettnang

Bürgerliches Brauhaus
Ravensburg

Härle-Brauerei
88376 Königseggwald

Brauerei Ott
88427 Bad Schussenried

14 **Was gibt es zum/zu/im ...?** What is there for/to/in ...? Ask the right questions for the answers below.

a. _____ ?

Zum Abendessen gibt es eine kalte Platte.

b. _____ ?

Zu trinken gibt es Bier, Wein, Sekt und Mineralwasser.

c. _____ ?

Im Theater gibt es ein Drama von Molière.

d. _____ ?

Im Rathauskeller gibt es deutsche Spezialitäten.

ANSWERS P. 154

15 Translate the following sentences into German.

a. What is there for breakfast?

_____

b. Is there a theatre in Ravensburg?

_____

c. There is cake or ice cream.

_____

d. There are many good restaurants in Leipzig.

_____

ANSWERS P. 154

16 Separable verbs – put them together again.

For example: **Wir steigen in fünf Minuten aus.**
▶ **Wir wollen in fünf Minuten aussteigen.**

a. Der Bus fährt nicht ab.

▶ Der Bus kann nicht _____

b. Mein Mann steigt in Brüssel um.

▶ Mein Mann muß in Brüssel _____

c. Die Maschine fliegt um 8 Uhr ab.

▶ Die Maschine muß um 8 Uhr _____

d. Wir kommen morgen abend an.

▶ Wir möchten morgen abend _____

e. Ich steige am Theater aus.

▶ Ich will am Theater _____

ANSWERS P. 154

17 Word building. Try to make up at least ten new words by combining the nouns below; they're all about food and drink. Provide your new words with their correct genders.

Suppe – Teller – Abend – Kinder – Kloß – Schwein – Steak – Restaurant – Bohnen – Essen – Wild – Platte – Salat – Kartoffel – Kalb – Keller – Wein – Mosel

_____

_____

_____

_____

_____

_____

_____

_____

_____

_____

ANSWERS P. 154

KEY WORDS

To use yourself:

Wo kann man hier ...	Where can you get a ...
gut	good
billig	cheap
schnell	quick
italienisch	Italian
vegetarisch	vegetarian
... essen?	... meal?
Was gibt es ...	What is there ...
zum Frühstück?	for breakfast?
zum Mittagessen?	for lunch?
zum Abendessen?	for supper?
zu trinken?	to drink?
Gibt es auch ...	Are there also ...
deutsche Spezialitäten?	German specialities?
vegetarisches Essen?	vegetarian dishes?
Was ist die Spezialität ...	What's the speciality ...
des Tages?	of the day?
des Hauses?	of the house?
Was können Sie (mir) empfehlen?	What can you recommend (me)?
Ist der (Wein) trocken?	Is it (the wine) dry?

Mainly to read and understand:

mit Selbstbedienung	with self-service
der Kinderteller	children's portion/dish
die Vorspeise	starter
die Hauptspeise/das Hauptgericht	main dish
die Beilage	side dish
die Nachspeise	dessert
das Rind/Schwein/Kalb	beef/pork/veal
der Braten	roast
das Hähnchen	chicken
die Forelle	trout
das Gemüse	vegetables
der Reis	rice
die Kartoffel	potato
Der Wein ist ...	The wine is ...
herb	very dry
trocken	dry
fruchtig	fruity
lieblich/süßlich	sweetish

DID YOU KNOW?

Mealtimes

In Germany the main meal of the day is lunch, served around one o'clock. If possible, Germans stick to their hot **Mittagessen**, even at work (many firms provide a canteen, **die Kantine**). The evening meal (**Abendessen** or **Abendbrot**) is served around seven p.m. and usually consists of slices of cold meat, sausage or cheese on bread.

Specialities

It's not all **Bratwurst, Sauerkraut, Kartoffeln** and **Bier** – nowadays German cuisine is much more sophisticated. There aren't any national specialities as such, but a great many regional dishes. Over the years, foreign influences have also inspired German cooking. This is partly due to the arrival of immigrant workers from Southern Europe, and also to the fact that the Germans are very keen travellers. In restaurants many German dishes are still rather rich, plentiful and meat-based, but there is also an increasing trend towards **leichte Kost** (light food) as well as vegetarian food (**vegetarisches Essen**). Some restaurants have introduced no-smoking zones (**Nichtraucherzonen**).

Local and regional specialities are far too numerous to be mentioned in detail. Generally, you might find that North Germans put sugar on the most unexpected dishes, even on cabbage and fried potatoes. The **Eintopf** (stew) is a very popular example of **Hausmannskost** (home cooking). **Bohnen, Birnen und Speck** (*lit.* beans, pears and bacon), for example, might sound like a strange combination, but it is a popular stew with a somewhat unusual sweet-sour-smoky aroma. **Aalsuppe** (eel soup) is based on the same principle, combining fresh eel, ham, different kinds of meat, vegetables and fruit. It's well worth trying **Räucherfisch**, freshly smoked fish, in one of the many **Räuchereien** (smokeries) in coastal resorts along the Baltic and North Sea.

Traditional South German and Austrian cooking offers a rich variety of non-meat dishes based on flour. **Dampfnudeln mit Vanillesauce**, for example, are yeast dumplings served with custard, **Nockerln** are small flour or semolina dumplings, **Powidltascherl** are dumplings filled with prunes and dusted with cinnamon and sugar. In Switzerland you could try cheese specialities such as **Raclette**, melted cheese served with potatoes, or a **Fondue**, melted cheese seasoned with wine, garlic and **Kirsch** served in a special pot, together with cubes of white bread to dip in. There is also the meat fondue, cubes of meat cooked in hot fat or broth. A **Rösti** consists of fried grated potatoes sometimes with a crispy cheese topping and served with fried egg and green salad. Also bear in mind **Spätzle** and **Maultaschen** – both are classic Swabian pasta dishes. In the spring, **Spargel** (asparagus) is a must: some restaurants offer up to 100 different dishes, all based on fresh **Spargel**.

Wines

Best known are wines from the Rhine area: **Rheingau, Rheinpfalz** and **Rheinhessen**, the birthplace of **Liebfraumilch**. Many of them are aromatic and full-bodied. The wines grown on the banks of the **Mosel** and its tributaries, the **Saar** and the **Ruwer**, have a lighter, fruitier taste. It's well worth trying wines from other areas, too. **Frankenwein** (from Franconia, an area south of Frankfurt), as well as the **Badische Weine** (from **Baden**, the southernmost German wine region) tend to be drier than the Rhine and Moselle wines and are often very aromatic. The even drier **Württemberger** is said hardly to leave its region of origin, **Baden-Württemberg**, because the winegrowers like it so much that they want to keep it to themselves.

AND FINALLY...

18 Your turn to speak. Study the menu on the right. On the recording you will be asked to order several items – Tom will prompt you.

SUPPEN
Bouillon mit Ei
Tomatensuppe
Kartoffelsuppe
 	
BEILAGEN
Reis
Nudeln
Salzkartoffeln
Pommes frites
Gemischter Salat
	HAUPTGERICHTE
	½ Brathähnchen mit
	   Kartoffelsalat
	Rinderbraten mit
	   Zwiebeln
	Schweineschnitzel mit
	   grünem Gemüse
	Forelle blau mit
	   Salatplatte

WEINE
weiß
Ihringer Vulkanfels
   (süßlich)
Alter Salzberg (herb)
rot
Sonnenberger Trollinger
   (herb)

ANSWERS

EXERCISE 1
(a) the 'September' **(b)** the 'Jever Böön' **(c)** 'Hofrestaurant'
(d) the 'September' **(e)** 'Le Buffet' and 'Hofrestaurant'
(f) all of them, except the 'September'

EXERCISE 2
No. 1: Café Cather No. 2: Gotische Weinstube St. Nicolai
No. 3: Schloßkeller Freiberg

EXERCISE 3
(a) Hertie SB-Restaurant **(b)** Braustüble **(c)** McDonald's
(d) Fischhaus Heilbronner

EXERCISE 5
(a) Steak **(b)** Kartoffeln, Salat **(c)** Steak **(d)** dunkles Bier
(e) ein kleines Bier

EXERCISE 6
Tages instead of Abends; Gulasch instead of Gulaschsuppe; cross out 'und' leaving Was kostet das'; zwölf Mark 85 instead of elf Mark 80; Fisch instead of Fischsuppe; Freitag instead of Mittwoch; kalte instead of heiße; Und zu trinken? instead of whole sentence; Bier instead of Mineralwasser

EXERCISE 7
(a) Gemischte Salatplatte mit Schafskäse (mixed salad platter with sheep cheese) **(b)** Wildsuppe mit Brot (venison soup with bread) **(c)** ½ Brathähnchen mit Bratkartoffeln und Salat (half a roast chicken with fried potatoes and salad) or Putenbrust mit Käse-Schinkenfüllung und Salzkartoffeln (turkey breast with a cheese and ham filling and potatoes) **(d)** Fischfilet mit Pommes frites und Buttererbsen (fish fillet with French fries and butter peas)
(e) Frische Walderdbeeren mit Sahne (fresh wild strawberries with cream)

EXERCISE 8

	Fleisch	kein Fleisch
kalt	Salami	Käse; Brot; Walderdbeeren; Kartoffelsalat
warm	**Kalbschnitzel;** **Putensteak;** **Wildschweingulasch**	**Buttererbsen;** **Klöße;** **gebackene Forelle; Rotkraut**

EXERCISE 11
The descriptions from the top to the bottom of the list should run as follows: dry; elegant with a touch of sweetness; mild; medium dry; full-bodied but mild

EXERCISE 12
(a) he's drinking his second bottle of wine **(b)** since lunchtime (noon) **(c)** you can eat as much as you like on Sundays **(d)** he will have to go back to New York quite soon **(e)** he hopes that he can manage to find his way out of the cellar and back to the hotel ...

EXERCISE 14
(a) Was gibt es zum Abendessen? **(b)** Was gibt es zu trinken? **(c)** Was gibt es im Theater? **(d)** Was gibt es im Rathauskeller?

EXERCISE 15
(a) Was gibt es zum Frühstück? **(b)** Gibt es ein Theater in Ravensburg? **(c)** Es gibt Kuchen oder Eis. **(d)** Es gibt viele gute Restaurants in Leipzig.

EXERCISE 16
(a) abfahren **(b)** umsteigen **(c)** abfliegen **(d)** ankommen
(e) aussteigen

EXERCISE 17
Here are some (but not all) possibilities: die Salatplatte; der Weinkeller; der Moselwein; die Bohnensuppe; der Kartoffelsalat; das Abendessen; der Kinderteller; das Kalbsteak; der Kartoffelkloß

11 LIKES AND DISLIKES

WHAT YOU WILL LEARN

▶ talking about your favourite foods and drinks
▶ discussing other likes and dislikes
▶ speaking about favourite travel destinations
▶ you will also be reading about holiday regions in Germany

BEFORE YOU BEGIN

Now that you have mastered two thirds of the course, you can relax and start thinking about some of the more conversational skills that you might like to develop in German. This unit will teach you how to talk about things you really enjoy doing by concentrating on a number of expressions, some of which are already familiar. The crucial thing to bear in mind is that idioms need to be treated as set phrases which cannot really be translated literally.

Wasserburg

Pronunciation notes

ng and nk

The **ng** as in **Ring** (ring) is pronounced as one nasal sound only and sounds just like the 'ng' in the English word 'ring'. The same rule applies to **ng** sounds in the middle of a word, such as in **singen** (to sing): don't be tempted to pronounce the **g** as a separate sound.

However, it's a different story with the **nk**: it should always be pronounced as two sounds, nasal + **k**, exactly as in English. Try practising the following words on the recording:
trinken (to drink); **danken** (to thank); **denken** (to think); **Frankreich** (France); **Lunge** (lung); **hängen** (to hang); **fangen** (to catch); **England**

Favourite foods and drinks

LISTEN FOR...

Was essen Sie gern?   What do you enjoy eating?
Was trinken Sie am liebsten?   What's your favourite drink?

Ruth	Was essen Sie gern?
Herr Hansen	Fleisch in jeder Variation, am liebsten Steaks.
Ruth	Und was trinken Sie am liebsten?
Herr Hansen	Westdeutsches Bier, am liebsten Königspils.

Was essen Sie gern(e)?   What do you enjoy/like eating? Note that **gern** or **gerne** (*lit.* with pleasure) can be added after any verb to express what you enjoy or like doing. For example:

Was trinken Sie gern(e)? What do you enjoy drinking? **Was kochen Sie gern(e)?** What do you enjoy cooking? **Was lesen Sie gern(e)?** What do you enjoy reading?

Fleisch in jeder Variation   all kinds of meat (*lit.* meat in every variation)

am liebsten Steaks (short for **ich esse am liebsten Steaks**) I like (eating) steaks best. More on **gern/lieber/am liebsten** in the grammar section in this unit.

Was trinken Sie am liebsten?· What do you like drinking best? What's your favourite drink?

(ich trinke) am liebsten Königspils I like (drinking) Königspils best. **(das) Königspils** short for König-Pilsener, a brand of beer. Note that there is **Flaschenbier** (bottled beer) and **Bier vom Faß** or **Faßbier** (*lit.* beer from the barrel, i.e. draught beer).

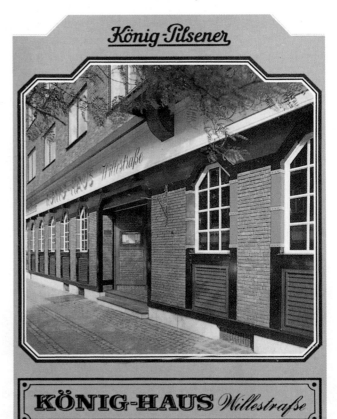

The König-Haus in Willestraße, Kiel

LISTEN FOR...
ich mag Fisch lieber   I prefer fish

Ruth	Essen Sie gerne Fisch?
Frau Bagan	Ja, gerne.
Ruth	Und Fleisch?
Frau Bagan	Ich mag Fisch lieber.
Ruth	Trinken Sie gerne Wein?
Frau Bagan	Ja, sehr gerne.
Ruth	Welchen Wein mögen Sie lieber: Rotwein oder Weißwein?
Frau Bagan	Ich mag Weißwein lieber.
Ruth	Und welche Sorte trinken Sie am liebsten?
Frau Bagan	Am liebsten Badischen.

ja, gerne   yes, I do (like it)

ich mag Fisch lieber or **ich mag lieber Fisch**   I like fish better, I prefer fish. Frau Bagan could just as easily have said: **ich esse Fisch lieber** or **ich esse lieber Fisch** I prefer eating fish. **Mag** is derived from the modal verb **mögen** to like (see below).

ja, sehr gerne   yes, very much

Welchen Wein mögen Sie lieber?   Which wine do you prefer? Again, Ruth could have asked: **Welchen Wein trinken Sie lieber?** Which wine do you prefer to drink?

welche Sorte   which kind; note that **welch-** (which) takes the same case endings as **der/die/das** etc. Examples: **das Fleisch ▶ welches Fleisch? dem Mann ▶ welchem Mann? die Kinder ▶ welche Kinder?**

(ich trinke/ich mag) am liebsten Badischen (Wein)   I like drinking/I like wines from Baden best. Baden is a famous wine region in Southwest Germany.

The modal verb **mögen** to like	
ich mag	wir mögen
du magst	ihr mögt
er/sie/es mag	sie/Sie mögen

PRACTICE

1 What could you say instead? Study the sentences below and then go back to the conversation about Frau Bagan's favourites and find the sentences that carry the same meaning but are worded slightly differently. Note them down.

a. Mögen Sie Fisch? ____________________

b. Ich esse lieber Fisch. ____________________

c. Mögen Sie Wein? ____________________

d. Welchen Wein trinken Sie lieber? ____________________

ANSWERS P. 170

e. Welche Sorte mögen Sie am liebsten? ____________________

2 Which answer fits? There's only one answer out of three that will fit each of the questions below. Check your answers on the recording.

New word:
der Champagner champagne

a. Was essen Sie gern?
Am liebsten Flaschenbier.
Nein, ich esse lieber Fleisch.
Ich esse gern Salat.

b. Was trinken Sie gern?
Ich trinke lieber Saft.
Ja, sehr gern.
Ich trinke gerne Wein.

c. Was essen Sie lieber, Fleisch oder Fisch?
Ich esse lieber Fisch.
Ja, gerne.
Am liebsten Badischen Wein.

d. Und was trinken Sie am liebsten?
Am liebsten Pizza.
Ich trinke am liebsten Champagner.
Ich trinke lieber Weißwein.

3 Favourite foods and drinks. On the recording, Tom is interviewing three people. Listen carefully and fill in the grid below.

	essen		trinken	
	gerne	**am liebsten**	**gerne**	**am liebsten**
Herr Blume				
Frau Matthei				
Herr Brand				

ANSWERS P. 170

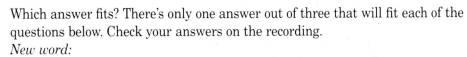

4 Match up the questions and answers below, then listen to the recording to check.

New word:

das Buch   book (*plural* **Bücher**)

Lesen Sie gerne?   *Ja, ich mag ...* _____

Kochen Sie gerne? _____

Was kochen Sie am liebsten? _____

Und was trinken Sie gerne? _____

Reisen Sie gerne? _____

Und wohin reisen Sie am liebsten? _____

Am liebsten nach Kanada.
Kalifornische Weine.
Ich koche sehr gerne.
Ja, ich mag Reisen.
Am liebsten koche ich Spaghetti.
Ja, ich mag Bücher.

5 Questions and answers. Here are the answers – now make up the questions and write them down. This exercise is slightly open-ended; there are several ways of phrasing your questions.

a. _____ ?

   Ja, ich esse gerne Fisch.

b. . _____ ?

   Ich esse am liebsten Forelle.

c. _____ ?

   Ja, ich trinke gerne Wein.

d. _____ ?

   Ich trinke lieber Weißwein.

e. _____ ?

   Am liebsten trinke ich Frankenwein.

POSSIBLE ANSWERS P. 170

6 Your turn to speak and tell Dorit about your own preferences. Tom will prompt you. These structures will come in useful:

ich/esse/trinke/gerne/sehr gerne/am liebsten

Frau Bagan asks Jessica whether she likes school

LISTEN FOR...

Gefällt dir die Schule?	Do you like school?
das Aufstehen	getting up (in the morning)

Frau Bagan	Gefällt dir die Schule?
Jessica	Ja, manchmal.
Frau Bagan	Und was gefällt dir?
Jessica	Alles eigentlich. Nur nicht das Aufstehen.
Frau Bagan	Gefällt dir Englisch?
Jessica	Ja.
Frau Bagan	Und gefällt dir Sport?
Jessica	Ja.
Frau Bagan	Und was gefällt dir am besten?
Jessica	Schwimmen.

Gefällt dir ...? Do you like ...? This is a very common phrase. It is formed with the verb **gefallen** to please; **dir** means 'to you' when you are talking to children and friends. **Es gefällt mir** is 'I like it' (*lit.* it pleases (to) me).

die Schule school

ja, manchmal yes, sometimes. A longer answer would be: **mir gefällt die Schule** or **die Schule gefällt mir** I like school. And in the negative: **mir gefällt die Schule nicht** or **die Schule gefällt mir nicht** I don't like school.

Was gefällt dir? What do you like? (*lit.* What pleases (to) you?)

alles eigentlich everything really

nur nicht das Aufstehen but not (the) getting up (in the morning) (**aufstehen** to get up); **das Aufstehen** getting up is a verb turned into a noun by placing the article **das** in front and giving it a capital letter.

am besten best (of all)

das Schwimmen swimming (from **schwimmen** to swim) is another verb turned into a noun.

7 A letter to a friend. Study the letter Kathrin has written to Gabi who has left Austria to work in Berlin. Compare the letter to the translation below. There are nine mistakes in the English text. Spot them and correct them. Note that Kathrin has written **Dich**, **Dir**, **Deine** and **Du** in capitals, as should be done in all letters.

New words: **endlich**   finally
vermissen   to miss
dich   you
der Kurs   course

> *Liebe Gabi!*
>
> *Viele Grüße aus Österreich. Wir vermissen Dich sehr. Wie gefällt Dir Berlin? Und wie gefällt Dir Deine neue Arbeit? Wir haben jetzt eine neue Kollegin, eine nette Frau. Und Karls Frau hat endlich das Baby – einen Jungen. Der Sommer hier ist wunderschön. Ich schwimme viel; und ich lerne jetzt Spanisch – jeden Mittwoch gehe ich in die Abendschule. Der Kurs gefällt mir gut, aber er macht viel extra Arbeit.*
> *Bitte schreibe mir bald, Deine Kathrin*

> *Dear Gabi,*
>
> *Many greetings from Switzerland. We miss you very much. How do you like Berlin? And how do you like your new house? We have a new colleague now, a nice man. And Karl's wife has finally had the baby – a girl. Spring here is wonderful. I do a lot of jogging, and I am learning Spanish now – every Tuesday I go to evening classes. I like the course and it does not make much extra work.*
> *Please come soon, Your Kathrin*

ANSWERS P. 170

8 Preferences. On the recording Erich is talking to a female friend about her preferences. Listen carefully and mark up the questionnaire below.

Gefällt dir Berlin?	ja	nein	manchmal
Gefällt dir die Schule?	ja	nein	manchmal
Gefällt dir Englisch?	ja	nein	manchmal
Gefällt dir Sport?	ja	nein	manchmal
Gefällt dir Schwimmen?	ja	nein	manchmal

ANSWERS P. 170

9 It's time for you to ask a few questions. Turn to the recording to ask a friend some questions. These phrases will come in useful:

Gefällt dir ...?
Was gefällt dir ... am besten?

New word:
die Jazzmusik   jazz music

CONVERSATIONS

 More likes and dislikes

LISTEN FOR...

Gefällt es Ihnen?	Do you like it? (*polite form*)
ruhig	quiet
segeln	to sail
spazierengehen	to go for a walk

Ruth	Gefällt es Ihnen an der Schlei?
Frau Bagan	Ja, sehr. Es ist so ruhig hier, und das Wasser ist so schön. Man kann herrlich segeln, und man kann spazierengehen und aufs Wasser schauen, den Wind und die Wellen genießen.

Gefällt es Ihnen an der Schlei?   Do you like it by the Schlei? **Die Schlei** is a picturesque sea inlet north of Kiel close to the Danish border. Note that Ruth is addressing an adult and therefore uses the polite form of address **Ihnen** (to you). She could also have asked: **Gefällt Ihnen die Schlei?** Do you like the Schlei?

ruhig   quiet

man kann herrlich segeln   there is great sailing (*lit.* one can sail wonderfully). Do not confuse **man** meaning 'one' or 'you' or 'people in general' with **der Mann** meaning 'man' which sounds exactly the same in spoken German.

spazierengehen   to go for a walk. More activities are: **wandern** or **Wanderungen machen** to hike; **radeln** or **radfahren** to cycle; **bergsteigen** to climb mountains.

aufs Wasser schauen short for **auf das Wasser schauen** to gaze at (*lit.* look onto) the water

der Wind   wind

die Welle   wave

genießen   to enjoy

Frau Bagan by the Schlei

LISTEN FOR...

das Meer	the sea
in den Bergen	in the mountains

Ruth	Was gefällt Ihnen besser, Norddeutschland oder Süddeutschland?
Frau Bagan	Mir gefällt Norddeutschland besser. Ich mag das Meer. Und ich mag nicht in den Bergen leben.

Was gefällt Ihnen besser?   What do you prefer? Note that **gefallen** can be combined with **gut/besser/am besten** depending on your order of preference:

mir gefällt Bonn	**(sehr gut)**	I like Bonn (very much)
mir gefällt Köln	**besser**	I like Cologne better
mir gefällt Berlin	**am besten**	I like Berlin best (of all)

ich mag nicht in den Bergen leben   I don't like living in the mountains (**der Berg** mountain); **in den Bergen** is the dative plural (see Grammar summary p. 235).

Am bayerischen Bodensee

PRACTICE

10 Preferences. On the recording, several people are being asked about their preferences. Make a ring round the countries/regions or towns they prefer.

a. Frau Sahler	Norddeutschland	Süddeutschland
b. Herr Sahler	Hamburg	München
c. Frau Martini	Bayern	Schleswig-Holstein
d. Herr Mohr	das Meer	die Berge
e. Frau Kohl	Irland	Schottland

ANSWERS P. 170

11 Study the advertisement for the **Genfersee** (Lake Geneva), also called 'the Swiss Riviera', and mark the statements that correspond directly to passages in the text.

WEITE UND WÄRME AM GENFERSEE
◆ ◆ ◆
SYMPHONIE DER FARBEN
◆ ◆ ◆
ABENDSONNENPANORAMA
◆ ◆ ◆
STILLE SEEN
◆ ◆ ◆
RENDEZVOUS MIT DER NATUR
◆ ◆ ◆
ROMANTISCHE BERGE
◆ ◆ ◆
SOMMERSONNE UND SPORT
◆ ◆ ◆
WANDERN   SEGELN   RADFAHREN
◆ ◆ ◆
BALLONFLIEGEN   EDLE WEINE
◆ ◆ ◆
GRANDE CUISINE

New word:
genießen   to enjoy

a. Man kann Wanderungen machen.
b. Man kann Sprachen lernen.
c. Man kann schöne Souvenirs kaufen.
d. Man kann die Weine genießen.
e. Man kann radfahren.
f. Man kann kochen.
g. Man kann segeln.
h. Man kann gut essen.

SCHWEIZER RIVIERA

Genfersee Gebiet Verkehrsbüro
Avenue d'Ouchy 60
CH-1006 Lausanne
Tel. 0041-21-617 72 04 – Fax 0041-21-617 30 80

ANSWERS P. 170

12

An Englishman in Munich. On the recording Mr Marks tells Dorit about his likes and dislikes. Listen to him and make a ring round the answers that apply.

a. Does Mr Marks like his work?

     yes   no   sometimes

b. Does he miss England?

     yes   no   sometimes

c. He likes Munich because there are so many …

     theatres/restaurants/concerts/shops/lakes/nearby mountains
     (*Mark four attractions*)

ANSWERS P. 170

13

Your turn to speak. But first of all study the letter Herr Riedel has written about himself. When you've finished, turn on the recording and pretend you are Herr Riedel. Dorit will ask you a few questions about yourself. Try to use as many phrases from the text as possible.

> *Mein Name ist Riedel. Mein Vorname ist Markus. Ich wohne in Dresden und arbeite dort in einem Museum. Die Arbeit gefällt mir gut, aber ich mag nicht in Dresden leben. Die Stadt ist mir zu groß. Ich komme aus Naumburg, das ist eine kleine Stadt nicht weit von Dresden. Naumburg ist so ruhig, und man kann schön spazierengehen. Mir gefällt Naumburg besser …*

The river Elbe in Dresden

The use of *gefallen*

You use the verb **gefallen** if you want to say that you like something. The most important forms of **gefallen** are used in phrases such as these:

Gefällt es Ihnen?
> Do you like it? (*lit.* pleases it (to) you?)

Wie gefällt es Ihnen hier?
> How do you like it here? (*lit.* how pleases it (to) you here?)

Gefällt dir die Schule? Do you like school?

Was gefällt dir besonders? What do you like especially?

Was gefällt dir besser? What do you like better?

Note that both **Ihnen** and **dir** mean 'to you'. You use **Ihnen** with adults and **dir** with children and friends.

If you want to say that *you* like something, you use **gefallen + mir**:

Es **gefällt** **mir hier.** I like it here.

Ulm **gefällt** **mir (gut).** I like Ulm.

Die Stadt **gefällt** **mir gut.** I like the town a lot.

Norddeutschland **gefällt** **mir besser.** I like North Germany better.

And if you don't like something you just add **nicht**:

Es **gefällt** **mir hier nicht.** I don't like it here.

Ulm **gefällt** **mir nicht.** I don't like Ulm.

Die Stadt **gefällt** **mir nicht.** I don't like the town.

German Bread Museum, Ulm

The use of *gern, lieber, am liebsten*

Another way of saying you like something is to use **gern** or **gerne**.

Ich esse **gern** **Steaks.** I like eating steaks.

Ich trinke **gern** **Kaffee.** I like drinking coffee.

Ich fahre **gern** **in den Süden.** I like going to the South.

If you *prefer* something, or if you would rather do something else, you use **lieber**:

Ich esse **lieber** **Fisch.** I prefer eating fish.

Ich nehme **lieber** **den Zug.** I prefer to take the train.

Ich möchte **lieber** **Wein.** I'd rather have wine.

And if you like something *best*, you use **am liebsten**:

Ich esse **am liebsten** **Fleisch.** I like eating meat best.

Ich reise **am liebsten** **nach England.** I like going to England best.

Ich möchte **am liebsten** **Kuchen.** I'd like some cake most of all.

And if you don't like something, you'll need to insert **nicht**:

Ich esse **nicht gern** **Steaks.** I don't like eating steaks.

Ich trinke **nicht gern** **Kaffee.** I don't like drinking coffee.

Remember: When expressing preferences, **gefallen** is followed by **gut/besser/am besten**:

Ulm **gefällt mir** **gut** .

Köln **gefällt mir** **besser** .

Berlin gefällt mir **am besten** .

... whereas other verbs combine with **gern/lieber/am liebsten** :

Ich trinke **gern** **Saft.**

Ich trinke **lieber** **Tee.**

Ich trinke am **liebsten** **Kaffee.**

14 Complete the answers to these questions.

Here are two examples:

Was essen Sie gern? ▶ *Ich esse gern* Suppe.
Kochen Sie gern? ▶ Ja, *ich koche gern.*

a. Was trinken Sie gern?

_____ Wein.

b. Was trinken Sie am liebsten?

_____ kalifornischen

Wein.

c. Wohin reisen Sie gern?

_____ nach

Südeuropa.

d. Und wohin reisen Sie am liebsten?

_____

nach Griechenland.

e. Schwimmen Sie gern?

Ja, _____

f. Lesen Sie gern?

Ja, _____

g. Und was lesen Sie am liebsten?

_____

Science Fiction.

h. Welche Musik mögen Sie lieber, Pop oder Jazz?

_____ Jazz.

ANSWERS P. 170

Weekly market in Ulm

15 Match up questions and answers.

Ja, sehr gern   **Am liebsten in den Süden**
Chinesische Gerichte   **Süddeutschland**
Am liebsten Moselwein **Nicht gut, leider**
In Süddeutschland

a. Wie gefällt es Ihnen in Kiel?

_____

b. Was gefällt Ihnen besser, Norddeutschland oder Süddeutschland?

_____

c. Reisen Sie gern?

_____

d. Und wohin reisen Sie am liebsten?

_____

e. Was essen Sie gern?

_____

f. Und was trinken Sie am liebsten?

_____

g. Wo arbeiten Sie lieber, in Norddeutschland oder in Süddeutschland?

_____

ANSWERS P. 170

KEY WORDS

Mainly to understand:

Expressions with
gern(e)*/lieber/am liebsten:

Was essen/trinken Sie gern?	What do you like eating/drinking?
... lieber?	What do you prefer eating/drinking?
... am liebsten?	What do you like eating/drinking best?

Welche Sorte trinken Sie gern?	Which sort do you like (drinking)?
... lieber?	Which sort do you prefer (drinking)?
... am liebsten?	Which sort do you like (drinking) best?

Welchen Wein mögen Sie lieber?	Which wine do you prefer?
... am liebsten?	Which wine do you like best?

Phrases with **gefallen +**
gut/besser/am besten

Gefällt dir/Ihnen die Arbeit?	Do you like the work?
Gefällt es dir/Ihnen in Ulm?	Do you like it in Ulm?

Was gefällt dir/Ihnen?	What do you like?
Was gefällt dir/Ihnen besser?	What do you like better?
Was gefällt dir/Ihnen am besten?	What do you like best?

To use yourself:

Expressions with
gern(e)*/lieber/am liebsten

Ich esse gerne Steaks	I like (eating) steaks
Ich esse lieber Fisch	I prefer (eating) fish
Ich esse am liebsten Salate	I like (eating) salads best

Ich mag (gern) Wein (trinken)	I like wine
Ich mag lieber Bier (trinken)	I prefer beer
Ich mag am liebsten Champagner (trinken)	I like champagne best

Ich reise/koche/lese gerne	I enjoy travelling/cooking/reading
... lieber	I prefer ...
... am liebsten	I like ... best (of all)

Phrases with **gefallen +**
gut/besser/am besten

Mir gefällt Ulm (gut)	I like Ulm
Mir gefällt es sehr gut	I really like it
Mir gefällt es in Ulm	I like it in Ulm
Mir gefällt München besser	I prefer Munich
Mir gefällt Kiel am besten	I like Kiel best (of all)
Man kann segeln/spazierengehen/wan-dern	You can sail/go for walks/go for hikes
Es ist ruhig hier	It's quiet here

* Remember you can say **gern**
or **gerne**.

Flensburg harbour

Popular holiday areas in Germany

(See map on page 249.)

1 *The North Sea* **die Nordsee**
Famous for its bracing climate, much recommended by doctors. The most popular resorts are on the East Frisian and North Frisian Islands (**Ostfriesische und Nordfriesische Inseln**); most famous and fashionable is the island of **Sylt**, close to the Danish border.

2 *The Baltic Sea* **die Ostsee**
The climate is milder, the sea and dunes less spectacular than those on the North Sea coast. There are a number of well-established seaside resorts such as Warnemünde, Kühlungsborn, Ahrenshoop and Binz. One can also come across rather futuristic resorts like Damp 2000.

3 *Lüneburg Heath* **die Lüneburger Heide**
A stretch of beautiful heath and moorland between Hamburg and Hanover. One of the few areas with a significant number of sheep in Germany. **Celle** and **Lüneburg** are the most famous towns with beautiful historic centres.

4 *The Mecklenburg Lakes* **die Mecklenburgische Seenplatte**
A vast area of hilly woodland with numerous lakes to cater for a wide range of recreational activities.

5 *The Spree Forest* **der Spreewald** (near Berlin)
A maze of waterways, dykes, weirs and small islands, ideal for boating and hiking.

6 *The Harz Mountains* **der Harz**
A wooded range of hills popular for hiking in summer and skiing in winter. Its highest peak, the **Brocken**, is the setting for the famous Walpurgis night (**Walpurgisnacht**) in Geothe's drama *Faust*.

7 *The Eifel and the Moselle Valley* **die Eifel und das Moseltal**
The Eifel, a hilly area close to the Belgian and Luxembourg borders, is one of the oldest and most interesting landscapes in Germany. Famous are its lakes (**Maare**) in volcanic craters. The climate and scenery are rather rugged. The Moselle Valley south of the Eifel Mountains is more romantic, with steep vineyards stretching down to the meandering Moselle river.

8 *The Erz Mountains* **das Erzgebirge**
Wild and scenic mountain range along the border with the Czech Republic, once famous for its silver and iron ore mines. Nowadays a popular tourist area for hiking, winter sports, spas and traditional crafts.

9 *The Rhine* **der Rhein**
The Rhine is one of Europe's largest, most famous and most polluted rivers. Avoid the industrial areas on the Upper Rhine around **Karlsruhe** and **Ludwigshafen** and on the Lower Rhine north of Cologne (**Köln**) – the scenic bits (hills, vineyards, castles) are between **Bonn** and **Mainz**.

10 *The Odenwald* **der Odenwald**
A large forest (the Germanic hero **Siegfried** was killed here, according to the legend). There are many nature reserves and spas.

11 *The Black Forest* **der Schwarzwald**
One of the most famous German holiday areas. It has beautiful villages and spas, clean air, a mild climate, and good hiking and skiing.

12 *Lake Constance and the Alps* **der Bodensee und die Alpen**
Lake Constance (it takes its English name from the city of **Konstanz** on its southern shore) is one of the biggest lakes in western Europe. It is surrounded by the Federal Republic, Austria and Switzerland. It is famous for its mild climate and has many resorts. The German Alps can be divided into the **Allgäu** Alps just east of Lake Constance and – further east, south of Munich – the Bavarian Alps (**Bayerische Alpen**). The highest Alpine peak in Germany is the **Zugspitze** (2963 metres).

13 *The Bavarian forest* **der Bayerische Wald**
A large stretch of woodland, close to the border with the Czech Republic. It has plenty of well-marked hiking and cross-country skiing trails and abundant wildlife.

AND FINALLY...

16 Your turn to speak again. Imagine you're on a holiday in Freiburg in the Black Forest; you are talking to someone who wants to know how you are enjoying your hotel, the food and the service. You will need some of the following phrases:

es gefällt mir/gut/sehr gut/nicht so gut/ich mag

ANSWERS

EXERCISE 1
(a) Essen Sie gerne Fisch?　**(b)** Ich mag Fisch lieber
(c) Trinken Sie gerne Wein?　**(d)** Welchen Wein mögen Sie lieber?　**(e)** Welche Sorte trinken Sie am liebsten?

EXERCISE 3

	essen		trinken	
	gerne	am liebsten	gerne	am liebsten
Herr Blume	vegetarische Gerichte	Salate	Wein	Rotwein
Frau Matthei	deutsche Spezialitäten	Schnitzel mit Kartoffelsalat	Bier	Pils
Herr Brand	norddeutsche Gerichte	Fisch	Whiskey	Kaffee

EXERCISE 5
(a) Essen Sie gerne Fisch?　**(b)** Was essen Sie am liebsten?
(c) Trinken Sie gerne Wein?　**(d)** Was trinken Sie lieber, Rotwein oder Weißwein?　**(e)** Welche Sorte trinken Sie am liebsten?

EXERCISE 7

The correct text is as follows: Many greetings from Austria. We miss you very much. How do you like Berlin? And how do you like your new job? We have a new colleague now, a nice woman. And Karl's wife has finally had the baby – a boy. Summer here is wonderful. I do a lot of swimming and I am learning Spanish now – every Wednesday I go to evening classes. I like the course, but it makes a lot of extra work. Please write to me soon, your Kathrin

EXERCISE 8
Berlin: manchmal; Schule: ja; Englisch: ja; Sport: nein; Schwimmen: nein

EXERCISE 10
(a) Süddeutschland　**(b)** Hamburg　**(c)** Schleswig-Holstein
(d) das Meer　**(e)** Schottland und Irland (she likes both)

EXERCISE 11
These statements correspond to the text: **a**; **d**; **e**; **g**; **h**

EXERCISE 12
(a) sometimes　**(b)** sometimes
(c) theatres/concerts/lakes/nearby mountains

EXERCISE 14
(a) Ich trinke gern ...　**(b)** Ich trinke am liebsten ...
(c) Ich reise gern ...　**(d)** Ich reise am liebsten ...
(e) Ich schwimme gern ...　**(f)** Ich lese gern ...
(g) Ich lese am liebsten ...　**(h)** Ich mag lieber ...

EXERCISE 15
(a) Nicht gut, leider　**(b)** Süddeutschland　**(c)** Ja, sehr gern
(d) Am liebsten in den Süden　**(e)** Chinesische Gerichte
(f) Am liebsten Moselwein　**(g)** In Süddeutschland

12 YOUR TOWN AND THE WEATHER

WHAT YOU WILL LEARN

▶ asking for information about a specific town
▶ talking about your home town
▶ understanding weather forecasts and commenting on the weather
▶ you will also read about holiday areas in Austria and Switzerland

BEFORE YOU BEGIN

There's only a handful of nouns to watch out for in this unit and they will be useful in connection with any town: **Rathaus** (town hall), **Museum**, **Kirche** (church) and the various words for 'cathedral' such as **Münster**, **Kathedrale** and **Dom**. Next come adjectives such as **alt** (old), **neu** (new), **romantisch** (romantic), **modern** (modern) and **historisch** (historic). As far as the weather is concerned, it's up to you to decide how much detail you want to absorb at this stage. You might just like to stick to a few basics such as **Sonne** (sun) and **Regen** (rain) and come back to this topic later. Before you start, think about your own town and ask yourself what terms you would need to describe it. As you progress through this unit, draw up a list of words that will be especially useful to you. Then come back to the same question at the end of the unit and try to answer it in German.

Glücksburg Castle

Pronunciation notes

Words ending with **b** are pronounced as if they ended in **p**.
Words ending with **d** are pronounced as if they ended in **t**.
Words ending with **g** are pronounced as if they ended in **k**.
Listen to these examples on the recording:
lieb (dear); **gelb** (yellow); **Hund** (dog); **Bad** (bath); **Tag** (day); **Burg** (castle)
Watch out:
When the word has extra letters at the end (for example a plural ending), the sound reverts to the one you would expect. For example:
Hund (**d** pronounced as **t**) but **Hunde** (**d** pronounced as English **d**).
The letters **dt** are always pronounced as **t**, for example **Stadt**, plural **Städte**.

At the tourist office: sights in Freiburg

LISTEN FOR...

Münster	minster, cathedral
Musikhochschule	music academy
Wanderungen	walks

Ruth	Haben Sie Informationen über Freiburg?
Frau Hildenstein	Ja.
Ruth	Was gibt es dort alles zu sehen?
Frau Hildenstein	Zum Beispiel das Münster, dann die Musikhochschule; ein sehr schöner Rathausplatz ist dort mit dem alten und dem neuen Rathaus; die alte und die neue Universität, dann das Augustinermuseum. Dann kann man sehr schöne Wanderungen machen von Freiburg aus in den Schwarzwald.

die Information (usually *plural* **Informationen**) information. Note that in spoken German, endings such as **-en** sometimes get swallowed or reduced to **-n** as illustrated in this conversation.

Was gibt es dort (alles) zu sehen? What is there to see there? (**alles** all, everything is just a filler). You might also like to ask: **Was gibt es dort zu machen?** What is there to do there? (or more simply **Was kann man dort sehen?** What can one see there? and **Was kann man dort machen?** What can one do there?). Quite often, in a conversation such as this, you will also come across the rather long word: **die Sehenswürdigkeiten** things worth seeing, sights.

Freiburger Münster

das Münster the minster, cathedral. The **Freiburger Münster** is a very famous Gothic cathedral dating back to the 13th century. Other words for cathedral: **der Dom, die Kathedrale.** The word for church is **die Kirche.**

die Musikhochschule academy of music

der Rathausplatz the town hall square (**das Rathaus** town hall; **der Platz** square)

die Universität university

das Augustinermuseum museum founded by the Augustinian monks. Note that the plural of **das Museum** is **die Museen.**

dann kann man sehr schöne Wanderungen machen then you can go on very beautiful hiking tours

1 Top eight in Leipzig. On the recording Dorit is being asked about famous sights in Leipzig. Listen to the interview and mark the sights mentioned on the map below. There should be eight sights altogether.

New words:
die Kantate
cantata
die Oper
opera; opera house
das Konzert
concert
das Gewandhaus
famous concert hall
in Leipzig

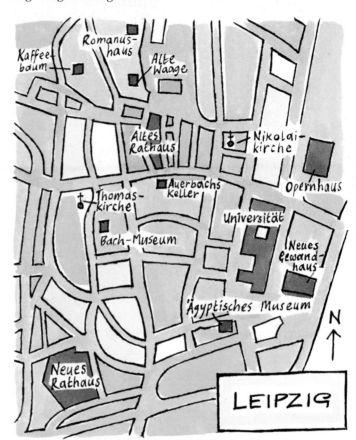

ANSWERS P. 186

2 Now listen to the interview again, and this time write down the German names of each place described by the clues below. You should come up with the names of five buildings.

a.   oldest church in Leipzig _____

b.   church of Johann Sebastian Bach _____

c.   for opera fans _____

d.   you'll find lots of information on Bach here _____

ANSWERS P. 186   e.   and this is the place for egyptologists _____

3 Your turn to speak. Now you are in Leipzig, asking for information on the area. Turn to the recording, where Tom will prompt you. You will need:

Haben Sie Informationen ...?
Was gibt es dort zu sehen?
Gibt es dort auch ...?

ANSWERS P. 186

▶ *Rainer Schilz comes from a big city in Northern Germany – he tells us more about it*

LISTEN FOR...

Einwohner	inhabitants
Fluß	river
Nachtleben	nightlife

Herr Schilz Ich komme aus einer Großstadt in Norddeutschland. Die Stadt hat ungefähr zwei Millionen Einwohner. Sie liegt an einem Fluß – an einem großen Fluß: an der Elbe. Sie ist bekannt für ihr Nachtleben. Da gibt es zum Beispiel eine Straße, die heißt Reeperbahn, mit vielen Bars, Klubs, Diskotheken und so weiter. Mir gefällt es in der Stadt. Die Atmosphäre ist immer liberal und tolerant.

die Großstadt big city; **die Hauptstadt** capital

ungefähr zwei Millionen Einwohner approximately two million inhabitants

sie liegt an einem Fluß it's (situated) by a river; **sie** refers to the feminine noun **die Stadt**; **liegt** is from **liegen** to lie, be situated. Similarly **Konstanz liegt an einem See** Constance is (situated) by a lake. **Brighton liegt am Meer** Brighton is (situated) by the sea.

die Elbe the river Elbe

By the Alster

bekannt für ihr Nachtleben well known for its (**ihr** *lit.* her – because it's **die Stadt**) nightlife (**das Nachtleben** nightlife). Instead of **bekannt**, you'll often come across **berühmt** famous.

die Reeperbahn name of a street famous for its nightlife

die Bar bar

der Klub club

die Diskothek or **Disko** disco

die Atmosphäre atmosphere

immer always

liberal liberal

tolerant tolerant

4 The city in Conversation 2 was in fact Hamburg. Here are some statements about Hamburg which are all wrong. Correct them, in writing, by going back to the original text. You can pick up expressions from the original, but you might also like to be a little more enterprising. We have given you one example. Your own answers could be slightly different.

a. Hamburg ist eine kleine Stadt.

> *Hamburg ist eine Großstadt.*

b. Hamburg liegt an der Donau.

c. Die Stadt hat kein Nachtleben.

d. Die Reeperbahn ist eine Straße mit vielen Kirchen und Museen.

e. Rainer Schilz gefällt es nicht in der Stadt.

f. Die Atmosphäre ist schlecht.

POSSIBLE ANSWERS P. 186

5 On the recording Erich will tell you about sights and events in Berlin. Listen carefully and mark the eight attractions that are actually mentioned.

a. Gedächtniskirche
Memorial church

b. Schloß Charlottenburg
Charlottenburg Palace

c. Rathaus Schöneberg
Schöneberg Town Hall

d. Grüne Woche
Agricultural Week

e. Bach-Tage
Bach Festival

f. Oktoberfest
October Festival

g. Zoologischer Garten
Zoological Gardens

h. Grunewald
Grunewald Forest

i. Wannsee
Lake Wannsee

j. Fernsehturm
TV Tower

k. Pergamon-Museum

l. Schloß Sanssouci
Sanssouci Palace

ANSWERS P. 186

6 Your turn to speak. On the recording Dorit is trying to guess your home town. She will ask you whether it's a big city, how many inhabitants it has, and whether it's by a river. Pretend you're from Dublin. Here are some snippets of information that might come in useful:

Dublin: Großstadt; Hauptstadt von Irland; ungefähr 800 000 Einwohner; liegt an der Liffey; Nationalgalerie; Nationalmuseum; zwei Universitäten; viele schöne Kneipen

CONVERSATION 3

> ◗ *The quiet life: Ursula asks Irene about life in a small town*

LISTEN FOR...

Dorf village
intimer more intimate
Leute people

Ravensburg
-Stadt der
Türme und Tore
Ravensburg
Städtisches Verkehrsamt
Kirchstraße 16
Tel. (07 51) 82-3 24, Fax 82-4 66

WEINGARTEN
erleben . . .
• größte
  Barock-
  basilika
  Deutschlands
• **Jubiläumsausstellung „900-
  Jahre Heilig-Blut-Verehrung"**
  vom 7.5.-28.8.94
• Alamannenmuseum – hist.
  Spezialmuseum
Info: Verkehrsamt Weingarten, Tel. (07 51) 4 05-1 25

Ursula	Irene, woher kommst du?
Irene	Ich komme aus Memmingen. Das ist zirka 50 Kilometer von Ulm.
Ursula	Ist das ein Dorf?
Irene	Nein, das ist kein Dorf. Es ist größer als ein Dorf. Memmingen ist eine Kleinstadt.
Ursula	Und gefällt es dir dort, oder möchtest du lieber in einer Großstadt wohnen?
Irene	Nein, mir gefällt es sehr gut dort. Ich möchte nicht in einer Großstadt wohnen. Es ist viel intimer in einer Kleinstadt, man kennt mehr Leute. Es ist ruhiger und nicht so hektisch.

das Dorf village

größer als ein Dorf bigger than a village. You use **als** (than) for comparisons, e.g.
London ist größer als München London is bigger than Munich;
Ulm ist kleiner als Köln Ulm is smaller than Cologne. More on comparisons on the grammar page in this unit – see also grammar section in Unit 8.

Isny in the Allgäu region

die Kleinstadt small town

es ist viel intimer in einer Kleinstadt it's much more intimate in a small town.

man kennt mehr Leute one knows more people

kennen to know people or places. But remember **ich weiß nicht** I don't know (from **wissen** to know [a fact]).

nicht so hektisch not so hectic

7 Carola has just moved from Berlin to Lübeck. Study her letter and then try to answer the questions below by using passages from the letter. Your answers could vary slightly.

> *Lübeck ist eine alte Hansestadt in Norddeutschland. Mit seinen 215 000 Einwohnern ist Lübeck keine Kleinstadt, aber auch keine Großstadt. Das Leben hier ist natürlich viel ruhiger als in Berlin. Ich finde, die ganze Stadt ist ein Museum. Man kann schön in der Altstadt spazierengehen, man kann wunderbar einkaufen, die Leute sind freundlich, und es gibt viele interessante Kirchen und Museen.*

New vocabulary:
Ich finde   *here* I think (also, of course = I find)

a. Ist Lübeck ein Dorf? _____

b. Wo liegt Lübeck? _____

c. Wie ist das Leben in Lübeck? _____

d. Wie sind die Leute? _____

e. Wo kann man spazierengehen? _____

f. Kann man auch gut einkaufen? _____

POSSIBLE ANSWERS P. 186

8 On the recording you will hear an interview about Bielefeld. Listen a few times and jot down the most important information under the key points below. Your answers can be in English and/or German.

a. Name der Stadt _____

b. groß/klein? _____

c. Einwohner _____

d. Sehenswürdigkeiten _____

e. Atmosphäre _____

POSSIBLE ANSWERS P. 186

9 Imagine you're from Brighton and Erich is asking you about it. You'll tell him that it's a seaside town in Southern England, quiet in the winter and hectic in the summer. Tom will prompt you. You will practise:

ich komme aus ...
am Meer
im Winter/im Sommer
ruhig/hektisch
es gefällt mir

And what about the weather?

LISTEN FOR...

Wetter	weather
windig	windy
Regen	rain

Ruth	Wie ist denn das Wetter hier in Kiel?
Frau Mohn	Im Winter ist es hier sehr kalt und windig.
Ruth	Und im Sommer?
Frau Mohn	Im Sommer ist es heiß und trocken. Und Regen haben wir oft im Frühjahr und im Herbst.

das Wetter the weather

windig windy (**der Wind** wind); the directions are **Nord, West, Ost** (East), **Süd.**

der Regen rain. Note the word order: Frau Mohn wants to emphasize the word 'rain' and therefore puts it at the beginning of the sentence; the usual word order would have been: **Und wir haben oft im Frühjahr und im Herbst Regen.**

Note that in Germany temperatures are always given in centigrade (**Celsius**). To convert to Fahrenheit multiply the centigrade figure by 9, divide by 5 and add 32. So **23 Grad Celsius** would be 73 degrees Fahrenheit. Or use the conversion table below:

Fahrenheit (°F)	212	104	86	68	59	50	41	32
Celsius (°C)	100	40	30	20	15	10	5	0

100°C = 212°F

30°C = 86°F
20°C = 68°F
15°C = 59°F
10°C = 50°F
5°C = 41°F
0°C = 32°F

▶ Weather terms

You will probably not need to use a lot of weather terms, but it is always useful to understand the gist of the weather forecast if you are travelling. Here is a list of the terms introduced by Dorit, Erich and Tom on the recording:

das Klima climate
die Vorhersage forecast
Höchsttemperaturen highest temperatures
Tiefsttemperaturen (also **Tiefstwerte**) lowest temperatures
bis morgen abend till tomorrow evening

die Sonne the sun
sonnig sunny
heiter bright, fair
trocken dry

die Wolke cloud
bewölkt cloudy
das Gewitter thunderstorm

der Wind wind
schwacher Wind light wind
starker Wind strong wind

der Nebel fog
neblig foggy

der Regen rain
der Schauer shower
naß wet
Niederschläge rain- or snowfall
es regnet it's raining

der Schnee snow
das Eis ice
das Glatteis black ice
der Frost frost
unter Null below freezing
es schneit it's snowing

PRACTICE

10 Some of the pictures below have got mixed up and no longer correspond to the captions. Put them straight.

a. Schnee und Glatteis, Temperaturen unter Null

b. sonnig und warm, Höchsttemperaturen 35 Grad

c. Nebel

d. bewölkt, Gewitter

e. starker Wind aus Nordost

f. Schauer

11 Something's wrong here too. Three of the five forecasts below contain contradictions. Can you spot the words or phrases that are wrong?

a. Die Vorhersage bis zum Wochenende: heiter und neblig, Regenschauer.

b. Sonnig und warm, Temperaturen unter Null.

c. Sonnig und heiter, schwacher Wind aus Südwest.

d. Die Vorhersage bis gestern abend: heiter und trocken, schwache Winde aus Südost.

e. Die Vorhersage bis morgen abend: Schneeschauer, Tiefstwerte minus 5 Grad.

12 Study the weather forecast below and mark the right boxes.

New vocabulary:
in der Mitte in the middle, i.e. between North and South Germany
in der Nacht zum Sonntag on Saturday night and early Sunday morning

> **Vorhersage: Am Samstag in Norddeutschland heiter bis wolkig, keine Niederschläge. Im Süden und in der Mitte stark bewölkt und Niederschläge. Höchsttemperaturen sieben bis zwölf Grad. Tiefsttemperaturen in der Nacht zum Sonntag um drei Grad. Im Norden leichter Frost bis minus drei Grad. Schwacher Wind aus Ost bis Nordost.**

a. Where is the weather going to be better?

in North Germany ☐

in South Germany ☐

b. What will the highest temperature be?

7–12 degrees ☐

3 degrees ☐

c. Where could you expect light frost at night?

in the south ☐

in the north ☐

d. Where is the wind coming from?

west to northwest ☐

east to northeast ☐

ANSWERS P. 186

13 Turn to the recording and listen to the weather report for Southern Bavaria and the Danube region. Pick out the main messages and note them down in German or English or both.

New word:
die Höhe height

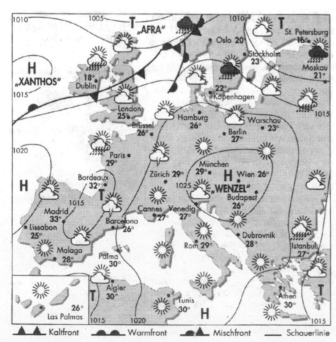

heute **(a)** _____

morgen nachmittag und abend

(b) _____

Höchsttemperaturen

(c) _____

In den Alpen in 2000 Meter Höhe

(d) _____

(e) _____ Wind aus

(f) _____

ANSWERS P. 186

Making comparisons

You use **als** (than) when you compare two *different* things:

Memmingen ist kleiner als Ulm.
Memmingen is smaller than Ulm.

Bier ist billiger als Wein.
Beer is cheaper than wine.

Remember that short adjectives with an **a**, **o** or **u** usually have an umlaut (**ä, ö** or **ü**) in the comparative (see also grammar section in Unit 8). For example:

München ist groß, aber London ist größer als München.
Munich is big, but London is bigger than Munich.

Irene ist elf Jahre alt. Mark ist vier Jahre älter als Irene.
Irene is eleven years old. Mark is four years older than Irene.

You use **so ... wie** (as ... as) when you compare two *similar* things:

Hana ist so groß wie Jessica.
Hana is as big as Jessica.

Fritz ist so alt wie Franz.
Fritz is as old as Franz.

Der Rock ist so teuer wie die Hose.
The skirt is as expensive as the trousers.

· Munich

14 Make comparisons as in the example below.

Compare the skirt with the trousers (skirt 80 DM; trousers 100 DM). Use **billig**.

Der Rock ist billiger als die Hose.

a. Compare Munich (population: 1.5 million) with Ulm (population: 100,000). Use **groß**.

b. Compare Maria with Hans. Use **alt**.

c. Compare Gerda with Claudia. Use **dick** (fat).

d. Compare the village with the city. Use **ruhig**.

ANSWERS P. 186

15 More comparisons. You'll need the following adjectives, but not in that order:

~~hart~~ – hektisch – schwer – teuer – klein –

Das Brot ist so hart wie der Käse.

a. _____

b. _____

c. _____

d. _____

ANSWERS P. 186

KEY WORDS

Haben Sie Informationen über ...?	Have you got (any) information on ...?
Was gibt es dort zu sehen?	What is there to see (there)?
Was kann man dort sehen/machen?	What can you see/do there?
Man kann Wanderungen machen	One can go hiking

I come from ...
Ich komme aus ...
- einer Großstadt — a big city
- einer Kleinstadt — a small town
- einem Dorf — a village

Die Stadt liegt ... — The town is situated ...
- an einem Fluß — on a river
- am Meer — by the sea
- in den Bergen — in the mountains

Sie ist bekannt für ... — It is well known for ...
- ihr Nachtleben — its nightlife
- ihr Rathaus — its town hall

Sie hat ... Einwohner — It has ... inhabitants

Es gibt viele Sehenswürdigkeiten	There are many sights
das Opernhaus/die Oper	opera house
die Diskothek/Disko	disco
der Rathausplatz	town hall square
der Dom/die Kathedrale/das Münster	cathedral
das Schloß	palace, castle

Ulm ist größer als Memmingen — Ulm is bigger than Memmingen

Die Atmosphäre ist ... — The atmosphere is ...
- ruhig — quiet
- hektisch — hectic
- liberal und tolerant — liberal and tolerant

... and see p. 179 for key words about the weather.

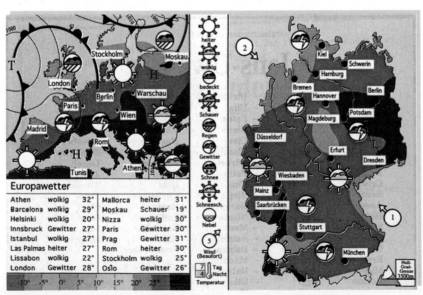

Holiday areas in Austria

Austria (**Österreich**) is a well-established holiday country and has much to offer, in terms of both culture and landscape: the Alps with their breathtaking scenery, tranquil lakes and picturesque mountain villages, as well as historic towns with ancient palaces, churches, monasteries and castles. The **Burgenland** in the east and **Vorarlberg** in the west offer a complete contrast of scenery, from Lake Neusiedl and the flat Pannonian Plains to the peaks of the Silvretta plunging down to the Rhine Valley and Lake Constance.

The **Salzkammergut** is within easy reach of **Salzburg**. The region offers numerous lakes, long stretches of valley and mountain walks. Salzburg itself – Mozart's birthplace – is an interesting city of music, art and architecture.

Other famous towns are **Innsbruck**, the capital of the Alps nestling at the foot of towering mountain ranges, and **Graz**, due south of Vienna, Austria's 'Little Italy' with its fine Italian Renaissance architecture. And there is of course Vienna itself (**Wien**), sumptuous capital of Austria, once the Imperial residence. Its principal sights are many splendid buildings, beautifully restored, the museums and the art galleries. You can succumb to the old-world charms of an elegant café, visit the famous **Staatsoper** or relax in a tavern in one of the quaint old wine villages on the outskirts of Vienna.

Holiday areas in Switzerland

Switzerland (**die Schweiz**) is another very popular holiday country. Some 65 percent of the population speak German. Some Swiss German dialects are not easy to understand, but the Swiss will speak standard German to foreigners.

For the holiday-maker, Switzerland offers great diversity concentrated in a small space. You can find valleys and mountain passes, orchards, vineyards and Alpine meadows, waterfalls, lakes, gorges, and in the southernmost region even palm trees and tropical fruits. Like Austria, Switzerland is a popular holiday area all the year round, boasting some of the world's most famous skiing resorts such as **St. Moritz**, **Zermatt**, **Davos**, **Arosa** and **Gstaad**. The Swiss Alps, running from the west to the east of the country, are rugged and spectacular, whereas the landscape in the south at the head of Lake Maggiore is much more gentle, with a distinctly Mediterranean touch. Thermal spas such as **Rheinfelden**, **Baden**, **Bad Ragaz** and **Vals** offer various cures and health treatments.

AND FINALLY...

16 Pretend you're from London and speaking to a lady from Dresden; you start talking about each other's cities. Tom will prompt you. Here are some useful expressions:

Woher kommen Sie? Ich komme aus ...
Was kann man dort sehen/machen ...?
es gibt ...
die Atmosphäre ist ...

Dresden: Zwinger, Semperoper, Theaterplatz, Geschäfte, Restaurants, Cafés

London: Buckingham Palast; Tower; Madame Tussaud's; Museen; Opern; Westminster Abtei (Abbey)

ANSWERS

EXERCISE 1
Nikolaikirche; Thomaskirche; Opernhaus; Neues Gewandhaus; Bach-Museum; Ägyptisches Museum; Altes Rathaus; Neues Rathaus

EXERCISE 2
(a) Nikolaikirche **(b)** Thomaskirche **(c)** Opernhaus **(d)** Bach-Museum **(e)** Ägyptisches Museum

EXERCISE 4
(b) Hamburg liegt an der Elbe. **(c)** Die Stadt ist bekannt für ihr Nachtleben. **(d)** Die Reeperbahn ist eine Straße mit vielen Bars, Klubs und Diskotheken. **(e)** Rainer Schilz gefällt es in der Stadt. **(f)** Die Atmosphäre ist liberal und tolerant.

EXERCISE 5
b; a; e; f; g; i; j; k

EXERCISE 7
(a) Nein, Lübeck ist eine alte Hansestadt. **(b)** Lübeck liegt in Norddeutschland. **(c)** Das Leben ist viel ruhiger als in Berlin. **(d)** Die Leute sind freundlich. **(e)** Man kann in der Altstadt spazierengehen. **(f)** Ja, man kann wunderbar einkaufen.

EXERCISE 8
(a) Bielefeld **(b)** groß (big) **(c)** zirka (around) 300 000 **(d)** nicht viel (not many) **(e)** ruhig, fast so wie in einer Kleinstadt (almost as in a small town; provincial)

EXERCISE 10
a/F; b/C; c/B; d/E; e/D; f/A

EXERCISE 11
(a) it's got to be either fair (heiter) or foggy with rain (neblig, Regenschauer) **(b)** if it's sunny and warm the temperatures can't be below zero (unter Null) **(d)** you can't have a forecast for yesterday evening (gestern abend); forecasts **(c)** and **(e)** are OK

EXERCISE 12
(a) North Germany **(b)** 7–12 degrees **(c)** in the north **(d)** east to northeast

EXERCISE 13
(a) sonnig **(b)** Gewitterschauer **(c)** 23 bis 27 Grad **(d)** um 13 Grad **(e)** schwacher **(f)** Südwest bis West

EXERCISE 14
(a) München ist größer als Ulm. **(b)** Maria ist älter als Hans. **(c)** Gerda ist dicker als Claudia. **(d)** Das Dorf ist ruhiger als die Stadt.

EXERCISE 15
(a) Anna ist so klein wie Carola. **(b)** Felix ist so schwer wie Benjamin. **(c)** Das Kleid ist so teuer wie der Rock. **(d)** London ist so hektisch wie New York.

13 MORE ABOUT YOURSELF

WHAT YOU WILL LEARN

▶ talking about your daily life
▶ chatting about your hobbies
▶ describing the flat or house you live in
▶ you will also read about five famous figures in German legend and folklore

BEFORE YOU BEGIN

Conversations about daily routines follow a certain predictable sequence – getting up, breakfast, going to work etc. This means that you will already know which general activities are going to come up, and can therefore concentrate on the particulars; for example: when is he/she getting up? and how does he/she get to work?

Pronunciation notes

y (and **j**)

The pronunciation of **y** depends on the position of the letter: If it's positioned within a word, it sounds just like **ü**. For example **typisch** typical, or **Pyramide** pyramid.
If it's at the beginning or the end of a word, it's pronounced as in English, for example **Yoga** and **Hobby**.
There's only one exception: the word for **y** itself (**Ypsilon**), where the **y** gets pronounced as an **ü** even though it's at the beginning of the word. Listen for the following words on the recording:
Yoga, but **Ypsilon**.
Gymnasium, Rhythmus, typisch, Hymne, Pyramide, Pyjama, Sibylle.
Hobby, Lobby, Party.

Note that most words beginning with 'y' in English are spelt with a **j** when taken over into German: **Joghurt** (yoghurt), **Jacht** (yacht); the German **j** always sounds like an English 'y'.

A typical day for Frau Bagan

LISTEN FOR...	
ich stehe auf	I get up
wir frühstücken	we have breakfast
ich ruhe mich aus	I have a rest

Ruth Wie sieht Ihr typischer Tag aus?
Frau Bagan Normalerweise stehe ich um sieben Uhr auf. Wir frühstücken um halb acht und gehen etwa um acht aus dem Haus. Ich fahre mit dem Auto zur Schule, und ich habe etwa bis zwölf oder ein Uhr Schule. Danach gehe ich einkaufen, und dann mach' ich Essen. Dann ruh' ich mich etwas aus, und dann mach' ich Schularbeiten.

Wie sieht Ihr typischer Tag aus? What does your typical day look like? **aussehen** to look is a separable verb (details in grammar section in Unit 10). Another example: **sie sieht gut aus** she looks good.

normalerweise normally

aufstehen to get up is another separable verb; **ich stehe auf** I get up. **Wann stehen Sie auf?** When do you get up?

A note on word order: as we have seen, the general rule is that the verb comes in second place in a sentence. Study these examples in the text:

normalerweise stehe ich ... (usual word order: **ich stehe normalerweise ...**)
danach gehe ich ... then I go ... (usual word order: **ich gehe danach ...**)
dann mache ich ... then I do ... (usual word order: **ich mache dann ...**)
So if a sentence starts with a word or phrase other than the subject (here **normalerweise** rather than **ich**). the subject (here **ich**) is sent into third place, while the verb remains in second.

frühstücken to eat breakfast

mit dem Auto by car

ich fahre zur Schule I drive/travel to school; similarly **ich fahre zur Arbeit** I drive/travel to work; **ich fahre zum Büro** I drive/travel to the office.

danach gehe ich einkaufen after that I go shopping (**einkaufen** to shop is a separable verb). Frau Bagan could also have said: **danach kaufe ich ein**.

dann mach' ich Essen then I make the meal; **mach'** is short for **mache**. **(das) Essen machen** to make (*lit.* to do) the meal. Note that **machen** means 'to do' at least as often as 'to make'. Another example: **Was machen Sie heute?** What are you doing today? And further down in the text:
und dann mach' ich Schularbeiten and then I do school work. Remember that Frau Bagan is a teacher, hence her working hours and the need to do school work. A usual working day would start at around 8 a.m. or even earlier.

dann ruh' ich mich etwas aus then I rest a little (**ruh'** is short for **ruhe**; **ausruhen** to rest is another separable verb). Note that **mich** (myself) is not translated: **Ich ruhe mich aus** I rest.

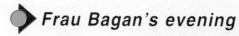

Frau Bagan's evening

LISTEN FOR...	
Nachrichten	news
Abendbrot	supper
wir unterhalten uns	we talk

Frau Bagan   Um sieben Uhr seh' ich Nachrichten, um halb acht kommt mein Mann nach Hause. Dann essen wir Abendbrot. Dann lese ich gerne, oder höre Musik, wir unterhalten uns über das, was am Tag geschehen ist, und gehen nicht vor elf Uhr zu Bett.

um sieben Uhr seh' (short for **sehe**) **ich Nachrichten**   at seven I watch the news (**sehen** *lit.* to see).

um halb acht kommt mein Mann nach Hause   at half past seven, my husband comes home

Abendbrot essen   to have supper

lesen   to read; e.g. **ich lese ein Buch** I read a book; **ich lese die Zeitung** I read the newspaper

Musik hören   to listen to music

wir unterhalten uns   we talk/chat

über das, was am Tag geschehen ist   about what has happened during the day (**geschehen** to happen); more on the past tense in the grammar section.

das, was   that which, or just what

zu Bett gehen   to go to bed

nicht vor elf Uhr   not before eleven

Kieler Nachrichten

UNABHÄNGIGE LANDESZEITUNG   FÜR SCHLESWIG- HOLSTEIN

DONNERSTAG, 13. JULI 1995 · NUMMER 161 · 28. WOCHE · 1,30 DM   KIELER ZEITUNG 1864 · KIELER NEUESTE NACHRICHTEN 1894

PRACTICE

1 Which verb? Write the correct verb into the gaps.

sehe – fahre – höre – mache – gehe – gehe – gehe – lese

a. Ich _____ um acht Uhr aus dem Haus.

b. Ich _____ mit dem Bus zur Arbeit.

c. Nach der Arbeit _____ ich einkaufen.

d. Danach _____ ich das Essen.

e. Um sieben Uhr _____ ich Nachrichten.

f. Und dann _____ ich ein Buch.

g. Oft _____ ich auch Musik.

ANSWERS P. 202 h. Um zehn Uhr _____ ich normalerweise zu Bett.

2 On the recording Herr Ott will tell you about his daily routine. Listen a few times and take brief notes in English.

New vocabulary:
die Mittagspause   lunch break

a. 6.30 _____

b. 7.30 _____

c. 8.00–12.00 _____

d. 12.00–13.00 _____

e. 13.00–16.30 _____

f. 19.00 _____

g. In the evening _____

ANSWERS P. 202 h. At 23.00 _____

3 Spot the mistakes. Compare the German text with the English translation and correct the mistakes made in the English translation. There are seven mistakes altogether.

> *Beate steht um sieben Uhr auf. Normalerweise trinkt sie nur eine Tasse Kaffee zum Frühstück. Sie geht um halb acht aus dem Haus und geht dann zu Fuß zum Büro. Dann arbeitet sie bis ein Uhr. Sie macht nur eine halbe Stunde Mittagspause. Um vier Uhr geht sie aus dem Büro. Dann geht sie durch den Park zurück nach Hause. Oft muß sie auch einkaufen. Um sechs Uhr macht sie das Abendessen. Abends geht sie gerne ins Kino.*

Beate gets up at eight o'clock. Normally she only drinks a cup of tea for breakfast. She leaves the house at half past eight and walks to the office. Then she works to one o'clock. She takes only an hour's lunchbreak. She leaves the office at four. Then she walks back home through the city centre. Often she has to do the shopping, too. At six she eats her supper. In the evening she likes to go to the theatre.

ANSWERS P. 202

4 On the recording you will hear Rainer talk about his daily routine. Listen a few times and tick the right boxes below.

New vocabulary:

daheim at home   **das Musikgeschäft** music shop

a. Wann steht Rainer auf?
　　um acht Uhr
　　um neun Uhr

b. Wie kommt Rainer zur Arbeit?
　　mit dem Fahrrad
　　mit der U-Bahn

c. Wo arbeitet Rainer?
　　in einem Büro
　　in einem Musikgeschäft

d. Wann arbeitet er?
　　von 10 bis 18 Uhr
　　von 11 bis 17 Uhr

e. Hat er Mittagspause?
　　nein
　　ja
　　manchmal

f. Und was macht er abends? (*mark two options*)
　　er geht in die Kneipe
　　er geht zur Abendschule
　　er hört daheim Musik

ANSWERS P. 202

5 An interview with Andreas. On the recording Andreas is interviewed about his daily routine. Listen to the recording and complete the transcript below.

Dorit: Wann stehen Sie auf?

Andreas Ich (**a**) ——————— um sechs Uhr (**b**) ——————— .

Dorit: Und was machen Sie dann?

Andreas: Ja, ich (**c**) ——————— Frühstück und (**d**) ——————— die Zeitung.

Dorit: Wann gehen Sie normalerweise aus dem Haus?

Andreas: Normalerweise (**e**) ——————— ich um sieben Uhr aus dem Haus.

Dorit: Und wie kommen Sie zur Arbeit?

Andreas: Ich (**f**) ——————— mit der U-Bahn.

Dorit: Wann sind Sie im Büro?

Andreas: Ich bin um halb acht (**g**) ——— und arbeite dann bis drei Uhr nachmittags.

Dorit: Was machen Sie nach der Arbeit?

Andreas: Nach der Arbeit (**h**) ——————— ich (**i**) ——————— , oder ich muß
(**j**) ——————— .

Dorit: Wann essen Sie Abendbrot?

Andreas: Normalerweise (**k**) ——————— ich um sechs Uhr Abendbrot.

Dorit: Und was machen Sie abends?

Andreas: Abends (**l**) ——————— ich (**m**) ——————— oder
(**n**) ——————— Musik.

Dorit: Wann gehen Sie zu Bett?

Andreas: Normalerweise (**o**) ——————— ich um zehn Uhr
(**p**) ——————— .

ANSWERS P. 202

6 Your turn to speak. This time you are being interviewed about your daily routine. You'll practise a number of phrases from the previous exercise.

▶ Life after work in Memmingen

LISTEN FOR...

es ist nicht viel los	there's not much going on
unternehmen	to undertake
Ausflüge	excursions
Kegeln	bowling, skittles

Ursula	Und was machst du so am Abend? Nach der Arbeit?
Irene	Ja, es ist natürlich nicht viel los in Memmingen. Es gibt ein kleines Theater, es gibt ein paar Kneipen ... Aber ich habe viele gute Freunde, und wir unternehmen oft was zusammen.
Ursula	Was zum Beispiel?
Irene	Im Sommer machen wir Ausflüge oder gehen zum Baden, im Winter fahren wir Ski. Und ab und zu gibt es auch mal eine Party. Und jede Woche treffen wir uns einmal zum Kegeln. Und nach dem Kegeln gehen wir dann noch ein Bier trinken – manchmal auch mehr. Meistens bin ich vor zwei Uhr nie zu Hause.

es ist nicht viel los there's not much going on. The opposite would be:
es ist immer viel los there's always a lot going on

unternehmen to do, to undertake

Ausflüge plural of **der Ausflug** day trip, excursion

wir gehen zum Baden we go bathing, or (more simply) **wir gehen baden**.
Similarly **wir gehen schwimmen** we go swimming, **wir gehen tanzen** we go dancing, **wir gehen kegeln** we go bowling.

im Winter fahren wir Ski in winter we go skiing; **Ski fahren** (to ski) is always two words.

ab und zu gibt es auch mal eine Party every now and then there is a party, **mal** is a filler word which has no particular meaning.

jede Woche treffen wir uns einmal zum Kegeln we meet up once every week to go bowling/to play skittles. **Wir treffen uns** *lit.* we meet one another; similarly **wir sehen uns** we see one another, **wir lieben uns** we love one another.

meistens bin ich vor zwei Uhr nie zu Hause mostly I am never home before two o'clock (**nie** never; **zu Hause** (at) home)

◢ Frau Oswald's hobbies

Ruth Und was machen Sie nach der Arbeit?
Frau Oswald Ja, Hausarbeit, zum Teil auch mach' ich meine Hobbys, Sport, zum Beispiel Schwimmen, Waldlauf. Dann interessiere ich mich vor allem für Sprachen. Ich interessiere mich für Reisen – der Ferne Osten, Südamerika.

die Hausarbeit   housework

das Hobby   hobby

der Sport   sport

zum Beispiel Schwimmen   for example swimming

der Waldlauf   jogging (on woodland paths)

ich interessiere mich für ...   I'm interested in ...

vor allem   above all

der Ferne Osten   the Far East

... and here are some more hobbies and pastimes: **Briefmarkensammeln** stamp collecting; **Fotografieren** photography; **Fernsehen** television

◢ Frau Bagan's weekend

LISTEN FOR...

Garten	garden
drinnen	inside
segeln	to sail

Ruth Was machen Sie am Wochenende?
Frau Bagan Am liebsten fahre ich an die Schlei. Ich arbeite gern im Garten, und wir gehen viel spazieren. Wenn es regnet, sind wir drinnen. Dann lese ich und höre Musik. Im Sommer segeln wir gerne. Wir segeln nach Dänemark ... Die Inseln sind wunderschön.

Was machen Sie am Wochenende?   What do you do at the weekend?

die Schlei   (as mentioned before) an inlet on the Baltic coast north of Kiel and close to the border with Denmark

der Garten   garden

wir gehen viel spazieren   we go for lots of walks; **spazierengehen** is not quite so serious as **wandern** (to hike).

drinnen   inside

segeln   to sail

Dänemark   Denmark

die Insel   island (plural **die Inseln**)

wunderschön   (very) beautiful

PRACTICE

7 What does Herr Berkenbusch do at the weekend? Listen to the interview on the recording and mark the correct statements below. Sometimes you can mark several.

a. In the summer, he enjoys
- [ ] working in the garden;
- [ ] sailing on Lake
- [ ] Constance; hiking in the mountains

b. If it's raining, he
- [ ] reads lots of books;
- [ ] listens to music;
- [ ] goes to the cinema.

c. In the winter, he likes
- [ ] skiing in the mountains;
- [ ] going to lots of parties;
- [ ] playing skittles with friends.

ANSWERS P. 202

8 Study the letter and decide which of the statements below are true or false.

New words:

das Studium   (university) studies   **die Medizin**   medicine   **zu Ende**   finished

> *Ich heiße Anita und bin 24 Jahre alt. Ich studiere Medizin und interessiere mich vor allem für Hals-, Nasen- und Ohrenmedizin. In zwei Jahren ist mein Studium zu Ende. Ich habe viele Hobbys: ich interessiere mich für Sprachen, Reisen, Musik und Theater. Am Abend lerne ich immer, und am Wochenende fahre ich in die Berge oder an einen See. Samstagabend gehe ich mit Freunden in eine Kneipe oder ins Kino. Manchmal gibt es auch eine Party.*

a. Anita ist vierundzwanzig.

b. Sie studiert Sprachen.

c. Sie muß noch drei Jahre studieren.

d. Ihre Hobbys sind Sprachen, Reisen, Musik und Theater.

e. Am Abend lernt sie immer – aber nicht am Samstagabend.

f. Am Wochenende macht sie Ausflüge.

ANSWERS P. 202

g. Am Samstagabend geht sie mit Freunden ins Theater.

9 **Was sind Ihre Hobbys?**   What are your hobbies? Take notes. On the recording, Sylvia and Mathias are being interviewed about their hobbies. Write them down in German.

Sylvia's Hobbys: _____

Mathias' Hobbys: _____

And on the recording Tom comments: **na, denn Prost**; **Prost** or **Prosit** means 'cheers' as you raise your glass with friends.

ANSWERS P. 202

10

Match these lonely hearts' advertisements – who would suit whom?

A **Romantikerin, mit kleiner Tochter, sucht den Mann fürs Leben**

B Patricia, 18 Jahre jung, sucht Freund bis Mitte 20

C Dame von Welt, 39 Jahre, liebt Shakespeare und Bach, sucht reifen Partner

D Wo ist die Frau für mich, bin 35 Jahre jung, aktiv, dynamisch und liebe Sport

E Attraktiver Arzt sucht romantische Sie auch mit Kind

F Boy, 24 Jahre, sucht Girl bis 20

G TENNIS ... SKIFAHREN ... SCHWIMMEN ... WO IST DER DYNAMISCHE PARTNER FÜR DIES UND VIELES MEHR??

H Akademiker, Ende 50, sucht kultivierte Dame bis Ende 30

_____ goes with _____ ; _____ goes with _____

ANSWERS P. 202

_____ goes with _____ ; _____ goes with _____

11

Wer ist es? Who is it? Who are we talking about? Study the clues below.

New vocabulary:
geboren born
gestorben died
die Kindheit childhood
still quiet
danach after that
der akademische Posten academic post
die Entdeckung discovery
der Nobelpreis Nobel prize
die Persönlichkeit personality

> **Geboren in:** Ulm, 14.3.1879
> **Gestorben in:** Princeton, 18.4.1955
> **Kindheit:** Ulm; München; sehr stilles Kind, sehr schlechter Schüler
> **Danach:** Italien; Schweiz; studiert in Bern, bekommt keinen akademischen Posten; arbeitet im Patentamt Bern
> **1905** revolutionäre Entdeckung; über Nacht weltberühmt
> **1921** Nobelpreis
> **1933** Emigration nach USA
> **Persönlichkeit:** viel Humor; liebt Musik; Pazifist

ANSWERS P. 202

12

Your turn to speak and talk about your hobbies. You'll practise:

meine Hobbys sind ...
ich interessiere mich (auch) für ...
Sprachen
Sport
Hausarbeit
Schwimmen
Musik
Garten

CONVERSATION

3

 Rainer Schilz talks about his flat in Hamburg

LISTEN FOR...

Altbauwohnung	flat in an old (as opposed to a modern) building
Blick	view
Vorort	suburb

Herr Schilz   Ich heiße Rainer Schilz, und ich bin Lehrer an einem Gymnasium in Hamburg. Ich wohne im Stadtzentrum, und zwar in einer großen Altbauwohnung. Die Wohnung hat vier Zimmer, Küche und Bad. Außerdem hab' ich noch einen Balkon, und von dort hat man einen sehr schönen Blick auf die Stadt und natürlich auch auf den Fluß. Vorher habe ich in einem Vorort gewohnt, und zwar in einer Neubauwohnung. Die Wohnung war kleiner, aber auch billiger. Die Wohnungen im Stadtzentrum sind für mich etwas teuer.

das Gymnasium   grammar school (and *not* gymnasium)

das Stadtzentrum   city centre

die Altbauwohnung   flat in an old building. These are quite sought after because of their character and generous proportions. Note that when describing a house or a flat in Germany, all rooms are counted, except kitchen and bathroom. So a **Dreizimmerwohnung** would probably have two bedrooms and one living room and 'translate' as a two-bedroom flat.

die Küche   kitchen

außerdem   besides

der Balkon   balcony

von dort hat man einen sehr schönen Blick auf die Stadt   from there one has a beautiful view over the city

vorher habe ich in einem Vorort gewohnt   before that I lived (*lit.* I have lived) in a suburb (**der Vorort** suburb). Details on the past tense used here are explained on the grammar page in this unit.

die Neubauwohnung   modern flat

die Wohnung war kleiner   the flat was smaller; **war** corresponds directly to the English 'was'. More on this tense in the grammar section of Unit 14.

PRACTICE

13 Study the three ads below in the left-hand column advertising flats for rent. Then take a look in the right-hand column where three people are looking for accommodation. Try to match them up – but be warned, they won't all fit.

New vocabulary:

das Appartement (*abbreviation* **App.**)   apartment   **der Keller**   cellar
vermieten (*abbreviation* **verm.**)   to let   **die Garage**   garage
die Kochecke   cooking facility   **kalt**   cold; (here) exclusive of heating bills
qm   square metres   **die Zuschrift** (*abbreviation* **Zuschr.**)   reply

1
Schöne 3-Zimmer-Wohnung 100 qm, Balkon, Garage, Keller, Garten, Nähe Ravensburg zu vermieten. DM 1150.- kalt Tel (07585) 2531

a
Student sucht Zimmer mit Dusche und Kochecke.
Tel (0751) 3421

2
2-Zimmer-Appartement 80 qm,
Stadtmitte,
DM 1000,- kalt
Zuschr. RZ 1309

b
Junger Arzt sucht Einzimmerwohnung. Zuschriften RZ 1378

3
1-Zimmer-App. 30 qm
Dusche/WC/Kochecke zu verm.
DM 550.- Keine Studenten!
Zuschriften RZ 6531

c
Familie sucht große Wohnung mit Garten und Garage bei Ravensburg.
Tel. (07502) 22331

ANSWERS P. 202

14 Who lives where? On the tape, Silke, Sven and Eckhard talk about their homes. Mark the table below.

	Silke	Sven	Eckhard
Zweizimmerwohnung			
Dreizimmerwohnung			
Haus			
Balkon			
Garten			
Keller			
Garage			
Altbauwohnung			
Neubauwohnung			
im Stadtzentrum			
in einem Vorort			

ANSWERS P. 202

15 Your turn to describe to Erich how you live. He's rather inquisitive and will ask you lots of questions. You'll need some of the words below:

Haus – Küche – Bad – Zimmer – Wohnung – Garten – Garage – Vorort

GRAMMAR AND EXERCISES

The perfect tense

When talking about the past, Germans often use the perfect tense. Here is an example from Conversation 3: **ich habe gewohnt** I have lived. Most verbs form the perfect tense with **haben** + a verb form called the past participle. In the example above, **gewohnt** is the past participle of **wohnen**.

As a rule, the past participle is formed like this: You take the **-en**[*] ending
off the infinitive: **wohn-en**   **arbeit-en**
so that you are left with
the stem: **wohn-**   **arbeit-**
then you add **ge-** to the
beginning: **ge-wohn**   **ge-arbeit**
and **-t**[**] to the end: **ge-wohn-t**   **ge-arbeit-et**

[*]or **-n** if the infinitive just ends in **n**, for example **klettern** to climb.
[**]or **-et** if the stem ends in **t** or **d**.

Here are all the forms of **wohnen** in the perfect tense:

ich habe	**gewohnt**	I have lived
du hast	**gewohnt**	you have lived
er/sie/es hat	**gewohnt**	he/she/it has lived
wir haben	**gewohnt**	we have lived
ihr habt	**gewohnt**	you have lived
sie/Sie haben	**gewohnt**	they/you have lived

In English, all verbs form their perfect tenses with 'have', but in German, a group of verbs use **sein** (to be) instead of **haben**. These verbs nearly always have something to do with movement or a change of state. Here is an example **reisen** (to travel):

ich bin	**gereist**	I have travelled
du bist	**gereist**	you have travelled
er/sie/es ist	**gereist**	he/she/it has travelled
wir sind	**gereist**	we have travelled
ihr seid	**gereist**	you have travelled
sie/Sie sind	**gereist**	they/you have travelled

Weak and strong verbs

Most verbs in German are 'weak' verbs, forming their past participle according to the pattern above: **ge** + stem + **(e)t**. However, there is a small but important group of so-called 'strong' verbs, which follow different patterns and are best learnt by heart. One of them cropped up in Conversations 1:
geschehen to happen.
Es ist geschehen it has happened. Sometimes the English and German verbs are closely related and change in a similar way, for example:

trinken   to drink
ich habe getrunken   I have drunk
singen   to sing
ich habe gesungen   I have sung
sinken   to sink
ich bin gesunken   I have sunk
kommen   to come
ich bin gekommen   I have come

Note that most past participles of strong verbs still take **ge-** at the beginning, but they end in **-en** rather than **-t**.

Word order: all past participles go to the end of the phrase, while the first verb takes up its usual position.
Ich habe die Zeitung gelesen.   I have read the paper.

Important note on translation: generally, the Germans use the tenses more loosely than the English. Quite often, you'll need to translate sentences such as **ich habe gelebt** with 'I lived' rather than 'I have lived' to make them sound right in English. However, this shouldn't pose any problems and will usually become clear from the context.

16 Write the perfect tense forms of the verbs **kaufen** (to buy) and **machen** (to make, do) in the spaces below. Both **kaufen** and **machen** are weak verbs which use **haben** to form the perfect tense. Their stems are **kauf-** and **mach-**.

ich _____ I have bought

du _____ you have bought

er/sie/es _____ he/she/it has bought

wir _____ we have bought

ihr _____ you have bought

sie/Sie _____ they/you have bought

ich _____ I have made

du _____ you have made

er/sie/es _____ he/she/it has made

wir _____ we have made

ihr _____ you have made

sie/Sie _____ they/you have made

ANSWERS P. 202

17 And now for a piece of detective work. Here is a selection of past participles, some are weak and some strong. Try to fit them into the sentences below. Then translate the sentences into English.

> gemacht – gelesen – gearbeitet – gehört – gekauft

a. Ich habe ein schönes Buch _____

_____

b. Er hat eine neue Jacke _____

_____

c. Wo haben Sie Urlaub _____?

_____

d. Wir haben von 9 bis 5 Uhr im Büro _____

_____

e. Sie hat gestern viel Musik _____

ANSWERS P. 202

18 Informed guesswork. Translate these sentences into English. They all contain strong verbs. Look at the stem to help you recognize the past participle and remember that many German verbs undergo changes that are similar to their English counterparts. Before translating the sentences, write out each past participle form, for example in **a: gesprochen**. Underline the verbs that take **haben** rather than **sein** to form the perfect tense.

a. Ich habe mit meinem Bruder gesprochen.

_____

b. Er ist zwei Kilometer geschwommen.

_____

c. Die Kinder haben zwölf Stunden lang geschlafen.

_____

d. Sie hat einen großen Preis gewonnen.

_____

e. Ich bin um acht Uhr gekommen.

_____

f. Wir sind mit dem Bus gefahren.

ANSWERS P. 202

KEY WORDS

Hobbies and pastimes

Was machen Sie ...	What do you do ...
am Wochenende?	at the weekend?
nach der Arbeit?	after work?
am Abend?	in the evening?

Meine Hobbys sind ...	My hobbies are ...
Sport	sport
Schwimmen	swimming
Waldlauf	jogging through the woods
Wandern	hiking
Segeln	sailing
Skifahren	skiing

Ich interessiere mich für ...	I am interested in ...
Sprachen	languages
Reisen	travelling
Musik	music

Wir machen Ausflüge	We go on excursions
gehen ein Bier trinken	go for a beer
treffen uns in einer Kneipe	meet up in a pub
hören Musik	listen to music
lesen ein Buch/die Zeitung	read a book/the paper

A typical day

Ich stehe um sieben (Uhr) auf	I get up at seven
gehe um acht aus dem Haus	leave the house at eight
mache Mittagspause	take my lunchbreak
gehe einkaufen	go shopping
mache (das) Essen	get the meal
gehe zu Bett	go to bed

How you live

Ich wohne ...	I live ...
im Stadtzentrum	in the city centre
in einem Vorort	in a suburb
in einer Altbauwohnung	in an old flat
in einer Neubauwohnung	in a new flat
in einem Haus	in a house

Die Wohnung hat	The flat has ...
vier Zimmer	four rooms (= three bedrooms)
Küche und Bad	kitchen and bathroom
einen Garten und eine Garage	a garden and a garage

Figures in legend and folklore

Wilhelm Tell

Legendary Swiss patriot and rebel, a famous crossbow marksman who reputedly saved his home district from Austrian oppression. According to tradition, a cruel Austrian governor forced Tell to shoot an apple off his own son's head from a distance of 80 paces. Tell is said to have killed the tyrant and initiated the movement which fought for an independent Switzerland.

Die Lorelei

Name of a steep cliff on the Rhine near St. Goar, dangerous to boatmen and celebrated for its echo. During the Romantic period this gave rise to the story of a beautiful siren sitting on the rock, combing her long blond hair and luring sailors to their deaths with her sweet song.

Das Donauweibchen

A beautiful nymph living in the Danube near Vienna. She once saved many fishermen's lives by warning them of an impending flood. Thereafter, she often visited them, until a young man fell deeply in love with her. He rowed out every night looking for her, but one morning the boat was found empty, and the nymph never returned.

Rübezahl

A moody, capricious giant living in the wild Silesian mountains and said to rule the vast underground kingdom of the **Riesengebirge**. Having fallen hopelessly in love with a princess, he kidnapped her and showered her with earthly riches, but she made her escape after asking him to count turnips (**Rüben**) as part of his courtship. This experience increased his fascination and irritation with mankind: **Rübezahl** was sometimes the great benefactor, but more often the frightening gnome who played cruel jokes on the lonely wanderer, sometimes with deadly consequences.

Frau Holla

Her realm is the **Meißner**, the highest peak in Lower Hesse. When she makes her beds, the feathers fly about and turn into snow. And when she's cooking, water vapours form into huge clouds shrouding the whole mountain. Frau Holla (sometimes known as Frau Holle) used to be a virtuous girl married to a drunkard and good-for-nothing who ruined and subsequently left her. But a goddess took pity on Frau Holla and gave her the whole mountain as a present. Ever since she has been said to help poor women in the area and punish lazy husbands.

AND FINALLY...

19 Your turn to speak and talk about your daily routine, your hobbies and where you live. Here's a letter written by Boris. Study it closely before turning to the recording where you pretend you are Boris.

New vocabulary: **die Eltern** parents

Ich heiße Boris Berner, und ich wohne in einer kleinen Zweizimmerwohnung in der Stadtmitte von Köln. Ich arbeite bei einer Bank und stehe immer um sechs Uhr auf. Ich gehe um sieben Uhr aus dem Haus und fahre mit dem Bus zur Arbeit. Mittagspause ist von eins bis zwei. Ich arbeite bis drei Uhr nachmittags, dann gehe ich einkaufen. Manchmal gehe ich auch im Park spazieren. Meine Hobbys sind Kochen, Popmusik und Fernsehen. Am Wochenende fahre ich zu den Eltern.

ANSWERS

EXERCISE 1
(a) gehe (b) fahre (c) gehe (d) mache (e) sehe (f) lese (g) höre (h) gehe

EXERCISE 2
(a) gets up, has breakfast, reads the paper (b) leaves the house (c) works (d) has lunch break (e) works (f) has supper (g) reads or goes to cinema (h) goes to bed

EXERCISE 3
gets up at *seven*; drinks a cup of *coffee*; leaves at half past *seven*; takes *half an hour's* lunchbreak; walks back home through the *park*; at six she *gets* her supper; in the evening she likes to go to the *cinema*.

EXERCISE 4
(a) um neun Uhr (b) mit dem Fahrrad (c) in einem Musikgeschäft (d) von 10 bis 18 Uhr (e) ja (f) er geht in die Kneipe oder er hört daheim Musik

EXERCISE 5
(a) stehe (b) auf (c) esse (d) lese (e) gehe (he actually says geh') (f) fahre (g) im Büro (f) gehe (again he says geh') (i) spazieren (j) einkaufen (k) esse (l) lese (m) gerne (n) höre (o) gehe (p) zu Bett

EXERCISE 7
(a) working in the garden; sailing on Lake Constance (b) listens to music or goes to the cinema (c) going to lots of parties

EXERCISE 8
True: a; d; e; f

EXERCISE 9
Sylvia: Sport, Schwimmen, Waldlauf, Sprachen, Reisen
Mathias: Segeln, Skifahren, Kegeln, Biertrinken

EXERCISE 10
A with E; B with F; C with H; D with G

EXERCISE 11
The person in question was Albert Einstein

EXERCISE 13
1/c; 3/b; a can't go to '3' because the owner doesn't want a student

EXERCISE 14
Silke: Dreizimmerwohnung; in einem Vorort; Altbauwohnung; Balkon; Garage; Sven: Haus; in einem Vorort; Garten; Keller; Eckhard: Zweizimmerwohnung; Neubauwohnung; im Stadtzentrum

EXERCISE 16
ich habe gekauft; du hast gekauft; er/sie/es hat gekauft; wir haben gekauft; ihr habt gekauft; sie/Sie haben gekauft. Ich habe gemacht; du hast gemacht; er/sie/es hat gemacht; wir haben gemacht; ihr habt gemacht; sie/Sie haben gemacht

EXERCISE 17
(a) gelesen; I (have) read a nice book. (b) gekauft; He (has) bought a new jacket. (c) gemacht; Where did you go (have you gone) on holiday? (d) gearbeitet; We (have) worked in the office from 9 to 5. (e) gehört; She (has) listened to a lot of music yesterday.

EXERCISE 18
(a) gesprochen (b) geschwommen (c) geschlafen (d) gewonnen (e) gekommen (f) gefahren.
Translations (literal translations in brackets): (a) I spoke (have spoken) to my brother. (b) He swam (has swum) two kilometres. (c) The children (have) slept for 12 hours. (d) She (has) won a big prize. (e) I came (have come) at eight o'clock. (f) We went (have gone) by bus. You should have underlined: gesprochen; geschlafen; gewonnen

14 MORE ABOUT THE PAST

▶ understanding what people have done during their holidays
▶ talking about past events in more detail
▶ you will also read about German history

BEFORE YOU BEGIN

Once you have mastered the basic tools for understanding the past tenses, it will be much easier to conduct a more detailed conversation. You can also begin to extend your reading skills by looking at newspapers, magazines and perhaps even books. The most important thing is to sample subject areas that you are already familiar with in your own language and that you genuinely enjoy. If you are interested in world events, look at a German daily after you have seen or read the headlines in English; if you like women's magazines, pick up a German weekly or bi-monthly. And if you enjoy literature, start with a short story that you know in English, or get hold of a bilingual edition. Some children's books or comics are great fun to read too.

Pronunciation notes

l

Just like the **r**, the **l** is a real giveaway when it comes to detecting a typical German trying to speak another language – or a foreigner trying to speak German. Generally speaking, the German **l** sounds flatter and lighter than the English l. Listen to the recording and practise the following words with Tom; all of them will crop up again in the course of Unit 14:

alleine (alone); **Teil** (part); **Nepal** (Nepal); **persönlich** (personally); **Berlin**; **Leute** (people); **einmal** (once).

Agnes tells Ruth about her trip to India

LISTEN FOR...

Wo bist du gewesen?	Where have you been?
alleine	alone
wir haben uns getroffen	we met up
gemeinsam	together

Ruth	Agnes, wo bist du im letzten Urlaub gewesen?
Agnes	Ich bin nach Indien gefahren.
Ruth	Und bist du alleine gereist?
Agnes	Zum Teil. Meine Freundin fuhr schon eine Woche vorher weg, und wir haben uns in Delhi getroffen und sind von da aus gemeinsam weitergereist. Und nach etwa vier Wochen haben sich unsere Wege wieder getrennt, und ich bin nach Sri Lanka und sie ist nach Nepal gefahren.

Wo bist du im letzten Urlaub gewesen? Where were you (*lit.* Where have you been) on your last holiday? **Sein** (to be) is a strong verb, and its past participle is **gewesen**. It belongs to the group of verbs that take **sein** rather than **haben** to form the perfect tense.

ich bin nach Indien gefahren I went to India (*lit.* I have gone to India). Note that **fahren** is a verb of motion and uses **sein** to form the perfect tense.

... bist du alleine gereist? ... did you travel alone? (*lit.* Have you travelled alone?) **reisen** (to travel) is another verb of movement and uses **sein** for the perfect tense.

alleine or **allein** alone

zum Teil partly

meine Freundin fuhr ... weg my girl friend left ...; **fuhr** is a different past form of **fahren** which is called the imperfect tense. This new tense will be discussed on the grammar page in this unit. **Wegfahren** is a separable verb (**weg** away, **fahren** to go).

vorher before that, earlier

wir haben uns in Delhi getroffen we met in Delhi (*lit.* we have met one another in Delhi).

... und (wir) sind von da aus gemeinsam weitergereist and from there we travelled on together (*lit.* and from there we have travelled on together) (**gemeinsam** together); **weitergereist** is the past participle of **weiterreisen** (to travel on, continue one's journey) which is a separable verb: **weiter + reisen**. Here is an example in the present tense: **ich reise morgen weiter** I travel on tomorrow. Note that in separable verbs, the **ge-** forming the past participle remains tagged on to the main verb *after* the prefix: **weiter+ge+reist**.

haben sich unsere Wege ... getrennt our paths separated (*lit.* our paths have separated) (**der Weg** path; **(sich) trennen** to separate). **Wir haben uns getrennt** we have separated; note that **sich** and **uns** are not translated.

wieder again, once more

PRACTICE

1 True or false? Here's a summary of Conversation 1 in English. It contains three mistakes. Spot them and put them right.

ANSWERS P. 218

Agnes went to India on her last holiday. She travelled partly on her own. Her boy friend left one week before and they met up in Sri Lanka. After four weeks they separated again. Agnes travelled to Delhi and her friend went to Nepal.

2 Choose the correct forms from the list below. But be careful, it contains infinitives as well as past participles and five of the forms will in fact be unsuitable.

> machen – essen – sein – gegessen – gebadet – baden – gewesen – fahren –
> gemacht – gefahren

a. Wo bist du im Urlaub _____?

b. Ich bin nach Italien _____

c. Was hast du dort _____?

d. Ich habe im Meer _____

ANSWERS P. 218

e. Und ich habe viel zu viel Spaghetti _____

3 On the recording, Gesine is being interviewed about her last summer holiday. Listen to the interview and write the answers to the questions below in the boxes provided, in German. The letters in the numbered boxes will give you the name of a country which is sometimes called the 'Bavaria of the North'.

a. Where did Gesine go last summer? ☐☐☐[7]☐☐☐

b. Had she been there before? [9]☐☐☐☐

c. What did she do there? ☐☐[8]☐☐☐☐☐☐☐☐☐☐☐

d. Where did she first learn English? ☐[1]☐[2]☐[3]☐☐☐☐

e. And where else after that? ☐☐☐☐☐☐[10]☐☐☐☐☐☐

f. But she learnt her best English by listening to ... songs. ☐[4]☐☐

g. And how was the Guinness? ☐☐☐[5]☐☐☐☐, ☐☐☐☐☐ ☐☐[6]

ANSWERS P. 218

Now write down the letters in boxes 1–10. ☐☐☐☐☐☐☐☐☐☐
1 2 3 4 5 6 7 8 9 10

4 Your turn to speak and practise the perfect tense through repetition – but with a difference. Dorit is making up a tall story and you will outdo her by making up another tall story with the help of Tom. To give you an example of the pattern, here's the beginning of the script:

(a) *Dorit:* 'Ich bin in Paris gewesen'

(b) *Tom:* 'Rom'

(c) pause, so you say: 'Und ich bin in Rom gewesen!'

(d) *Erich:* 'Und ich bin in Rom gewesen!'

More about Agnes' trip to India

LISTEN FOR...	
Wie hat das geklappt?	How did that work out?
angenehmer	more pleasant
zu zweit	with someone else

Ruth	Bist du dann alleine gereist?
Agnes	Dann bin ich alleine gereist. Ja.
Ruth	Wie hat das geklappt?
Agnes	Das hat ganz gut geklappt. Eh – natürlich ist es angenehmer, wenn man zu zweit reist, aber im großen und ganzen hat das ganz gut geklappt.

Wie hat das geklappt? How did that work out? (*lit.* How has that worked out?) (**klappen** to work (out))

das hat gut geklappt That worked out well (*lit.* That has worked out well)

ganz gut quite well

angenehmer more pleasant (**angenehm** pleasant)

wenn man zu zweit reist if one travels with someone else; **zu zweit** with someone else (**zweit** from **zwei** two). Note the word order: after conjunctions such as **wenn** (if), **weil** (because) and **daß** (that) the verb has to go right to the end of the clause.

im großen und ganzen on the whole

How did Agnes travel – and how was the food?

LISTEN FOR...	
geschmeckt	tasted
aufpassen	to be careful
keine rohen Früchte	no raw fruit

Ruth	Und wie bist du gefahren? Mit dem Bus? Mit dem Zug?
Agnes	Meistens mit dem Bus oder auch mit dem Zug.
Ruth	Ehm. Und das Essen?
Agnes	Das Essen hat mir persönlich nicht so gut geschmeckt. Ehm – das ist halt das übliche Curry, und Curry und nochmal Curry. Und vor allem mit den Früchten muß man sehr aufpassen, denn man darf also keine rohen Früchte essen.
Ruth	Mhm. Aber du bist nicht krank geworden?
Agnes	Ich nicht, aber meine Freundin war ziemlich krank.

meistens   mostly

das Essen hat mir nicht so gut geschmeckt   I did not particularly enjoy the food (*lit.* the food has not tasted so good to me (**schmecken** to taste). **Das Essen schmeckt gut** The food tastes good.

persönlich   personally

nochmal(s)   again

mit den Früchten muß man sehr aufpassen   with the fruit one must be very careful; **aufpassen** (to be careful, watch out) is a separable verb, e.g. **ich passe immer auf** I am always careful; **du paßt auf** you are careful. **Passen Sie auf!** Be careful! Watch out!

man darf also keine rohen Früchte essen   so one must not eat any raw fruit (*lit.* one may eat no raw fruits)

Du bist nicht krank geworden?   You did not become ill? (*lit.* You have not become ill?); **werden** (to become) is another strong verb that takes **sein** to form the perfect tense: **ich werde krank** I become ill; **ich bin krank geworden** I became ill (*lit.* I have become ill)

ich nicht   (here) I didn't

ziemlich   rather

5 Here is a summary of Conversations 2. Check it through carefully, spot the three mistakes and correct them.

    a. Agnes ist dann alleine gereist.

    b. Das hat nicht gut geklappt.

    c. Agnes ist meistens mit dem Auto gefahren.

    d. Das Essen hat Agnes nicht geschmeckt.

    e. Mit den Früchten muß man sehr aufpassen.

    f. Agnes ist nicht krank geworden.

ANSWERS P. 218   **g.** Agnes' Freundin war auch nicht krank.

6 The cartoon refers directly to one of Agnes' statements in Conversations 2. Write it down as a caption.

ANSWERS P. 218

7 On the recording Sissy talks about her holidays. Listen several times, then answer the questions in English.

    a. What did Sissy do?

    _____

    _____

    b. Did she travel on her own?

    _____

    _____

    c. How did that work out?

    _____

    _____

    d. What happened?

    _____

    _____

    e. What's Sissy's conclusion at the end of the conversation?

    _____

ANSWERS P. 218   _____

8 Three options, but two are wrong! Make a ring round the correct participles.

    a. Wo bist du im letzten Urlaub ...?   gelebt – gewesen – gegessen

    b. Ich bin nach Deutschland ...   gefahren – geklappt – gearbeitet

    c. Wie hat das ...?   gesungen – gehört – geklappt?

    d. Ich habe in einem schönen Hotel ...   gereist – gewohnt – gesunken

ANSWERS P. 218   **e.** Und das Essen hat sehr gut ...   geschehen – geschmeckt – getrunken

9 Lisa's trip to Sri Lanka. Study her letter below and fill in the correct past participles.

New vocabulary:
Asien   Asia

Im letzten Urlaub bin ich nach Sri Lanka (**a**) —————————————— (**fahren**). Das

war meine erste Reise nach Asien. Ich bin mit meinem Freund (**b**) ——————————

(**reisen**). Er ist schon zweimal in Indien (**c**) —————————————— (**sein**).

Unsere Reise hat sehr gut (**d**) —————————————— (**klappen**),

und es war wunderschön auf Sri Lanka. Meistens sind wir mit dem Bus (**e**) ——————

—————————————— (**fahren**), aber manchmal auch mit dem Zug. Das

Essen hat mir gut (**f**) —————————————— (**schmecken**). Aber mein Freund

ist sehr krank (**g**) —————————————— (**werden**).

ANSWERS P. 218   Er war eine Woche im Bett!

9 Your turn to speak. Pretend you are Lisa and answer Erich's questions on your holiday. You went to Sri Lanka with a friend, had a good time, travelled by bus and liked the food.

Herr Schuster spent his Easter in Berlin

Ruth	Was haben Sie an Ostern gemacht?
Herr Schuster	Ostern bin ich mit einer Gruppe englischer Studenten nach Berlin gefahren.
Ruth	Und warum? Was haben Sie da gemacht?
Herr Schuster	Eh, wir haben deutsche Firmen besichtigt.
Ruth	Und wie hat's den Studenten gefallen?
Herr Schuster	Oh, die Studenten waren begeistert; es war sehr schön in Berlin.

(an) Ostern at Easter; similarly **(an) Weihnachten** at Christmas (also **zu Ostern/Weihnachten**)

mit einer Gruppe englischer Studenten with a group of English students; **englischer Studenten** is the genitive case (see p. 237) (**die Gruppe** group; **der Student** student).

warum why

wir haben deutsche Firmen besichtigt we looked round German firms (*lit.* we have looked round German firms), **besichtigen** to look round. Another example: **wir haben die Kathedrale besichtigt** we looked round the cathedral (*lit.* we have looked round the cathedral).

Wie hat's den Studenten gefallen? How did the students like it? (*lit.* how have the students liked it?). **Gefallen** is a strong verb, and the past participle is the same as the infinitive: **gefallen**. Some more examples: **Wie hat es Ihnen gefallen?** How did you like it? (*lit.* How have you liked it?); **es hat mir sehr gut gefallen** I liked it (*lit.* have liked it) very much; **es hat uns sehr gut gefallen** we liked it (*lit.* have liked it) very much.

die Studenten waren begeistert the students were thrilled (more on **waren** on the grammar page in this unit).

View from the Kurfürstendamm of the Kaiser Wilhelm Memorial Church

More on Herr Schuster's Berlin visit

LISTEN FOR...

die Leute	the people
Besuch	visit
gegessen	eaten

Ruth	Wie war das Wetter?
Herr Schuster	Ah, das Wetter war wunderbar. Die Leute waren sehr freundlich – rundrum, es war ein schöner Besuch.
Ruth	Mhm. Und was haben Sie sonst noch alles gemacht? Abends zum Beispiel?
Herr Schuster	Ja, abends sind wir an den Kudamm gegangen, das ist eine der schönsten Straßen in Berlin. Wir haben gegessen dort, wir sind in Diskotheken gegangen, wir sind ins Kino gegangen, ins Theater gegangen. Die Studenten haben natürlich auch in Tanzlokalen getanzt, und ab und zu haben sie auch schon mal zu viel getrunken und sind dann – ich glaube einmal – zu spät ins Hotel gekommen.

wunderbar   wonderful

die Leute waren sehr freundlich   The people were very friendly

rundrum   (more correctly **rundum**) altogether (*lit.* all round)

der Besuch   visit (**besuchen** to visit)

Was haben Sie sonst noch alles gemacht?   What else did you do? (*lit.* What have you otherwise everything done?).

der Kudamm: short for **Kurfürstendamm**, Berlin's famous boulevard with many fashionable shops, cafés and restaurants

wir haben gegessen   we ate (*lit.* we have eaten); **essen** to eat is a strong verb, and its past participle is **gegessen**.

wir sind gegangen   we went (*lit.* have gone); **gehen** to go is another strong verb, and its past participle is **gegangen**. Note that **gehen** uses **sein** to form the perfect tense.

das Tanzlokal   place to dance – this is now a rather old-fashioned word

zu spät   too late

sie sind ... gekommen   they came (*lit.* they have come); **kommen** to come is another strong verb using **sein** to form the perfect tense. Its past participle is **gekommen**.

ich glaube   I believe, I think

11 Study the last two conversations until you are thoroughly familiar with them. Then fill in the missing past participles. We have given you the infinitives that need to be transformed.

a. (machen) Was haben Sie an Ostern _____ ?

b. (fahren) Ich bin nach Berlin _____

c. (gefallen) Wie hat's Ihnen _____ ?

d. (gehen) Wir sind ins Kino _____

e. (tanzen) Die Studenten haben _____

f. (trinken) Ab und zu haben sie zu viel _____

ANSWERS P. 218 **g.** (kommen) Einmal sind sie zu spät ins Hotel _____

12 Copycats. Mathias loves to do everything that Jessica has already done. For example, if she says: **Ich bin gestern nach Ulm gefahren**, he will say: **Und ich fahre heute nach Ulm**. Continue the same pattern with the sentences below.

a. *Jessica:* Ich bin gestern nach Paris gereist.

Mathias: _____

b. *Jessica:* Ich habe gestern eine Party gemacht.

Mathias: _____

c. *Jessica:* Ich habe gestern den Eifelturm besichtigt.

Mathias: _____

d. *Jessica:* Ich bin gestern in eine Disko gegangen.

Mathias: _____

e. *Jessica:* Ich habe gestern getanzt.

Mathias: _____

f. *Jessica:* Ich habe gestern Champagner getrunken.

ANSWERS P. 218 *Mathias:* _____

13 On the recording a young man is being asked what he did last week. Listen to his replies and match up the pictures with the appropriate day of the week in the diary, in other words fill in **a**, **b**, etc. but obviously not in that order.

ANSWERS P. 218

14 In the letter below, Hannes is talking about his recent Christmas holiday. Fill in the missing words from the box underneath the letter and listen to the recording to check your answers.

Weihnachten (a)_____ ich in Spanien. Ich bin mit einer Spanierin

verheiratet, und ihre Familie wohnt in der Nähe von Barcelona. Wir sind oft nach

Barcelona (b) _____ und haben die Stadt (c) _____ .

Abends (d) _____ wir dann mit der Familie zusammen; wir haben schön

(e) _____ und viel Wein (f) _____ . Das Wetter

(g) _____ schön, und es hat uns sehr gut (h) _____ .

ANSWERS ALSO ON P. 218

waren – gegessen – gefallen – gefahren – getrunken – besichtigt – war – war

15 Your turn to speak and talk about your last Christmas break. You'll be practising some of the verbs from the previous exercise. Tom will prompt you.

The imperfect tense

There are two main verbs that you will often hear in the imperfect tense: **sein** (to be) and **haben** (to have).

Here are two examples of the imperfect tense of **sein** from this unit:

Meine Freundin war krank.

   My girl friend was ill.

Die Studenten waren begeistert.

   The students were thrilled.

The complete pattern of **sein** and **haben** in the imperfect runs like this:

sein		to be
ich	war	I was
du	warst	you were
er/sie/es	war	he/she/it was
wir	waren	we were
ihr	wart	you were
sie/Sie	waren	they/you were

haben		to have
ich	hatte	I had
du	hattest	you had
er/sie/es	hatte	he/she/it had
wir	hatten	we had
ihr	hattet	you had
sie/Sie	hatten	they/you had

The imperfect of **sein** and **haben** is worth learning as it is so frequently used. Otherwise, you'll probably get by with just using the perfect tense with the other verbs. You should, however, try to recognize the imperfect when you hear it or come across it in newspapers and books. In conversational German, you will nearly always hear a mix of both tenses. Generally speaking, North Germans seem to make more use of the imperfect tense than South Germans.

Weak verbs

The imperfect of weak verbs is formed as follows. Remove the **-en** from the infinitive: **wohn-en**
Replace it with **-te**: ▶ **wohn-te**
Add the appropriate ending:

ich	wohnte	I	lived
du	wohntest	you	lived
er/sie/es	wohnte	he/she/it	lived
wir	wohnten	we	lived
ihr	wohntet	you	lived
sie/Sie	wohnten	they/you	lived

This corresponds to the English pattern 'I play ▶ I played'.

Strong verbs

The imperfect forms of strong verbs follow different patterns that will need to be looked up in the dictionary. One example from this unit is **fahren ▶ fuhr**:

Meine Freundin fuhr weg.   My girl friend left.
Sometimes there are similarities between English and German verb forms:

ich kam   I came

wir sangen   we sang

sie tranken   they drank

Here are all the imperfect forms of **trinken** (to drink) and **kommen** (to come):

ich	trank	kam
du	trankest*	kamest*
er/sie/es	trank	kam
wir	tranken	kamen
ihr	tranket*	kamet*
sie/Sie	tranken	kamen

* These forms sound somewhat antiquated and are seldom used. You would normally use the perfect forms.

16 **War** or **waren**? Complete the sentences below using the correct imperfect forms of **sein**, then translate the sentences into English.

a. Ich _____ krank.

_____

b. Das Wetter _____ schlecht.

_____

c. Er _____ gestern hier.

_____

d. Wir _____ im Theater.

_____

e. Anita und Marion _____ zu Ostern

in Berlin.

_____

ANSWERS P. 218

17 **Hatte** or **hatten**? Complete the sentences below using the correct imperfect forms of **haben**, then translate the sentences into English.

a. Meine Freundin _____ einen

großen Hund.

_____

b. Wir _____ ein Haus am Meer.

_____

c. Ich _____ ein neues Auto.

_____

d. Peter _____ den Schlüssel.

_____

e. Gisela, Manfred und Martin _____

einen schönen Urlaub.

_____

f. _____ Hans eine gute Reise?

_____

ANSWERS P. 218

18 Write out all the imperfect forms of the verb **machen**, following the example of **wohnen** on the previous page.

ich _____ I made

du _____ you made

er/sie/es _____ he/she/it made

wir _____ we made

ihr _____ you made

sie/Sie _____ you/they made

ANSWERS P. 218

19 Study the list of strong verbs on the Key words page, then translate the sentences below into English.

a. Er fand das Haus.

_____

b. Wir schliefen bis zehn Uhr.

_____

c. Peter brachte mir ein Buch.

_____

d. Ich vergaß die Adresse.

_____

e. Sie fanden das Hotel.

_____

f. Sie trank ein Glas Bier.

_____

g. Wir flogen nach Timbuktu.

_____

ANSWERS P. 218

KEY WORDS

To understand:

Wo bist du/sind Sie im letzten Urlaub gewesen?	Where did you go for your last holiday?
Was haben Sie Ostern/Weihnachten gemacht?	What did you do at Easter/Christmas?
Wie hat das geklappt?	How did that work out?
Wie hat es Ihnen gefallen?	How did you like it?
Wie war das Wetter?	What was the weather like?

To use yourself:

Ich bin nach Indien/Berlin gefahren	I went to India/Berlin
Wir haben uns in Delhi getroffen	We met up in Delhi
Wir haben die Stadt besichtigt	We looked round the town
Wir haben dort ...	There we ...
gegessen	ate
getrunken	drank
getanzt	danced
Wir sind in Diskotheken/ins Theater gegangen	We went to discotheques/to the theatre
Das hat (ganz) gut geklappt	It worked out (quite) well
Es hat uns gut gefallen	We liked it very much
Wir waren begeistert	We were thrilled
Das Wetter war schön/wunderbar	The weather was fine/wonderful

Here is a list of strong or irregular verbs you will find useful:

Infinitive	*Imperfect*	*Past Participle*	
bringen	brachte	gebracht	to bring
finden	fand	gefunden	to find
fliegen	flog	geflogen	to fly
haben	hatte	gehabt	to have
helfen	half	geholfen	to help
kommen	kam	gekommen	to come
sein	war	gewesen	to be
schlafen	schlief	geschlafen	to sleep
trinken	trank	getrunken	to drink
vergessen	vergaß	vergessen	to forget

DID YOU KNOW?

Notes on German history

Germany has nearly always had a strong regional tradition. It used to consist of many different, often tiny states which formed various alliances amongst – and against – each other. The First German Empire (**Reich**) flourished in the Middle Ages under the successors of Charlemagne (**Karl der Große**) and the **Hohenstaufen** emperors. It covered a huge area comprising Germany, Austria, parts of France and Italy and areas of what is now Poland, the Czech and Slovak Republics and Hungary. The emperors of this **Reich** saw themselves as successors to the Roman Empire and called their realm 'Holy Roman Empire of the German Nation'. Officially, the Holy Roman Empire lasted until 1806 when Napoleon dissolved it, but it had begun to decline a long time before, especially after the devastating Thirty Years' War (1618–1648).

Prussia and the Second German Empire of 1871

After the Thirty Years' War Prussia and Austria emerged as the two most powerful states within the Holy Roman Empire, and their rivalry continued over the next two centuries. Under Bismarck Prussia fought a final war against the Austrians and defeated them in 1866. Bismarck then founded a German Empire without Austria in 1871. The Prussian king Wilhelm became its emperor (**Kaiser**) and Bismarck chancellor. Austria meanwhile remained a powerful empire on its own. The dual monarchy of Austria and Hungary was founded in 1867, and Austria actually became Germany's ally in the First World War (1914–1918).

Germany between the wars

After the First World War the **Kaiser** (Wilhelm II) abdicated, and Germany became a republic. Politics during the Weimar Republic became increasingly fractured and polarized, while the country's economic decline continued. In 1933 the National Socialists under Adolf Hitler came to power, and the dark period of the infamous Third Reich began. Hitler annexed Austria and invaded Poland in 1939. This led to the Second World War.

Postwar Germany

After its surrender in 1945 Germany and its capital Berlin were divided into four 'zones' occupied by Britain, the United States, France and the Soviet Union. In 1949 the three western zones were merged, and the Federal Republic of Germany (FRG) was founded with Bonn as its capital. Soon after, the German Democratic Republic (GDR) was founded in the Soviet sector. Its capital was East Berlin. Berlin was now a divided city, its three western sectors remaining in close affiliation to Bonn, but surrounded, as it were, by East German territory. Increasing East–West tension culminated in the erection of the Berlin Wall by the East German government in 1961. However, in the wake of the changes in Eastern Europe and with the collapse of the Soviet Union, the Wall was opened in October 1989, and a year later the two German states reunited.

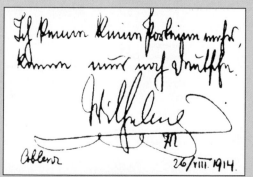

Kaiser Wilhelm II's handwriting

AND FINALLY...

20 Another chance to speak. Erich is asking you about your activities last week. Here is a selection of useful phrases. Use the imperfect for **haben** and **sein**, but otherwise stick to the perfect.

ich hatte ... eine Party
ich habe ... gearbeitet/getanzt/geschlafen

ich war ... krank/im Büro
ich bin ... gegangen

ANSWERS

EXERCISE 1
Here are the wrong sentences: her boy friend should read: her girl friend; they met up in Sri Lanka should read: they met up in Delhi; Agnes travelled to Delhi should read: Agnes travelled to Sri Lanka

EXERCISE 2
(a) gewesen   (b) gefahren   (c) gemacht   (d) gebadet
(e) gegessen

EXERCISE 3
(a) Irland   (b) nein   (c) Wanderungen   (d) Schule
(e) Abendschule   (f) Pop   (g) bitter, aber gut.
MYSTERY WORD: Schottland

EXERCISE 5
(b) Das hat ganz gut geklappt.   (c) Agnes ist meistens mit dem Bus gereist oder auch mit dem Zug.   (g) Agnes' Freundin war ziemlich krank.

EXERCISE 6
Man darf also keine rohen Früchte essen.

EXERCISE 7
(a) She went to Bali.   (b) No, with her boyfriend.
(c) It did not work out very well.   (d) He didn't like the food; the climate was too hot for him and he became ill.
(e) Next time she'll travel on her own.

EXERCISE 8
(a) gewesen   (b) gefahren   (c) geklappt   (d) gewohnt
(e) geschmeckt

EXERCISE 9
(a) gefahren   (b) gereist   (c) gewesen   (d) geklappt
(e) gefahren   (f) geschmeckt   (g) geworden

EXERCISE 11
(a) gemacht   (b) gefahren   (c) gefallen   (d) gegangen
(e) getanzt   (f) getrunken   (g) gekommen

EXERCISE 12
(a) Und ich reise heute nach Paris.   (b) Und ich mache heute eine Party   (c) Und ich besichtige heute den Eifelturm.
(d) Und ich gehe heute in eine Disko.   (e) Und ich tanze heute.
(f) Und ich trinke heute Champagner.

EXERCISE 13
Montag: **d**   Dienstag: **b**   Mittwoch: **e**   Donnerstag: **g**
Freitag: **f**   Samstag: **c**   Sonntag: **a**

EXERCISE 14
(a) war   (b) gefahren   (c) besichtigt   (d) waren
(e) gegessen   (f) getrunken   (g) war   (h) gefallen

EXERCISE 16
(a) Ich war krank (I was ill).   (b) Das Wetter war schlecht (The weather was bad).   (c) Er war gestern hier (He was here yesterday).   (d) Wir waren im Theater (We were in the theatre).   (e) Anita und Marion waren zu Ostern in Berlin (Anita and Marion were in Berlin at Easter).

EXERCISE 17
(a) Meine Freundin hatte einen großen Hund (My girl friend had a big dog).   (b) Wir hatten ein Haus am Meer (We had a house by the sea).   (c) Ich hatte ein neues Auto (I had a new car).   (d) Peter hatte den Schlüssel (Peter had the key).
(e) Gisela, Manfred und Martin hatten einen schönen Urlaub (Gisela, Manfred and Martin had a nice holiday).
(f) Hatte Hans eine gute Reise? (Did Hans have a good trip?)

EXERCISE 18
ich machte; du machtest; er/sie/es machte; wir machten; ihr machtet; sie/Sie machten

EXERCISE 19
(a) He found the house.   (b) We slept until 10 o'clock.
(c) Peter brought me a book.   (d) I forgot the address.
(e) They found the hotel.   (f) She drank a glass of beer.
(g) We flew to Timbuktu.

15 STATING YOUR INTENTIONS

WHAT YOU WILL LEARN

▶ inviting someone out
▶ responding to an invitation
▶ talking about future plans
▶ you will also read about papers, magazines, radio stations and TV programmes in German

BEFORE YOU BEGIN

Go out and celebrate! You have now reached the very last unit in the course and have acquired a whole range of new skills to activate and build on. Travelling to a German-speaking country would now, of course, be an excellent way to consolidate your knowledge. If you can't do that right now, try to see a German film with subtitles, tune into German radio and TV stations and look around for another challenge, such as Macmillan's *Breakthrough Further German*.

Pronunciation notes

... are not really necessary any more as all the important points have been covered. But how about trying out a couple of tongue twisters, as demonstrated on the recording:

Fischers Fritz fischt frische Fische (Fisher's Fritz fishes fresh fish)
In Ulm, um Ulm und um Ulm herum (In Ulm, around Ulm and all around Ulm)

▶ An invitation to a concert

LISTEN FOR...

Hast du Lust ...?	Do you feel like ...?
Was gibt es denn?	What's on?

Hermann	Ich geh' heute abend ins Konzert. Hast du Lust mitzugehen?
Cordula	Ja, gerne. Was gibt es denn?
Hermann	Klavierkonzerte, Tschaikowsky –
Cordula	Und wo?
Hermann	Das ist in der Stadthalle.
Cordula	Um wieviel Uhr denn?
Hermann	Um acht Uhr.
Cordula	O ja, gut. Wann treffen wir uns denn dann?
Hermann	Um halb acht im 'Bürgereck'.

ins Konzert   to a concert; **das Konzert** means both concert and concerto, as here in

das Klavierkonzert   piano concerto.

Hast du Lust mitzugehen?   Do you feel like coming/going along (too)? **Mitgehen** to come/go along is a separable verb. Your answer could be: **ja, ich komme mit** yes, I('ll) come along.

So this is how you issue invitations: **Hast du Lust, ins Kino zu gehen?** Do you feel like going to the cinema? Or in the polite form: **Haben Sie Lust, essen zu gehen?** Do you feel like going out for a meal? **Haben Sie Lust auf ein Glas Wein?** Do you feel like a glass of wine? Possible answers: **ich habe keine Lust** I don't feel like it, or: **tut mir leid, ich habe keine Zeit** (I'm) sorry, I have no time.

Was gibt es denn?   What's on?
die Stadthalle   municipal hall
um wieviel Uhr?   at what time?

Wann treffen wir uns denn dann?   When shall we meet then? (*lit.* When do we meet each other); **denn** and **dann** are fillers to make the sentence less abrupt, like 'then' in English.
(das) Bürgereck   name of a pub

Invitations

Haben Sie Lust auf einen Film?   Do you feel like a film? or:
Haben Sie Lust, ins Kino zu gehen?   Do you feel like going to the cinema?

1 Here's a bunch of people seeking fun and entertainment. Match them up with the sort of show they're looking for. You will also need to look at the top two advertisements on p. 220.

ANSWERS P. 233

2 On the recording Frau Birke is trying to invite Herr Stock out. What happens next? Answer the questions below, in English. Be as brief as possible.

New vocabulary: **das macht nichts** that doesn't matter **dick** fat

a. What's her first suggestion? _____

b. What's Herr Stock's excuse? _____

c. What happens if Herr Stock goes to the opera? _____

d. What's the title of the film mentioned by Frau Birke? _____

e. Why can't Herr Stock go to the cinema? _____

f. What idea does Frau Birke come up with next? _____

g. Why does Herr Stock object to this? _____

ANSWERS P. 233
h. So what's Frau Birke's final suggestion? _____

3 Your turn to invite and be invited. Turn to the tape where Tom will assist you. You will need the following expressions:

Haben Sie Lust/Zeit? **ich habe (keine) Lust/Zeit** **ja, gerne**

and you will also hear the title ***Das Dschungelbuch*** – *The Jungle Book*.

▶ Ingrid's plans for the day

LISTEN FOR...	
Friseur	hairdresser
abwaschen	to wash up
aufräumen	to tidy up

Hast du frei?   Have you got the day off?

heute hab' ich frei   I've got the day off

Gott sei Dank   thank goodness (*lit.* God be thanks)

der Friseur   hairdresser

Ursula	Ingrid, was machst du heute? Hast du frei, oder mußt du arbeiten?
Ingrid	Nein, heute hab' ich frei, Gott sei Dank. Heute morgen geh' ich erst mal einkaufen, und dann zum Friseur ... Ja, und dann ist schon Mittag. Ich werde etwas zu Hause essen, und dann abwaschen und die Wohnung ein bißchen aufräumen. Heute nachmittag gehe ich mit dem Hund spazieren, und dann so um vier werden ein paar Freundinnen zum Kaffee kommen. Um halb sechs kommt dann schon mein Mann von der Arbeit nach Hause. Heute abend machen wir nichts – wir sehen uns wahrscheinlich einen guten Film im Fernsehen an.

ich werde etwas zu Hause essen   I'll eat something at home. This is an example of the future tense. It is formed with **werden** + infinitive:

ich werde ... essen I will eat ... Note that the infinitive goes to the end. Also note that you do not necessarily have to use the future tense when stating future intentions. More often than not the Germans use the present tense (as do the English in many cases, using what is called the present continuous):

heute nachmittag gehe ich mit dem Hund spazieren this afternoon I am taking the dog for a walk (*lit.* I go walking with the dog). Also note that there is no present continuous in German, so 'I'm going to the cinema' would be translated as

ich gehe ins Kino.

You can also express something that may happen in the future by using modal verbs, for example: **ich muß mit dem Hund spazierengehen** (I have to take the dog for a walk) or **ich möchte mit dem Hund spazierengehen** (I'd like to take the dog for a walk). More details on the future tense are on the grammar page in this unit.

der Hund   the dog

abwaschen   to wash up; a separable verb: **ich wasche ab** I wash up.

aufräumen   to tidy up; another separable verb: **ich räume die Wohnung auf** I tidy up the flat.

kommt dann schon mein Mann von der Arbeit nach Hause   my husband comes home from work. Again the present tense is used for a future event.

heute abend machen wir nichts   this evening we're not doing anything (*lit.* we do nothing)

wir sehen uns wahrscheinlich einen guten Film an   we('ll) probably watch a good film; **ansehen** to watch is a separable verb.

4 Brigitte and Kurt are planning a party. On the recording, Brigitte is asking Kurt about all the jobs he promised to do. What has he done already? What's he still planning to do? Match up the tasks with the times.

a.	die Party ist	**A.**	vor vier Wochen
b.	abwaschen	**B.**	heute nachmittag
c.	einkaufen	**C.**	heute morgen
d.	Friseur gehen	**D.**	morgen abend
e.	Wohnung aufräumen	**E.**	morgen früh
f.	mit Hund spazierengehen	**F.**	morgen

ANSWERS P. 233

5 Informed guesswork. Study the TV schedule of the **ZDF** (**Zweites Deutsches Fernsehen**) below. Not all the words will be familiar to you. Nonetheless try to answer the questions below.

ZDF

13.00	**ZDF Sport extra**
	Tennis-ATP-Turnier
17.45	**Der Alte**
	Der Detektiv
19.00	**heute – Wetter**
19.25	**Herzsprung**
	Fernsehfilm der Woche
20.50	**Vor der Fußball-WM**
21.00	**auslandsjournal**
21.45	**heute-journal**
22.15	**Blutiger Sonntag**
	Ital. Spielfilm v. 1990
23.45	**Apropos Film**
00.15	**heute**
00.20	**Das kleine Fernsehspiel:**
	Bab el oued City

a. How many sports programmes could you watch? At what time are they on and what kind of sport would they offer?

_____

_____

b. What's the TV film of the week called?

_____

_____

c. Is there any other film on that night?

_____

d. When would you get the weather forecast?

_____

e. Which titles could be news or current affairs programmes?

_____

ANSWERS P. 233

6 Your turn to speak about your plans for the day. On the recording Erich will tell you what he is planning to do tomorrow; your task will be to do exactly the same things today. For example, he will say: **Ich werde morgen ins Kino gehen**. And then it's your turn to say: **Und ich gehe heute ins Kino**. You won't need any prompting as you'll be taking your cues from Erich.

CONVERSATION 3

 Herr Schilz's weekend plans

LISTEN FOR...

ein ruhiges Wochenende	a quiet weekend
wir spielen Karten	we play cards
faulenzen	to laze about

Herr Schilz Ich habe diese Woche viel gearbeitet, und ich möchte gern ein ruhiges Wochenende. Ich wohne mit meiner Freundin zusammen, und wir werden viel Zeit zu Hause verbringen. Wir kochen, spielen Karten, lesen, faulenzen ... Samstagabend gehen wir wahrscheinlich ins 'Quartier Latin'. Das ist meine Stammkneipe, und da treffen wir immer unsere Freunde. Am Sonntag wird's dann wohl etwas hektischer. Da kommen ein paar Freunde zu Besuch; die bringen auch ihre Kinder mit, und dann wird's wohl schon etwas lauter werden.

ich möchte ein ruhiges Wochenende   I'd like a quiet weekend

wir werden viel Zeit zu Hause verbringen   we'll spend a lot of time at home

wir spielen Karten   we'll play cards

faulenzen   to laze about, do nothing (**faul** lazy; also means rotten, foul)

Quartier Latin   name of a pub

meine Stammkneipe   my usual boozer (**die Stammkneipe** pub where one is a regular)

am Sonntag wird's (wird es) etwas hektischer   on Sunday it'll be (*lit.* it becomes) a bit more hectic

zu Besuch   for a visit (*cf* **besuchen** to visit; **ich besuche meine Schwester** I visit my sister)

die bringen auch ihre Kinder mit   they're bringing their children along too; **mitbringen** to bring along is a separable verb.

dann wird's wohl schon etwas lauter werden   then it will probably become a bit noisier (**laut** loud, noisy).

es wird ... werden   it will become ...

Note: 'become' is **werden**, and not **bekommen** (to receive)

7 It's Friday morning, and Wanda is telling you about her plans for the weekend. Listen to the recording and take down notes in the diary, in German.

Samstag, 4. August

bis 12 Uhr _____

dann _____

am Abend _____

_____

Sonntag, 5. August

am Morgen _____

am Nachmittag _____

_____

ANSWERS P. 233

8 Different sentences, identical meanings. Match them up!

A. Ich werde einkaufen.
B. Ich werde kochen.
C. Ich werde faulenzen.
D. Ich werde daheim bleiben.
E. Ich werde zum Essen gehen.

a. Ich werde nichts machen.
b. Ich werde das Essen machen.
c. Ich werde zu Hause sein.
d. Ich werde in die Geschäfte gehen.
e. Ich werde ins Restaurant gehen.

ANSWERS P. 233

9 Your turn to speak. Next week will be a little busy for the owner of this diary – pretend it's yours. Dorit will ask you about your plans. This time you can vary your responses and state your future intentions with three different phrases:

ich werde (I will)

ich möchte (I'd like to)

ich muß (I have to)

And what is Rainer Schilz going to do for his holiday?

LISTEN FOR...

toll	super, brilliant
eine Weile	a while
über Land	overland
man lernt Land und Leute kennen	one gets to know the country and the people

Ursula	Und Herr Schilz, was für Urlaubspläne haben Sie?
Herr Schilz	Ja, wir werden dieses Jahr unsere große Reise machen, und zwar fahren wir für sechs Wochen nach Südamerika.
Ursula	Das ist ja toll! Und wohin fahren Sie da?
Herr Schilz	Wir werden nach Rio fliegen und eine Weile dort bleiben. Von da fahren wir dann mit dem Bus über Land. Das ist am billigsten, und man sieht auch am meisten, und man lernt Land und Leute kennen.

Was für Urlaubspläne ...? What (kind of) holiday plans (**der Plan** plan) ...?

unsere große Reise our big trip

Südamerika South America

toll brilliant, super, great

wir werden eine Weile dort bleiben we'll stay there for a while

über Land overland

man sieht am meisten one sees the most;

am meisten (most) is the superlative of **viel** (much, a lot); the comparative is: **mehr** (more). For example:

man sieht viel one sees a lot;
man sieht mehr one sees more.

man lernt Land und Leute kennen one gets to know (*lit.* one learns to know) the country and the people

10 Six people in search of a holiday. Listen to the recording to find out what they want. Here's a selection of holidays they can choose from. Study it carefully and then make your recommendation in the spaces below.

A Schön und fit – attraktive Programme im Sporthotel 'Zur Post'. Fitneßcenter, Schwimmbad, Sauna, Solarium. Ein Hotel mit Stil und Komfort. Zuschr. unter A

B MORGENS TENNIS, MITTAGS SURFEN, ABENDS TANZEN. AKTIV SEIN RUND UM DIE UHR. INFO HAPPY-SURF. Zuschr. unter B

C Sprachferien in der Toskana. Romantisches Hotel. Schöne Natur. Zuschr. unter C

D schön sein von innen. yoga in der beautyfarm im berghotel ananda. Zuschr. unter D

E Aktives Reisen. Fahrrad. Trekking. Wandern. Bergsteigen in Kanada. Zuschriften unter E

F Ferien ohne Ozonloch! Portugal, privates Fischerhaus am Meer. Kein Massentourismus. Zuschr. unter F

G Studienreisen durch Griechenland. Zuschr. unter G

H Ferien auf dem Bauernhof. Bayern-Urlaub für die ganze Familie. Zuschr. unter H

I Klassische Rundreise durch Ägypten. Unsere Reiseführer informieren Sie über Land und Leute, Geschichte und Kultur. Zuschriften unter I

J Malen, Keramik, Musik, Kochen: Kreativurlaub in der Provence. Kleine Gruppen, Spezialprogramme für Kinder. Zuschr. unter J

ANSWERS P. 233

11 Your turn to ask Anke about her holiday plans – turn to the recording where Tom will prompt you. You will need the following questions:

Was für Urlaubspläne ... ?   Was werden Sie ... ?

Wohin fahren ... ?   Wie lange wollen Sie ... ?

▶ Agnes' future plans

LISTEN FOR...

Zukunft	future
Vertrag	contract
ungewiß	uncertain
freiberuflich	freelance

Ruth	Agnes, was für Pläne hast du für die Zukunft?
Agnes	Ich habe einen Vertrag bis nächstes Jahr im Juli hier in dieser Stadt und werde bis dahin arbeiten.
Ruth	Und danach?
Agnes	Eh, das ist noch ungewiß. Vielleicht werde ich freiberuflich arbeiten. Oder vielleicht werde ich auch etwas ganz anderes machen.

Was für Pläne hast du?   What plans have you got?

die Zukunft   the future

der Vertrag   contract

bis dahin   till then

danach   after that

Agnes

noch ungewiß   still uncertain; as in English, **un-** denotes the opposite, e.g. **gewiß** certain ▶ **ungewiß** uncertain; **glücklich** happy ▶ **unglücklich** unhappy; **klar** clear ▶ **unklar** unclear

vielleicht   perhaps

freiberuflich   freelance

etwas ganz anderes   something completely different

12 On the recording you will hear five people being asked about their future plans. Listen carefully and take notes (in German) about what they're doing in the grid below. Follow the example.

	Who?	*When?*	*What?*
a.	Anna	*nächstes Jahr*	*in Bonn studieren*
b.	Richard		
c.	Frau Braun		
d.	Herr Lange		
e.	Frau Columbus		

ANSWERS P. 233

13 Read and understand: Ursula, an Aries (**Widder**), and Michael, a Scorpio (**Skorpion**), have found the following horoscopes in a magazine. When you've read them, mark the right boxes below.

Widder

21. März–20. April

> Ihr Leben wird angenehmer, vor allem im Beruf. Auch die Arbeit wird leichter, und Sie können an Urlaub denken. Machen Sie eine große Reise und nehmen Sie einen netten Freund mit!

a. Is Ursula going to have a difficult time this month?
- yes
- no

b. Is her work going to be any easier from now on?
- yes
- no

c. Should she
- stay at home and work even harder
- go on holiday with a nice friend?

ANSWERS P. 233

Skorpion

24. Oktober–22. November

> Denken Sie manchmal an Ihre Zukunft? Machen Sie jetzt neue Pläne! Probieren Sie mal etwas ganz anderes. Vorsicht: Ende Oktober wird es wahrscheinlich Probleme in Ihrer Familie geben, aber danach wird das Leben wieder ruhiger.

d. Should Michael think about his future and change things?
- yes
- no

e. Are there going to be a lot of problems at work at the end of October?
- yes
- no

f. When will life be quieter again?
- in October
- in November

14 Your turn to have plans for the future. Turn to the recording of Conversation 5, where all will be revealed – or will it? Here are some useful phrases:

Ich werde ... (freiberuflich) ... arbeiten; ich werde ... etwas ganz anderes machen

GRAMMAR AND EXERCISES

The future

The future tense is formed with **werden** (which here has the meaning of 'will', 'shall' or 'be going to') plus the verb in the infinitive.

Ich werde etwas essen.
> I'll eat something.

Wir werden viel Zeit zu Hause verbringen.
> We'll spend a lot of time at home.

Ich werde im Sommer nach Portugal fahren.
> I'll go to Portugal in the summer.

Note that after **werden** the second verb goes to the *end* of the sentence.

Here are all the forms of **werden**:

ich	werde	I will/shall
du	wirst	you will
er/sie/es	wird	he/she/it will
wir	werden	we will/shall
ihr	werdet	you will
sie/Sie	werden	they/you will

Werden on its own often has the meaning of 'to become', 'to get'.

Ich werde krank.   I become/get ill.
Wir werden naß.   We're getting wet.

Very often the present is used to state future plans as in English:

Wir treffen uns heute abend.
> We're meeting up this evening.

Am Sonntag kommen ein paar Freunde.
> A few friends are coming on Sunday.

Wir fliegen im Sommer nach Rio.
> We're flying to Rio in the summer.

Or you could use **möchte** or **will** to say what you want to do in the future:

Heute abend möchte ich ausgehen.
> I'd like to go out tonight.

Ich will morgen zu Hause bleiben.
> I want to stay at home tomorrow.

A note of caution: do not confuse **ich werde** with **ich will**.

> **ich will** = I want (and *not* I will)
> *for instance* **Ich will fliegen** I want to fly
> **ich werde** = I will
> *for instance* **ich werde fliegen** I will fly

15 The sentences below contain various future intentions. Rewrite them using the correct forms of the verb **werden**. Then rewrite them again, using the present tense – but they will still have a future meaning.

a. Wir möchten im Sommer nach Portugal reisen.

_____

_____

b. Er will heute nachmittag ins Kino gehen.

_____

_____

c. Franziska möchte am Wochenende nach Berlin fliegen.

_____

_____

d. Sie wollen an Weihnachten durch Mexiko fahren.

_____

_____

ANSWERS P. 233

16 Translate into German using the correct form of **werden**.

a. I'm getting wet _____

b. She is getting old _____

c. The weather is getting hot _____

d. The coffee is getting cold _____

ANSWERS P. 233

KEY WORDS

Hast du/Haben Sie heute frei?	Have you got today off?
(Ja), heute habe ich frei	(Yes), I've got today off
Ich werde ...	I'll ...
einkaufen gehen	go shopping
zum Friseur gehen	go to the hairdresser
abwaschen	wash up
aufräumen	tidy up
spazierengehen	go for a walk
Heute abend machen wir nichts	This evening we're not doing anything
Hast du/Haben Sie Lust ...	Do you feel like ...
auf ein Glas Wein?	a glass of wine?
ins Kino zu gehen?	going to the cinema?
mitzugehen?	coming along too?
zum Essen zu kommen?	coming for dinner?
Ja, gerne	Yes, with pleasure
Nein, ich habe keine Lust	No, I don't feel like it
Morgen ...	Tomorrow ...
faulenzen wir	we'll laze about
spielen wir Karten	we'll play cards
kommen ein paar Freunde zu Besuch	a few friends will come to visit
Was für Urlaubspläne haben Sie?	What (kind of) holiday plans have you got?
Wir werden nach ... fahren/fliegen	We'll go/fly to ...
Ich werde ...	I'll ...
über Land fahren	travel overland
mir ein Auto mieten	rent a car
Was für Pläne hast du/haben Sie für die Zukunft?	What plans have you got for the future?
Vielleicht werde ich etwas ganz anderes machen	Perhaps I'll do something completely different

The German media

German newspapers and magazines

As many of their names suggest, most of the big German dailies evolved from regional papers: **Frankfurter Allgemeine Zeitung, Frankfurter Rundschau, Stuttgarter Zeitung, Süddeutsche Zeitung**. They still have a local section covering events in the region.

There is also quite a number of purely regional dailies with a considerable distribution in their area: their first section is dedicated to world news, while the second section covers local issues.

There are not many evening papers in Germany and no specific Sunday papers either. Many dailies, however, carry special weekend sections. The most widely read nationwide tabloid is **Bild**, which tries to appeal to the masses with a mix of scandal, sport and politics.

Three weeklies worth mentioning are **Die Zeit**, a serious paper with an in-depth analysis of political, cultural and economic issues; **Der Spiegel**, which modelled itself on the American *Time* magazine; and **Focus** which might be easiest to read as it has short articles and many diagrams and pictures.

There is also a plethora of other publications, from specialist interest to fashion magazines. One popular all-round magazine is **Stern**, another – geared to a mainly female readership – is **Brigitte**.

Many daily papers carry special advertising sections in their weekend issues, including job adverts, property ads, holiday pages and a lonely hearts section.

Radio stations and TV programmes

In Britain you can receive various German-speaking radio stations, such as **Deutsche Welle**, **Deutschlandfunk**, Radio Austria International, Swiss Radio International and the German Service of the BBC (or indeed a number of other stations such as **WDR** and **NDR**) on medium wave, digital, cable and short wave. All you need to know are the wavelengths and transmission times. If you have a satellite dish or cable TV you will of course also be able to watch TV programmes in German.

AND FINALLY...

18 A last chance to speak. And a last chance to invite Dorit out. Turn to the recording where Tom will prompt you. You'll need:

was machen Sie ...
heute/morgen/abend/übermorgen/danach
bis/wann .../haben Sie Lust/Zeit ...

ANSWERS

EXERCISE 1
(a) theaterstadel (21./22.5.) Collage Theater 'Du verstehst mich nicht' **(b)** theaterstadel (19.5.) Flamenco **(c)** E.D. (22.5 evening) 50er Oldie-Nacht **(d)** Bacchus (20.5.) Trad. Blues; or (30.5.) Blues **(e)** E.D. (27.5.) American Dream-Men Menstrip-Show **(f)** E.D. (22.5. afternoon) Jugenddisco

EXERCISE 2
(a) a glass of wine **(b)** no time – meeting in his firm **(c)** he gets earache **(d)** A man and a woman (Ein Mann und eine Frau) **(e)** he's already seen the film **(f)** to go out for a meal, perhaps Chinese **(g)** he's too fat **(h)** to go swimming ...

EXERCISE 4
a/D; b/B; c/E; d/A; e/F; f/C

EXERCISE 5
(a) 13.00 (tennis) and 20.50 (football) **(b)** 19.25 Herzsprung; **(c)** 22.15 Blutiger Sonntag **(d)** 19.00 **(e)** heute; auslandsjournal; heute-journal

EXERCISE 7
Samstag, 4. August: bis 12 Uhr arbeiten; dann schwimmen gehen; am Abend mit Freunden ins Kino. Sonntag, 5. August: am Morgen faulenzen; am Nachmittag kommt die Freundin zu Kaffee und Kuchen

EXERCISE 8
A/d; B/b; C/a; D/c; E/e

EXERCISE 10
Marianne: J Urs: H Lisa: E Florian: F Susanne: C
Alexander: I

EXERCISE 12
(b) im Sommer, drei Monate nach Sri Lanka **(c)** Weihnachten, Eltern in Köln besuchen d. Ostern, zu Hause bleiben **(e)** heute nachmittag, mit den Kindern in den Zoo gehen

EXERCISE 13
(a) no **(b)** yes **(c)** go on holiday with a nice friend **(d)** yes **(e)** no – but there might be problems at home **(f)** in November

EXERCISE 15
(a) Wir werden im Sommer nach Portugal reisen. Wir reisen im Sommer nach Portugal. **(b)** Er wird heute nachmittag ins Kino gehen. Er geht heute nachmittag ins Kino. **(c)** Franziska wird am Wochenende nach Berlin fliegen. Franziska fliegt am Wochenende nach Berlin. **(d)** Sie werden an Weihnachten durch Mexiko fahren. Sie fahren an Weihnachten durch Mexiko.

EXERCISE 16
(a) Ich werde naß. **(b)** Sie wird alt. **(c)** Das Wetter wird heiß. **(e)** Der Kaffee wird kalt.

REVIEW SECTION

The last 15 minutes at the end of the recording will give you a chance to review the most important points of the course through extra speaking practice. Each exercise corresponds to one unit in the book and is based on the key words of that particular unit. Usually, Tom will be there to prompt you.

EXERCISE 1

This is a simple pronunciation exercise practising common greetings and introductions. Before you start, have another look at the key words of Unit 1.

EXERCISE 2

You have just met and are having a first chat with Dorit about your family, your work and the languages you can speak. Tom will prompt you on the recording.

EXERCISE 3

You're trying to book a room at a hotel. You want a single room with a shower for one week. You will also need to find out the price of the room and to ask whether breakfast is included. Before you start, think carefully about all the phrases you will need.

EXERCISE 4

This time you are ordering a snack and a drink as well as some tea and cake. But first of all, you will get a chance to practise a number of generally useful phrases for the pub and restaurant.

EXERCISE 5

You will ask for directions and repeat the most important pieces of information given to you. And you will also have a short conversation with a bus driver to find out whether he's going to the city centre.

EXERCISE 6

The first part of the exercise will give you a chance to practise the times. In the second part, you will be talking to Dorit about holidays.

EXERCISE 7

You want to buy postcards, stamps and souvenirs.

EXERCISE 8

A visit to the doctor. You're Herr Maier, visiting the **Hals-, Nasen- und Ohrenärztin** (ear, nose and throat specialist).

EXERCISE 9

At a railway station. You want to go to Kassel tomorrow morning. Find out when there is a good connection and then buy a second class return ticket.

EXERCISE 10

You're at the restaurant ordering a full meal. First of all, you enquire about the speciality of the day, then you order trout with red cabbage and potatoes, a noodle soup as a starter and a bottle of mineral water. Tom will prompt you.

EXERCISE 11

You are from Boston, talking to an acquaintance in Munich. He will ask you whether you like it in Boston, and he'll also want to find out whether you like the theatre and the cinema.

EXERCISE 12

Comparing the weather in Scotland and South Germany. Have a quick look at the weather terms before setting out on this exercise.

EXERCISE 13

What are your hobbies and where do you live?

EXERCISE 14

You are telling Dorit about your last holiday, which was in Munich.

EXERCISE 15

An invitation. You are trying to persuade Erich to go out for the evening.

GRAMMAR SUMMARY

Below you will find a short summary of what we think are the most important grammar points occurring in this course. Some useful grammar terms will also be explained.

VERBS

infinitive	A verb is a word denoting action or being, e.g. I *am*, he *goes*, she *loves* him. The simplest form of the verb is called *infinitive*. In English this form is preceded by 'to': to love, to go, to be, etc. In German all verbs in the infinitive end in **-en** or **-n**, e.g. **gehen** (to go), **tun** (to do). These infinitive endings change according to the subject of the verb, i.e. who or what acts: **ich gehe** (I go), **du gehst** (you go), **er/sie/es geht** (he/she/it goes), **wir gehen** (we go), **ihr geht** (you go), **sie/Sie gehen** (they/you go).
stem	In the present tense (see 'tenses' below) these endings are the same for most verbs (see Unit 2 p. 28), but sometimes the vowel in the *stem*, or main part of the verb, changes in the **du**, **er**, **sie** and **es** forms, e.g. **sprechen** (to speak): **du sprichst**, **er/sie/es spricht**; **fahren** (to go, to drive): **du fährst**, **er/sie/es fährt**. These verbs are called *strong verbs* (see below).
no continuous	Remember that in English there are two ways of expressing an action, e.g. 'I eat' and 'I am eating'. In German there is only one: **ich esse**. This applies to all tenses.
tenses	A tense says *when* you are doing something, e.g. now (in the *present*), some time ago (in the *past*) or at some point sooner or later (in the *future*).
perfect	There are two ways of talking about the past in German: the *perfect* tense and the *imperfect* tense. The perfect tense is explained in Unit 13 p. 198. It is more widely used than the imperfect, so it is more important for you to learn. The perfect is formed with the present of **haben** or **sein**, plus the past participles e.g. **ich habe gewohnt**, **ich bin gereist** (I have lived, I have travelled).
past participles	**gereist** and **gewohnt** are the *past participles* of the verbs **reisen** and **wohnen**.
weak verbs	Weak verbs are formed by putting **ge-** in front and **-t** after the stem: **gereist**, **gewohnt**; there are also irregular forms: **ich bin gekommen** (I have come), **ich habe unterrichtet** (I have taught).
imperfect	The imperfect is used to describe actions which happened quite a long time ago, e.g. **vor zehn Jahren wohnte er in Ulm** (ten years ago he lived in Ulm). Weak verbs form their imperfect by inserting endings after the stem: **ich wohnte**, **du wohntest**, **er/sie/es wohnte**, **wir wohnten**, **ihr wohntet**, **sie/Sie wohnten** (see Unit 14 p. 214).
strong verbs	These are verbs such as **fahren: ich fuhr** (I drove), **du fuhrst** (you drove), **er/sie/es fuhr** (he/she/it drove), **wir fuhren** (we drove), **ihr fuhrt** (you drove), **sie/Sie fuhren** (they/you drove), which change their stem altogether. Note that closely related English verbs often do the same, e.g.

singen	**sang**	**gesungen**	(sing, sang, sung)
trinken	**trank**	**getrunken**	(drink, drank, drunk)

Dictionaries usually list all strong verbs.

use of the past tenses	Remember that the perfect in German often has to be the simple past in English (see Unit 13 p. 198):

Gestern habe ich bis elf Uhr geschlafen.   Yesterday I *slept* till eleven o'clock.

future	The future is formed in German with the present of **werden** and the infinitive of the verb, e.g. **ich werde gehen**, **du wirst gehen**, etc. (I'll go, you'll go, etc.) (see Unit 15 p. 230). In German you can often use the present tense to state future intentions:

Morgen fahre ich nach Hause.   Tomorrow I'll go home.

modal verbs	These are verbs such as **müssen** (must), **können** (can), **dürfen** (may), **wollen** (to want to), **sollen** (shall, is to). They are explained in Unit 9 p. 134.

separable verbs	These are verbs such as **anfangen** (to begin), **zumachen** (to shut), **aufhören** (to stop), etc. They consist of two parts, a short *prefix* (such as **an**, **auf**, **zu**, etc.) and then a verb. In the infinitive these two parts appear together, but otherwise they are split up: **ich fange an** (I begin), **wir machen zu** (we shut). In longer sentences the prefix goes right to the end:

Wir fangen um neun Uhr an.   We start at nine.

Wir hören um 12 Uhr auf.   We stop at 12.

Note: If there is also a modal verb, the separable verb is joined up again, e.g. **ich möchte aufhören** (I would like to stop), **wir wollen jetzt anfangen** (we want to start now). (See also p. 150)

NOUNS

A noun is the name of a person or thing, e.g. 'James', 'dog', 'book', 'fun'. In German all nouns have a capital initial letter: **da ist ein <u>Mann</u>** (there's a man); **siehst du die <u>Frau</u>?** (do you see the woman?).

genders	All German nouns are either masculine, feminine or neuter, i.e. they have a *gender*. You can tell the gender of a noun when it is used with the words for 'the' (**der/die/das**) and 'a' (**ein/eine/ein**).

articles	The following words are articles:

masculine:	**der/ein**	Mann	the/a man
feminine:	**die/eine**	Frau	the/a woman
neuter:	**das/ein**	Kind	the/a child

subject/object	In German the article often undergoes a change according to the function a noun has in a sentence. It can, for example, be the *subject* or the *object*. A subject is a person or thing that acts, e.g. '*the woman* is reading'. The object is the person or thing on the receiving end, e.g. 'the woman reads *the paper*'. Whereas in English 'the' or 'a' is used regardless of whether a noun is a subject or an object, in German the articles often change when a noun becomes an object, i.e. when its function or *case* is changed (see Unit 3 p.42).

cases   There are four cases altogether:

1. the *nominative*, e.g. **Der Mann ist hier.**   *The man* is here.
2. the *accusative*, e.g. **Ich sehe den Mann.**   I see *the man*.
3. the *genitive*, e.g. **das Foto des Mannes**   *the man's* photo/the photo *of the man*.
4. the *dative*, e.g. **Ich gebe dem Mann das Buch.**   I give *the man* the book/I give the book *to the man*.

Here are the nominative, accusative, genitive and dative forms for **der/die/das**:

	singular			plural
	masculine	feminine	neuter	all genders
nom.	der Mann	die Frau	das Kind	die Männer/Frauen/Kinder
acc.	den Mann	die Frau	das Kind	die Männer/Frauen/Kinder
gen.	des Mannes	der Frau	des Kindes	der Männer/Frauen/Kinder
dat.	dem Mann	der Frau	dem Kind	den Männern/Frauen/Kindern

Here are the forms for **ein/eine/ein**:

	masculine	feminine	neuter
nom.	ein Mann	eine Frau	ein Kind
acc.	einen Mann	eine Frau	ein Kind
gen.	eines Mannes	einer Frau	eines Kindes
dat.	einem Mann	einer Frau	einem Kind

The negative of **ein/eine/ein** is **kein/keine/kein** (no, none) and follows the same pattern. So do **mein** (my), **dein** (your) and **sein** (his).

PRONOUNS

Pronouns stand for a noun, e.g. '*Mary* loves *Fred* – *she* loves *him*'. Here are the nominative, accusative and dative pronouns:

nominative		accusative		dative	
ich	I	**mich**	me	**mir**	(to) me
du	you	**dich**	you	**dir**	(to) you
er	he	**ihn**	him	**ihm**	(to) him
sie	she	**sie**	her	**ihr**	(to) her
es	it	**es**	it	**ihm**	(to) it
wir	we	**uns**	us	**uns**	(to) us
ihr	you	**euch**	you	**euch**	(to) you
Sie	you	**Sie**	you	**Ihnen**	(to) you
sie	they	**sie**	them	**ihnen**	(to) them

Note that the dative is often translated by 'to' + pronoun in English, e.g.
er gab es mir   he gave it *to me*   **wir sagten es ihm**   we said it *to him*
Often you will find the dative form of pronouns in phrases such as **es gefällt mir, es schmeckt Ihnen, wie geht es dir?** etc.

PREPOSITIONS

Prepositions are words such as 'near', 'by', 'in', 'to', 'through', 'over', etc. (see Unit 5 p. 74). In German certain prepositions take certain cases, e.g. **aus** (out of, from) takes the dative:

Er kommt aus dem Norden.   He comes from the north.

And **durch** (through) takes the accusative:

Wir gehen durch den Garten.   We go through the garden.

prepositions with the dative

Prepositions which take *only* the dative:

von from, of	**seit** since, for
zu to, at	**mit** with
nach to, after	**gegenüber** opposite
bei at	**außer** except
aus out of, from	

prepositions with the accusative

Prepositions which take *only* the accusative:

durch through	**gegen** against, towards
entlang along	**ohne** without
für for	**um** around, at

prepositions with the dative or accusative

Prepositions which take the dative *or* the accusative:

in in, into	**neben** next to
an on, to, at	**zwischen** between
auf on, onto	**über** over, across
vor in front of, ago	**unter** under, below
hinter behind	

With these prepositions the accusative is used if there is *movement* to a place, e.g.

Er ging in <u>den</u> Garten.   He went *into* the garden.

The dative is used if there is *no movement*, e.g.

Er stand <u>im</u> (= **in dem**) **Garten.**   He was standing *in* the garden.

ADJECTIVES

comparison Adjectives are words such as 'good', 'bad', 'red', 'pretty', etc. (see Units 7 and 8 pp. 104 & 120). You use adjectives if you want to describe and compare things, e.g.

Das Kind ist groß. The child is tall.
Die Frau ist größer. The woman is taller.
Der Mann ist am größten. The man is tallest.

Be aware of the fact that adjectives, like articles, change if they are in front of the noun depending on the cases they are in, as shown in the table below.

	singular			plural
	masculine	feminine	neuter	all genders
nom.	der kleine Mann	die kleine Frau	das kleine Kind	die kleinen Männer
acc.	den kleinen Mann	die kleine Frau	das kleine Kind	die kleinen Männer
gen.	des kleinen Mannes	der kleinen Frau	des kleinen Kindes	der kleinen Männer
dat.	dem kleinen Mann	der kleinen Frau	dem kleinen Kind	den kleinen Männern
nom	ein kleiner Mann	eine kleine Frau	ein kleines Kind	kleine Männer
acc.	einen kleinen Mann	eine kleine Frau	ein kleines Kind	kleine Männer
gen.	eines kleinen Mannes	einer kleinen Frau	eines kleinen Kindes	von kleinen Männern
dat.	einem kleinen Mann	einer kleinen Frau	einem kleinen Kind	kleinen Männern

WORD ORDER

simple sentences with one verb In simple sentences (i.e. sentences which contain only one verb), the most important rule is that the main verb always goes in second position, e.g.

| Ich | _fahre_ nach London. | I travel to London. |
| Mein Haus | _ist_ groß. | My house is big. |

This rule also applies when the sentence begins with an expression of time, place, or even the object, e.g.

Im September	_fahre_	ich	nach London.	I'm going to London in
Nach London	_fahre_	ich	im September.	September
Das Auto	_nehme_	ich.		I take that car

sentences with two verbs In sentences with two verbs the second verb gets sent to the end.

| Ich möchte nach London gehen. | I want to go to London. |
| Ich habe | das Auto | gekauft. | I have bought the car. |

Grammar summary   239

VOCABULARY

A

ab off, away
ab departing
   ab Ulm 14.05 departing Ulm 14.05
ab und zu now and then
Abend (e) *m* evening
   abends in the evening
Abendessen (–) *n* supper
aber but
abfahren to depart
Abfahrt (en) *f* departure
Abflug (¨e) *m* departure (flight)
abwaschen to wash up
acht eight
Achtel (–) *n* one eighth
Adler (–) *m* eagle
Aha! (exclamation) I see!
Akademiker (–) *m* person with academic
   qualifications
allein or **alleine** alone
alles all; everything
   alles Gute all the best
(die) Alpen the Alps
also so; that is (to say)
alt old
Altbau (ten) *m* old building
Altbauwohnung (en) *f* flat in an old
   building
Altstadt (¨e) *f* old part of town
am (an + dem) at the
   am Bahnhof at the station
   am besten best
Ambulanz *f* casualty department
Amerika *n* America
amerikanisch American
Ampel (n) *f* traffic light
amüsant amusing
an at
an arriving
   Ulm an 13.05 arriving Ulm 13.05
anbieten to offer
andere other
   die andern the others
Anfang (¨e) *m* beginning
anfangen to begin
angenehm pleasant
Angestellte (n) *m*/*f* employee
ankommen to arrive
Ankunft (¨e) *f* arrival
anprobieren to try on
Anruf (e) *m* phone call
Anschluß (¨sse) *m* connection
Ansichtskarte (n) *f* picture postcard
Antwort (en) *f* answer
Apfel (¨) *m* apple
Apotheke (n) *f* chemist's

The *gender* of nouns is given
after the brackets:
m means masculine, *f* feminine
and *n* neuter

The plural of nouns is given in
brackets, for example
Zimmer (–) room ▶ no change in
plural: **Zimmer**
Mutter (¨) mother ▶ no change
except for an umlaut in stem
vowel: **Mütter**
Wurst (¨e) sausage ▶ add **e** and
stem vowel takes an umlaut:
Würste

Apparat (e) *m* telephone
   am Apparat on the telephone
Appetit *m* appetite
   guten Appetit! enjoy your meal
April *m* April
Arbeit (en) *f* work
arbeiten to work
arbeitslos unemployed
Art (en) *f* species; kind
Arzt (¨e) *m* doctor
Aschenbecher (–) *m* ashtray
Atmosphäre (n) *f* atmosphere
auch also; too
auf on; in
   auf dem ersten Stock on the first floor
   auf englisch in English
auf open
auf Wiederseh(e)n goodbye
Aufenthalt *m* stopover
aufhören to stop
aufmachen to open
aufpassen to be careful
aufräumen to tidy up
Aufschnitt *m* selection of cheeses
   (**Käseaufschnitt**) or sausage
   (**Wurstaufschnitt**)
aufstehen to get up
August *m* August
aus from; out of
Ausfahrt (en) *f* exit (*for vehicles*)
Ausgang (¨e) *m* exit (*for people*)
Auskunft (¨e) *f* information
Ausland *n* foreign countries
   im Ausland abroad
außer except
Ausstellung (en) *f* exhibition
Ausstieg (e) *m* exit (*in trams, buses or*
   trains)
Autobahn (en) *f* motorway

Abend (e) evening ▶ add **e**:
Abende
Bank (en) bank ▶ add **en**:
Banken
and so on.

If nothing is given in brackets,
there is no plural for that
particular word or it is hardly
ever used. For example:
Wasser water
If (*pl*) appears in brackets, the
word is used in the plural only.
For example:
Leute (*pl*) people

B

Bäckerei (en) *f* bakery
Bad (¨er) *n* bath
Bahn *f* train
Bahnhof (¨e) *m* station
Balkon (e) *m* balcony
Banane (n) *f* banana
Bank (en) *f* bank
Bankkauffrau *f* /**Bankkaufmann** *m* bank
   clerk
Bar (s) *f* bar
   bar in cash
Bauch (¨e) *m* belly
Bauchschmerzen (*pl*) stomach ache
Bär (en) *m* bear
Bauernhof (¨e) *m* farm
Baumwolle *f* cotton
bayerisch Bavarian
Bayern *n* Bavaria
Beamte (n) *m* **Beamtin (nen)** *f* state
   employee
bedeckt overcast
Bedienung (en) *f* waitress
begeistert enthusiastic; thrilled
bei near; at
beide both
Beilage (n) *f* side dish
Beispiel (e) *n* example
   zum Beispiel (z.B.) for example
Beitz (en) *f* (colloquial) pub
bekannt well known
bekommen to get
belegte Brote (*pl*) open sandwiches
Belgien *n* Belgium
beliebt popular
Benzin *n* petrol
bereits already
Berg (e) *m* mountain

Berghütte (n) *f* mountain cabin
bergsteigen to climb mountains
Beruf (e) *m* profession
  von Beruf by profession
berühmt famous
besetzt taken, occupied
besichtigen to look round, have a look at
besonders especially
besser better
Besserung: gute Besserung get well soon
beste/r/s best
bestimmt certainly
Besuch (e) *m* visit
besuchen to visit
bewölkt cloudy
bezahlen to pay
Bioladen (¨) *m* health food shop
Bier (e) *n* beer
bieten to offer
billig cheap
Birne (n) *f* pear
bis until; to
  bis jetzt so far
  bis dann till then
(ein) bißchen a bit, a little
bitte please; you're welcome; Beg your pardon
  Wie bitte? What did you say? Beg your pardon?
bitter bitter
blau blue
bleiben to stay
bleifrei unleaded
Blick (e) *m* view
bloß only
Blume (n) *f* flower
Blumenkohl (e) *m* cauliflower
Bluse (n) *f* blouse
Blut *n* blood
Bodensee *m* Lake Constance
Bootsfahrt (en) *f* boat trip
Bouillon (s) *f* clear broth
Braten (–) *m* roast
braten to fry
Brathähnchen (–) *n* roast chicken
Bratwurst (¨e) *f* fried/grilled sausage
Brauerei (en) *f* brewery
braun brown
BRD *f* (**Bundesrepublik Deutschland**) Federal Republic of Germany
breit broad, wide
Brief (e) *m* letter
Briefmarke (n) *f* stamp
bringen to bring; to take
Brot (e) *n* bread; loaf
Brötchen (–) *n* roll
Brücke (n) *f* bridge
Bruder (¨) *m* brother
Buch (¨er) *n* book
buchen to book
Burg (en) *f* castle

Bus (se) *m* bus
Butter *f* butter

C

Campingplatz (¨e) *m* campsite
Champagner (–) *m* champagne
China *n* China
Chinese *m* /**Chinesin** *f* Chinese
chinesisch Chinese
Chips (*pl*) crisps
Creme (s) *f* cream

D

da as, because; there; then
dahin (to) there
Dame (n) *f* lady
damit so that
danach after that
danke (schön) thank you (very much)
  vielen Dank many thanks
danken to thank
dann then
darf: Was darf's sein? Can I help you?
das the (*for neuter nouns*); that; this
Datum (Daten) *n* date
dauern to take (time)
  Wie lange dauert das? How long does that take?
dazu with it
DDR *f* (**Deutsche Demokratische Republik**) German Democratic Republic
denken to think, to believe
der the (*for masculine nouns*); that; this
deutsch German
Deutschland *n* Germany
Dezember *m* December
dick fat
die the (*for feminine nouns*); that; this
Dienstag (e) *m* Tuesday
dies this
diese/r/s this
Ding (e) *n* thing
Diskothek (en) *f* discotheque
Donnerstag (e) *m* Thursday
Doktor (en) *m* doctor
Dom (e) *m* cathedral
Doppelzimmer (–) *n* double room
Dorf (¨er) *n* village
dort there
dorthin (to) there
drüben: da drüben over there
drei three
dritte/r/s third
drüben: da drüben over there
du you (*familiar form singular*)
dumm stupid
dunkel dark
durch through
dürfen to be allowed to
durstig thirsty
Dusche (n) *f* shower
D-Zug (¨e) *m* (moderately) fast train

E

ebenfalls also
Ei (er) *n* egg
eigentlich in fact, really, actually
eilig in a hurry
Eilzug (¨e) *m* semi-fast train
einfach simple; single (ticket)
  nach Ulm einfach a single to Ulm
einlösen to cash
einmal once; one
  einmal Ulm einfach one single (ticket) to Ulm
ein/e a
  ein Mann a man
  eine Frau a woman
eins one
einsteigen to get on, board
Einwohner (–) *m* inhabitant
Einzelfahrschein (e) *m* single ticket
einzeln single
Einzelzimmer (–) *n* single room
Eis *n* ice; ice cream
elegant elegant
elf eleven
empfehlen to recommend
Ende *n* end
Endstation (en) *f* last stop, terminus
England *n* England
Engländer (–) *m* Englishman
Engländerin (nen) *f* Englishwoman
  ich bin Engländer/Engländerin I am English
englisch English
Entdeckung (en) *f* discovery
entfernt distant
entschuldigen to excuse
  entschuldigen Sie bitte excuse me please
Entschuldigung (en) *f* excuse
Entwerter (–) *m* ticket-cancelling machine
er he
Erdbeere (n) *f* strawberry
Erdbeertorte (n) *f* strawberry flan
sich erholen to rest, to relax
erreichen to reach
erst at first
erste/r/s first
erwarten to expect
es it
essen to eat
Etage (n) *f* floor
etwas something; some; a little
Europa *n* Europe
europäisch European
evangelisch protestant

F

fahren to travel, go (*by bus/tram/train*); to drive
Fahrer (–) *m* driver
Fahrgast (¨e) *m* passenger
Fahrkarte (n) *f* ticket

Fahrschein (e) *m* ticket
Fahrzeit (en) *f* journey time
Familie (n) *f* family
Familienzimmer (–) *n* family room
fangen to catch
Farbe (n) *f* colour
Faßbier (e) *n* draught beer (*lit.* barrel beer)
fast nearly, almost
faulenzen to laze about
Februar *m* February
Feiertag (e) *m* public holiday
Feld (er) *n* field
Fensterscheibe (n) *f* window pane
Ferien (*pl*) holidays
Ferienhaus (¨er) *n* holiday house
Ferienwohnung (en) *f* holiday flat
Ferne Osten *m* Far East
Fernamt *n* operator
Ferngespräch (e) *n* long-distance phone call
Fernsehen *n* television
fernsehen to watch television
Feuerwehr *f* fire brigade
Fieber *n* fever
finden to find
Firma (Firmen) *f* firm
Fisch (e) *m* fish
fischen to fish
fit fit
Flasche (n) *f* bottle
Fleisch *n* meat
fliegen to fly
Flug (¨e) *m* flight
Flughafen (Flughäfen) *m* airport
Flugschein (e) *m* air ticket
Flugticket (s) *n* air ticket
Flugzeit (en) *f* flying time
Flugzeug (e) *n* airplane
Fluß (Flüsse) *m* river
Forelle (n) *f* trout
Frage (n) *f* question
fragen to ask
Frankreich *n* France
französisch French
Frau (en) *f* wife; woman; Mrs
Fräulein (–) *n* Miss
frei free
freiberuflich freelance
Freitag (e) *m* Friday
Freizeit *f* spare time
Fremdenverkehrsamt (¨er) *n* tourist office
Freund (e) *m* friend; boy friend
Freundin (nen) *f* friend; girl friend
freundlich friendly
frisch fresh
Friseur (e) *m* hairdresser
Frost (¨e) *m* frost
Frucht (e) *f* fruit
Fruchtsaft (¨e) *m* fruit juice
früh early
Frühjahr *n* spring
Frühstück *n* breakfast

fünf five
für for
Fuß (¨e) *m* foot
    zu Fuß on foot
Fußball *m* football
Fußgängerzone (n) *f* pedestrian precinct

G

ganz quite
    ganz durch straight through
Gasse (n) *f* alleyway, lane
Gast (¨e) *m* guest
Gasthof (¨e) *m* country inn
Gaststätte (n) *f* pub/restaurant
Gastwirtschaft (en) *f* (basic) pub/restaurant
geben to give
gebietsweise in places
Geburtsdatum (-daten) *n* date of birth
Geburtstag (e) *m* birthday
gefallen to please
    es gefällt mir I like it
gegen against; round about
    gegen 7 Uhr round about 7 o'clock
gehen to go; to walk
    Wie geht es Ihnen? How are you?
    mir geht es gut I am well
gelb yellow
Geld (er) *n* money
Geldwechsel *m* exchange (*money*)
gemeinsam together
gemischt mixed
Gemüse (–) *n* vegetable
genial ingenious
Genie (s) *n* genius
genießen to enjoy
geöffnet open
Gepäck *n* luggage
Gepäckaufbewahrung *f* left luggage
geradeaus straight ahead
Gericht (e) *n* dish
gering few
gern with pleasure
Geschäft (e) *n* business; shop
Geschäftsreise (n) *f* business trip
Geschenk (e) *n* present
geschieden divorced
geschlossen shut
gesund healthy
Gesundheit *f* health; bless you!
Getränk (e) *n* drink
getrennt separately
Gewinnzahl (en) *f* winning number
gewiß certain/ly
Gewitter (–) *n* thunderstorm
gewittrig thundery
Glas (¨er) *n* glass
Glatteis *n* black ice
glauben to believe; to think
gleich immediately; equal
    gleich hier right here
Gleis (e) *n* platform

Glück *n* luck; happiness
glücklich happy
Gold *n* gold
golden golden
Gott (¨er) *m* god
    Gott sei Dank thank God
Gottesdienst (e) *m* service
Grapefruit (s) *f* grapefruit
grau grey
Grenze (n) *f* border
Griechenland *n* Greece
griechisch Greek
Grillwurst (¨e) *f* grilled sausage
groß big
    im großen und ganzen on the whole
Größe (n) *f* size
größer bigger
Großstadt (¨e) *f* big city
grün green
Gruppe (n) *f* group
Gruß (¨e) *m* greeting
    viele Grüße many greetings
grüßen to greet
Grüß Gott (*South German, Austrian*) hello
Gulasch *m* goulash
günstig reasonable (price)
Gurke (n) *f* cucumber
gut good
    guten Tag/Morgen/Abend good day/morning/evening
    gute Nacht good night
Gymnasium (Gymnasien) *n* grammar school

H

Haar (e) *n* hair
haben to have
half half
Hals (¨e) *m* throat; neck
Halsweh *n* or Halsschmerzen (*pl*) sore throat
halten to stop
Haltestelle (n) *f* stop
hart hard
hassen to hate
hängen to hang
hätte would have
    was hätten Sie gern? what would you like to have?
Haselnuß (Haselnüsse) *f* hazelnut
Hauptbahnhof (¨e) *m* main station
Hauptspeise (n) *f* main dish
Hauptstraße (n) *f* main street, high street
Haus (¨er) *n* house
Hausarbeit (en) *f* housework
Häuschen (–) *n* little house
Hausfrau (en) *f* housewife
Hausmannskost *f* home cooking
heilig holy
heiß hot (temperature)

Vocabulary

heißen to be called
  ich heiße Anton my name is Anton
heiter bright; fair
Hektik *f* frenzy
hektisch hectic
helfen to help
hell light (*colour*)
Hemd (en) *n* shirt
herb dry (*of wines*)
Herbst *m* autumn
Herr (en) *m* Mr; gentleman
herrlich wonderful
heute today
  heute morgen this morning
  heute abend this evening
hier here
hin und zurück return; there and back
hinter behind
hinüber down; across; over
historisch historical
Hobby (s) *n* hobby
Hochhaus (¨er) *n* high-rise building
Höchsttemperatur (en) *f* maximum
  temperature
hoffen to hope
Höhe (n) *f* height, altitude
holen to fetch
Honig *m* honey
Hose (n) *f* (pair of) trousers
Hotelführer (–) *m* hotel guide (book)
Hund (e) *m* dog

I

ich I
IC *m* *short for* InterCity train
ICE *m* *short for* InterCity Express train
ideal ideal
ihr you (*familiar form pl*)
Imbiß (sse) *m* snack
Imbißstube (n) *f* snack bar
immer always
Indien *n* India
Industrie (n) *f* industry
Information (en) *f* information
Ingenieur (e) *m* engineer
inklusiv inclusive(ly)
Inland *n* interior (of a country)
  im Inland at home
Insektenstich (e) *m* insect bite
Insel (n) *f* island
sich interessieren für to be interested in
international international
intim intimate
irisch Irish
Irland *n* Ireland
Italien *n* Italy
italienisch Italian

J

ja yes
Jacke (n) *f* jacket; cardigan
Jackett (s) *n* (men's) jacket
Jahr (e) *n* year

Jahrhundert (e) *n* century
Januar *m* January
Japan *n* Japan
japanisch Japanese
jawohl yes; indeed; certainly
jede/r/s each; every
jetzt now
Joghurt (e) *m* yoghurt
Jugendherberge (n) *f* youth hostel
Jugendliche *m*/*f* youth, youngster
Jugoslawien *n* Yugoslavia
Juli *m* July
Junge (n) *m* boy
Juni *m* June

K

Kaffee *m* coffee
Kaiser (–) *m* emperor
Kaiserin (nen) *f* empress
Kakao *m* cocoa
Kalb (¨er) *n* calf; veal
kalt cold
  kalte Karte (cold) snack menu
Kännchen (–) *n* small pot; jug
Kanne (n) *f* (tea/coffee) pot
Kantate (n) *f* cantata
Karotte (n) *f* carrot
Karte (n) *f* card; ticket; menu
Käse *m* cheese
Käsekuchen (–) *m* cheesecake
Käsesahnetorte (n) *f* rich cheesecake
Kasse (n) *f* cash desk
kaum scarcely
kegeln to play skittles; to go bowling
kein/e no; none
  kein Kind no child
  keiner nobody
kennen to know
Kind (er) *n* child
Kinder(fahr)karte (n) *f* children's ticket
Kindheit *f* childhood
Kino (s) *n* cinema
Kiosk (e) *m* kiosk
Kirche (n) *f* church
Kirsche (n) *f* cherry
klappen to work out
  es klappt gut it works well
klar clear
Klasse (n) *f* class
Klavier (e) *n* piano
Klee *m* clover
Kleid (er) *n* dress
klein small
Kleinstadt (¨e) *f* small town
kleinstädtisch small-town, provincial
klingen to sound
Klub (s) *m* club
Kneipe (n) *f* (colloquial) pub
Knödel (–) *m* dumpling
kochen to cook
Kollege (n) *m* colleague
Kollegin (nen) *f* colleague
komisch comical, funny

kommen to come
Konditorei (en) *f* patisserie
König (e) *m* king
Königin (nen) *f* queen
können can; to be able to
  könnte could
Konzert (e) *n* concert
Kopf (¨e) *m* head
Kopfsalat (e) *m* lettuce
Kopfschmerz (en) *m* headache
  ich habe Kopfschmerzen I've got a
  headache
kosten to cost
Kotelett (s) *n* cutlet; chop
kräftig strong; bright (*colours*)
krank ill
Krankheit (en) *f* illness
Krankenhaus (¨er) *n* hospital
Küche (n) *f* kitchen; cuisine
Kuchen (–) *m* cake
kühl cool
kultiviert cultured
Kultur (en) *f* culture
kulturell cultural
Kunst (¨e) *f* art
Kunsthalle (n) *f* large art gallery
Kurs (e) *m* exchange rate; course
kurz short

L

Lage (n) *f* location; situation
Lamm (¨er) *n* lamb
Land (¨er) *n* land; country; state
  auf dem Land in the country
landen to land
Landschaft (en) *f* landscape; scenery
Landung (en) *f* landing
lang (e) long
langsam slow(ly)
langweilig boring
Lärm *m* noise
laufen to run; to walk
laut loud, noisy
leben to live
Lebensmittelgeschäft (e) *n* food shop
Leberwurst (¨e) *f* liver sausage
ledig single
leer empty
Lehrer (–) *m* teacher
leicht light
leid: es tut mir leid I'm sorry
leider unfortunately
lesen to read
Leute (*pl*) people
lieben to love
lieber preferably
  ich nehme lieber Tee I'd rather have
  tea
liegen to lie, be (situated)
Liegewagen (–) *m* couchette
Linie (n) *f* (tram or bus) route
  schlanke Linie (slim) figure
links left

Lokal (e) *n* pub
Lotion (en) *f* lotion
Lotto *n* lottery
Luftpost *f* airmail
Lunge (n) *f* lung
Lust *f* pleasure; joy
   Haben Sie Lust ...? Do you feel like ...?
lustig jolly
lutschen to suck

M

machen to do; to make
Mädchen (–) *n* girl
mag: ich mag ... lieber I like ... better, I
   prefer ...
mager lean; skimmed (*milk*)
Mai *m* May
Mal (e) *n* time
   ein anderes Mal another time
   dreimal three times
malen to paint
man one
   man kann das nicht machen one can't
   do that
manchmal sometimes
Mann (¨er) *m* man; husband
Mantel (¨) *m* coat
Markt (¨e) *m* market
Marmelade (n) *f* jam
März *m* March
Maschine (n) *f* machine; plane
mäßig moderate
Medizin *f* medicine
Mehl *n* flour
Mehrfahrtenkarte (n) *f* ticket for several
   trips
meine my
meistens mostly
Mensch (en) *m* person; man
Messe (n) *f* trade fair; mass
Metzgerei (en) *f* butcher's
mieten to rent; to hire
Milch *f* milk
mild mild
Minute (n) *f* minute
mit with
mitgehen to come/go along (too)
Mittagessen (–) *n* lunch
Mittel (–) *n* remedy; means
Mittwoch *m* Wednesday
möchte: ich möchte gerne I'd like to
Modell (e) *n* model
mögen to like
Moment (e) *m* moment
   im Moment at the moment
Monat (e) *m* month
Montag *m* Monday
Morgen (–) *m* morning
morgen tomorrow
   morgen abend tomorrow evening
   morgen früh tomorrow morning
morgens in the morning
Mosel *f* Moselle river

Mosel(wein) *m* Moselle wine
Mund (¨e) *m* mouth
Museum (Museen) *n* museum
Musikhochschule (n) *f* academy of music
Müsli *n* muesli
müssen must; to have to

N

nach after; to
   nach London to London
   nach 6 Uhr after 6 o'clock
Nachmittag (e) *m* afternoon
nachmittags in the afternoon
Nachricht (en) *f* news
nächste/r/s next; nearest
   der nächste Zug the next train
   die nächste Bank the nearest bank
Nacht (¨e) *f* night
Nachtleben *n* nightlife
nachts at night
Nähe *f* proximity
   in der Nähe von near
Name (n) *m* name
naß wet
Nebel (–) *m* fog
Nebelfeld (er) *n* fog patch
neben next to
neblig foggy
nehmen to take
nein no
nennen to mention
nett nice
neu new
Neubau (ten) *m* new building
neun nine
nicht not
   nicht wahr? isn't that true?
Nichtraucher (–) *m* non-smoker
nie never
Niederlande *f* Netherlands
Niederschlag (¨e) *m* rainfall/snowfall
niederschlagsfrei free of rainfall or
   snowfall
Nobelpreis (e) *m* Nobel prize
noch still; as yet
   noch nicht not yet
Norden *m* north
normal normal
normalerweise normally
Notbremse (n) *f* emergency brake
Notruf (e) *m* emergency call
November *m* November
Nudeln (*pl*) noodles, pasta

O

oben above; on top
Ober (–) *m* waiter
   Herr Ober waiter
Ochse (n) *m* ox
Ochsenmaulsalat (e) *m* ox muzzle salad
oder or
offen open
Öffnungszeit (en) *f* opening hour(s)

oh je! oh weh! oh dear!
ohne without
Oktober *m* October
Öl (e) *n* oil
Orange (n) *f* orange
Ort (e) *m* place, town
Ortsnetzkennzahl (en) *f* area code
örtlich local; in places
Osten *m* east
Ostern *n* Easter
Österreich *n* Austria
österreichisch Austrian

P

Paar (e) *n* pair
Packung (en) *f* packet
Paket (e) *n* packet; parcel
Park (s) *m* park
Parkplatz (¨e) *m* parking space
Passagier (e) *m* passenger
passen to fit
passieren to happen
Patentamt (¨er) *n* patent office
Patrizier (–) *m* patrician
Pause (n) *f* break
Pension (en) *f* boarding house
perfekt perfect
persönlich personally
Persönlichkeit (en) *f* personality
Petersilie *f* parsley
Pfeffer *m* pepper
Pfingsten *n* Whitsun
Pfirsich (e) *m* peach
Pfund (e) *n* pound
Pilz (e) *m* mushroom
Pinte (n) *f* (colloquial) pub
Plakat (e) *n* poster
Plan (¨e) *m* plan
planen to plan
planmäßige Abfahrt scheduled departure
Platz (¨e) *m* square; seat; place
Platzkarte (n) *f* seat reservation
Polizei *f* police
Pommes (frites) (*pl*) chips
Portion (en) *f* portion
Portugal *n* Portugal
Postamt (¨er) *n* post office
Post *f* post office; mail
Postbeamte (n) *m* post office official
Postbeamtin (nen) *f* post office official
Posten (–) *m* post, position
Postkarte (n) *f* postcard
Präparat (e) *n* medication
Praxis *f* surgery
Preis (e) *m* price; prize
Preislage (n) *f* price range
preiswert good value; reasonable
Prestige *n* prestige
prima super
privat private
Probe (n) *f* trial; test
probieren to try (out)
Professor (en) *m* professor

Professorin (nen) *f* professor
Prosit! *or* Prost! *n* cheers! (enjoy your drink!)
Prospekt (e) *m* prospectus, brochure
Pullover (–) *m* pullover; sweater

Q

quer across
Querstraße (n) *f* crossroad

R

radeln *or* radfahren to cycle
Radio (s) *n* radio
Rathaus (¨er) *n* town hall
rauchen to smoke
Raucher (–) *m* smoker
rechts (on/to the) right
Reformhaus (¨er) *n* health food shop
Regen *m* rain
reif mature; ripe
Reis *m* rice
Reise (n) *f* journey
    gute Reise have a good journey
reisen to travel
Reisescheck (s) *m* traveller's cheque
reiten to ride
Rentner (–) *m* pensioner
Rentnerin (nen) *f* pensioner
reservieren to reserve
Rezept (e) *n* recipe; prescription
richtig right
Richtung (en) *f* direction
    in Richtung Ulm in the direction of Ulm
Rind (er) *n* beef; cattle
Rindfleisch *n* beef
Rippchen (–) *n* spare rib
Rock (¨e) *m* skirt
roh raw; fresh
rosa pink
Rostbraten *m* roast
rot red
Rotwein (e) *m* red wine
Rücken *m* back
Rückfahrkarte (n) *f* return ticket
Rufnummer (n) *f* (telephone) number
Ruhe *f* silence
ruhen to rest
Ruhetag (e) *m* day off
ruhig quiet
rund round
rundum all round
Russische Eier (*pl*) (*lit.* Russian eggs) egg mayonnaise
Rußland *n* Russia
russisch Russian

S

Saft (¨e) *m* juice
sagen to say; to tell
Sahne *f* cream
Salami *f* salami

Salat (e) *m* salad; lettuce
Salatplatte (n) *f* salad platter
Salz *n* salt
salzig salty
Salzkartoffeln (*pl*) boiled potatoes
Sammelkarte (n) *f* ticket for several trips
sammeln to collect
Samstag *m* Saturday
Sandale (n) *f* sandal
sauer sour
S-Bahn (en) *f* suburban train
Schaf (e) *n* sheep
scharf sharp; hot (*spicy*)
Schauer (–) *m* shower
Scheck (s) *m* cheque
Scheibe (n) *f* slice
    Fensterscheibe (n) *f* window pane
Schein (e) *m* (bank)note
schick chic, smart
Schiff (e) *n* ship
Schinken (–) *m* ham
schlafen to sleep
Schlafwagen (–) *m* sleeper
Schlafzimmer (–) *n* bedroom
schlank slim
schlecht bad
schließen to shut
Schließfach (¨er) *n* luggage locker
Schloß (¨sser) *n* palace, mansion; castle
schlucken to swallow
Schlüssel (–) *m* key
schmecken to taste
    schmeckt es Ihnen? are you enjoying your food?
Schmerz (en) *m* pain; ache
Schmuck *m* jewellery
Schnaps (¨e) *m* schnapps
Schnee *m* snow
schnell quick
Schnellimbiß (sse) *m* snack bar
Schnellzug (¨e) *m* (moderately) fast train
Schnitzel (–) *n* slice of pork *or* veal
Schokolade (n) *f* chocolate
schon already
schön beautiful, nice
schreiben to write
Schuh (e) *m* shoe
Schule (n) *f* school
Schüler (–) *m* pupil
Schülerin (nen) *f* pupil
Schwaben *n* Swabia
schwäbisch Swabian
schwach weak; light
schwarz black
Schwarzwald *m* Black Forest
Schweden *n* Sweden
Schwein (e) *n* pig; pork
Schweinebraten (–) *m* roast pork
Schweinshaxe (n) *f* knuckle of pork
Schweiz *f* Switzerland
schwer difficult; heavy
Schwester (n) *f* sister
schwierig difficult

schwimmen to swim
sechs six
See (n) *m* lake
segeln to sail
sehen to see
Sehenswürdigkeit (en) *f* sight
sehr very
Seife (n) *f* soap
Sekretär (e) *m* secretary
Sekretärin (nen) *f* secretary
sein to be
seit since; for
    seit 14 Jahren for 14 years
    seit November since November
Seite (n) *f* side; page
Sekt *m* sparkling wine
Sekunde (n) *f* second
Selbstbedienung *f* self-service
selbsttätig automatically
selbstverständlich of course
selten seldom
September *m* September
Serie (n) *f* series
sie she; they
Sie you (*polite form sing and pl*)
sieben seven
Silber *n* silver
Ski fahren, Ski laufen to ski
Skigebiet (e) *n* skiing resort/area
Socke (n) *f* sock
sogar even
Sohn (¨e) *m* son
sollen shall
    soll ich? shall I?
    ich sollte I should, I ought to
Sommer (–) *m* summer
sommerlich summery
Sonderangebot (e) *n* special offer
Sonderfahrkarte (n) *f* special ticket
Sonne (n) *f* sun
Sonnenblumenbrot (e) *n* sunflower bread
sonnig sunny
Sonntag *m* Sunday
sonst otherwise, else
    sonst noch etwas? anything else?
Sonstiges other items
Sorte (n) *f* sort; brand
Souvenir (s) *n* souvenir
Spanien *n* Spain
spät late
    zu spät too late
Spätzle *n* type of pasta popular in Swabia
spazierengehen to go for a walk
    ich gehe spazieren I'm going for a walk
Speise (n) *f* food; dish
Speisekarte (n) *f* menu
Spezialität (en) *f* speciality
speziell special
Spiel (e) *n* game; play
spielen to play
Spielzeug *n* toy(s)

Spirituosen *(pl)* spirits *(alcohol)*
Sport *m* sport
sportlich sporty; casual
Sprache (n) *f* language
Spray (s) *n* spray
sprechen to speak
Sprechstunde (n) *f* surgery hour(s)
Stadt (¨e) *f* town; city
Stadthalle (n) *f* civic hall
Stadtzentrum (Stadtzentren) *n* town centre
städtisch municipal
stark strong
Start (s) *m* start; takeoff
starten to start; to take off
Station (en) *f* stop
stehen to stand
Stein (e) *m* stone
Stelle (n) *f* post; job
sterben to die
Stern (e) *m* star
still quiet
stimmt so keep the change
Stock (Stockwerke) *m* floor, storey
Strand (¨e) *m* beach
Straße (n) *f* street
Straßenbahn (en) *f* tram
Streifenkarte (n) *f* ticket for several trips
Stück (e) *n* piece; play
   ein Stück Kuchen a piece of cake
   ein modernes Stück a modern play
Studium (Studien) *n* studies
Stunde (n) *f* hour
stürzen to fall
Süden *m* south
   im Süden in the south
   in den Süden to the south; south
Supermarkt (¨e) *m* supermarket
Suppe (n) *f* soup
süß sweet
süßlich sweetish

T

Tablette (n) *f* tablet, pill
Tag (e) *m* day
Tageskarte (n) *f* ticket valid for one day only
Tagessuppe (n) *f* soup of the day
Tagestour (en) *f* day trip
täglich daily
Tanne (n) *f* fir tree
Tante (n) *f* aunt
Tante-Emma-Laden (¨) *m* corner shop
tanzen to dance
Tanzlokal (e) *n* dance hall
Tarifzone (n) *f* fare stage
Taschentuch (¨er) *n* handkerchief
Tasse (n) *f* cup
Taxi (s) *n* taxi
TEE *m* short for Trans Europ Express (train)
Tee *m* tea
Teewurst (¨e) *f* smoked sausage spread

Teilnehmer (–) *m* subscriber
Telefon (e) *n* telephone
telefonieren to telephone
Teil (e) *m* part
   zum Teil partly
Tempo *n* speed
Termin (e) *m* appointment
teuer expensive
Theater (–) *n* theatre
Tiefstwert (e) *m* lowest temperature
Tier (e) *n* animal
Tisch (e) *m* table
Toast *m* toast
Tochter (¨) *f* daughter
Toilette (n) *f* toilet
toll super, brilliant
Tomate (n) *f* tomato
Topf (¨e) *m* pot
Torte (n) *f* gateau; flan
tragisch tragic
Traube (n) *f* grape
Traum (¨e) *m* dream
treffen to meet
trennen to divide
Trimm-Dich-Pfad (e) *m* keep fit trail
trinken to drink
trocken dry
trotzdem nevertheless
tschüs *(colloquial)* goodbye, cheerio
Tür (en) *or* Türe (n) *f* door
typisch typical

U

U-Bahn *f* underground (railway)
über over; via
überall everywhere
überhaupt at all
Uhr (en) *f* watch; clock
   um 6 Uhr at 6 o'clock
Umleitung (en) *f* diversion
umsteigen to change *(buses / trains)*
umwechseln to change
umziehen to move
und and
   und so weiter and so on
ungefähr approximately
ungewiß uncertain
unglücklich unhappy
Universität (en) *f* university
unklar unclear
unter under, below
   unter Null below zero
Unterführung (en) *f* underpass
unternehmen to do; to undertake
unterrichten to teach
Urlaub *m* holiday
   im Urlaub on holiday

V

vegetarisch vegetarian
verbannen to ban
Verbindung (en) *f* connection
verbringen to spend time

vereinzelt occasional
vereist icy
vergessen to forget
verheiratet married
verkaufen to sell
Verkäufer (–) *m* shop assistant
Verkäuferin (nen) *f* shop assistant
Verkehrsbüro (s) *n* tourist office
verkehren to run *(between places)*
vermissen to miss
verschieden various
verstehen to understand
Vertrag (¨e) *m* contract
viel much; many
vielleicht perhaps
Vollmilch *f* (unskimmed) milk
volltanken to fill up (the tank)
von of; from
vor in front of
vor allem above all
vorher before that
Vorhersage (n) *f* forecast
vorläufig in the near future; for the time being
vormittags in the morning
Vorname (n) *m* first name
Vorort (e) *m* suburb
Vorsicht *f* attention; caution
Vorverkauf *m* advance sale
   im Vorverkauf in advance *(ticket)*

W

wahrscheinlich probably
Wald (¨er) *m* wood; forest
Waldlauf (¨e) *m* jogging on woodland paths
Wagen (–) *m* car
wandern to hike
Wanderung (en) *f* hiking tour
wann when
Währung (en) *f* currency
wäre: das wäre gut that would be good
warten to wait
warum why
was what
   was für Kuchen? what kind of cake?
Wasser *n* water
Wechsel (–) *m* change
wechselhaft changeable
wechseln to change
wecken to wake
Weg (e) *m* way; path
weg away
weich soft
Weihnachten *n* Christmas
weil because
Wein (e) *m* wine
weiß white
weiter further
welche/r/s which
   welcher Tag which day
Welle (n) *f* wave
Welt (en) *f* world

wenig few
werden to become
  es wird dunkel it's getting dark
  ich werde gehen I'll go
wesentlich substantially
Westen *m* west
Westdeutschland *n* West Germany
Wetter *n* weather
wichtig important
wie how
  wie geht's? how are things?
wieder again
(auf) Wiederschauen (*South German*)
  goodbye
(auf) Wiedersehen goodbye
wieviel how much
Wild *n* game
Wildsuppe (n) *f* venison soup
Willkommen *n* welcome
Winter (–) *m* winter
Wintergarten (¨) *m* conservatory
wir we
wirklich really
Wirtschaft (en) *f* (basic) pub/restaurant
wissen to know
wo where
Woche (n) *f* week
Wochenende (n) *n* weekend
woher where from
wohin where to
wohnen to live

Wohnung (en) *f* flat, apartment
Wolke (n) *f* cloud
wolkig cloudy
Wolle (n) *f* wool
wollen to want
Wort (¨er) *n* word
wünschen to wish
würde would
Wurst (¨e) *f* sausage
Würstchen (–) *n* small sausage
Würstchenbude (n) *f* sausage stall

Z

Zahn (¨e) *m* tooth
Zahnpasta (en) *f* toothpaste
Zahnschmerzen (*pl*) toothache
zart delicate
zehn ten
Zeit (en) *f* time
  zur Zeit at the moment
Zeitschrift (en) *f* magazine
Zeitung (en) *f* newspaper
Zentrum (Zentren) *n* centre
ziemlich rather
Zimmer (–) *n* room
Zimmernachweis *m* accommodation
  bureau
Zinn *n* pewter
zirka approximately
Zitrone (n) *f* lemon
Zoo (s) *m* zoo

zu shut
zu to
  zur Bank to the bank
  zum Hauptbahnhof to the main
  station
zu too
  zu groß too big
zu Hause at home
(zu) Ostern/Weihnachten at
  Easter/Christmas
zu zweit with someone else
Zucker *m* sugar
Zug (¨e) *m* train
Zukunft *f* future
zumachen to shut
zurück back
zusammen together
Zuschlag (¨e) *m* surcharge
zwar: und zwar and that is to say, to be
  more precise
zwei two
zweimal twice
  zweimal Bonn einfach two single
  tickets to Bonn
zweite/r/s second
Zwiebel (n) *f* onion
Zwiebelrostbraten (–) *m* roast beef with
  onions
zwischen between
zwo two
zwölf twelve

INDEX

Popular holiday areas in Germany

(Numbers refer to notes on page 169.)

OTHER TITLES IN THE BREAKTHROUGH

LANGUAGE SERIES FROM MACMILLAN

GERMAN FOR BEGINNERS ▼▼

Breakthrough German Activity Book - Practice for beginners
Breakthrough German Teacher's Guide
Breakthrough German Teacher's Cassettes
Breakthrough Video German

OTHER GERMAN COURSES ▼▼

Breakthrough Further German
Breakthrough Business German

FRENCH FOR BEGINNERS ▼▼

Breakthrough French
Breakthrough French Activity Book - Practice for beginners
Breakthrough French Teacher's Guide
Breakthrough French Teacher's Cassettes
Breakthrough Video French

OTHER FRENCH COURSES ▼▼

Breakthrough Further French
Breakthrough Business French

SPANISH FOR BEGINNERS ▼▼

Breakthrough Spanish
Breakthrough Spanish Activity Book - Practice for beginners
Breakthrough Spanish Teacher's Guide
Breakthrough Spanish Teacher's Cassettes
Breakthrough Video Spanish

OTHER SPANISH COURSES ▼▼

Breakthrough Further Spanish
Breakthrough Business Spanish

OTHER LANGUAGES FOR BEGINNERS ▼▼

Breakthrough Italian   Breakthrough Greek
Breakthrough Russian   Breakthrough Arabic
Breakthrough Japanese

Titles are available in most larger bookshops. Your bookshop will be pleased to order for you any title not in stock.

In case of difficulty please call 01256 29242 and ask for Macmillan Direct.